TRADITIONAL NAVAJO TEACHINGS

A TRILOGY

VOLUME I

Sacred Narratives and Ceremonies

Robert S. McPherson and Perry Juan Robinson

Robert S. McPherson is Professor of History Emeritus at Utah State University—Blanding Campus and author of numerous books about the history and cultures of the Four Corners Region.

Perry Juan Robinson is from the highly traditional area of Piñon, Black Mesa, Arizona, with a strong family heritage of practicing medicine people. He has been a member of the Navajo Nation Medicine Men Association for over twenty years and continues to work as a hataałii.

Cover Art: Charles Yanito
Cover Design: Chris Monson
Interior Design: Chris Monson and Kerin Tate
Map Design: Erin Greb
Copyediting and Indexing: Kerin Tate

Other books of related interest by the author:
Traders, Agents, and Weavers: Developing the Northern Navajo Region
        (University of Oklahoma Press)
Both Sides of the Bullpen: Navajo Trade and Posts of the Upper Four Corners
        (University of Oklahoma Press)
Viewing the Ancestors: Perceptions of the Anaasazi, Mokwič, and Hisatsinom
        (University of Oklahoma Press)
Under the Eagle: Samuel Holiday, Navajo Code Talker
        (University of Oklahoma Press)
Dineji Na'nitin: Navajo Traditional Teachings and History
        (University Press of Colorado)
Navajo Tradition, Mormon Life: The Autobiography and Teachings of Jim Dandy
        (University of Utah Press)
Along Navajo Trails: Recollections of a Trader, 1898-1948
        (Utah State University Press)
A Navajo Legacy: The Life and Teachings of John Holiday
        (University of Oklahoma Press)
Navajo Land, Navajo Culture: The Utah Experience in the Twentieth Century
        (University of Oklahoma Press)
The Journey of Navajo Oshley: An Autobiography and Life History
        (Utah State University Press)
Sacred Land, Sacred View: Navajo Perceptions of the Four Corners Region
        (University Press of Colorado)
The Northern Navajo Frontier, 1860-1900: Expansion through Adversity
        (University of New Mexico Press)

Contents

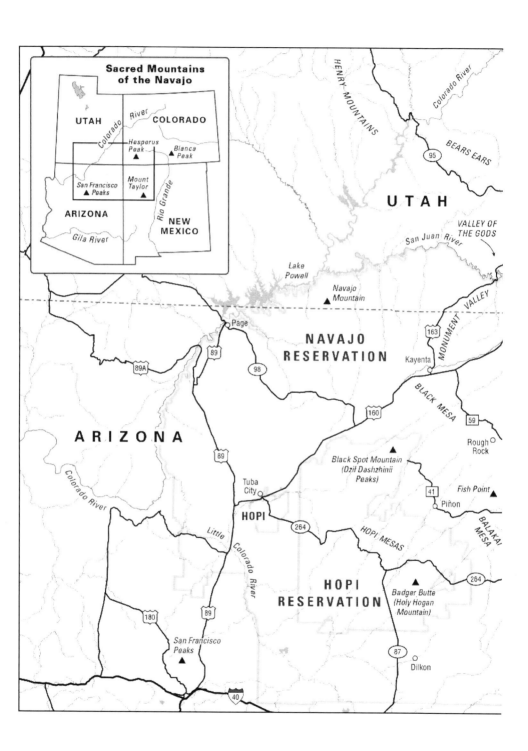

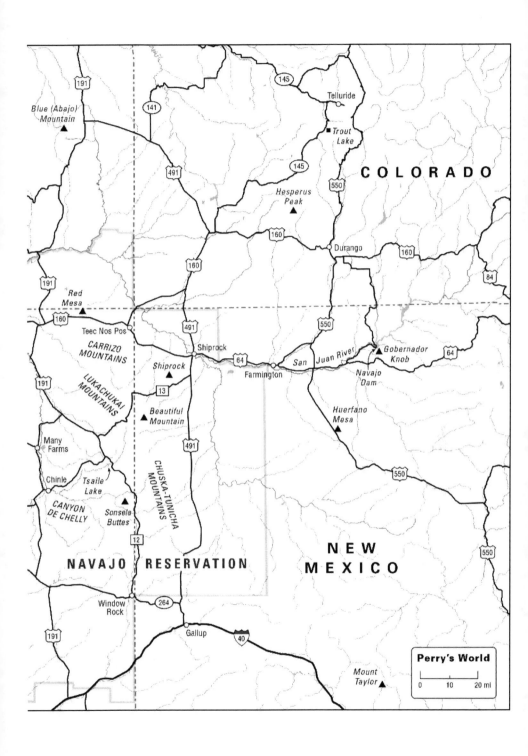

INTRODUCTION

Into the Táchééh

I sat in my office that late September day in 2017, working at my desk and enjoying the newfound freedom of having retired three months previous. Even though I continued to go to the university on a daily basis as an emeritus faculty member, all of the teaching, grading, and official college responsibilities were over; I could dictate my own comings and goings. The phone rang. It was Rick Hendy, Behavioral Health Director from the Utah Navajo Health System (UNHS) organization that provided medical services both on and off the Utah portion of the Navajo Reservation. I had known Rick for a number of years as a casual acquaintance and was aware of his interest in Navajo traditional perspective, especially as it interfaced with western medicine. His approach to mental health infused thought and practices from both cultures; he, in turn, knew of my interest in Native American teachings and history. Our views coincided, so he hoped that there were some things we could accomplish together. He asked if I was interested in pursuing a project, I said that I was, and so we agreed to meet a few days later when he would bring along a friend and coworker—Navajo medicine man Perry Juan Robinson.

We met on September 27 in my small adobe office called "Walden" that perches on a rock shelf overlooking Westwater Canyon with Elk Ridge and the Bears Ears in the distance. In Navajo culture, the sweat lodge (táchééh) is a place where not only physical cleansing occurs, but also intense teachings are given. A great deal of traditional lore is shared there, uninterrupted by the distractions of modern society. For months to come, Walden became that place for me, where Perry opened up the world of the People's beliefs and practices. Following introductions, Rick began with his proposal: Perry and I would create a number of entries about Navajo practices to post on the UNHS website to help patients understand how western and Navajo medicine was compatible. Perry was to provide the content, I would handle the interviewing and writing, and Rick would see that the information was loaded onto an appropriate computer platform and

1

placed online for those interested. The project seemed worthwhile, so I
offered to do it without pay, while Rick would cover Perry's salary, and
Perry could outline the information and limits of the interviews. Indeed,
Perry was to steer the project in the direction that he felt best, with Rick and
I agreeing that he was to determine subject matter, depth of information to
be shared, the best approach to presenting it, and final approval of anything
to be made public. We would try to get together once a week to conduct
interviews while keeping Rick informed of our progress and sending him
topically organized subjects with suggested headings. None of us were sure
where this project would go, other than a few open-ended goals.

On October 10 we had our first recorded interview. There were a
number of things that bubbled to the surface immediately. First was the long
line of medicine people from whom Perry descended. His father, Juan
Robinson, was born in 1920, died June 24, 1974, and had practiced
traditional medicine all of his life and had performed as a Road Man in the
Native American Church. Perry's mother—Alice Nez Robinson (March 9,
1922–November 6, 2018)—was a medicine woman, as were Perry's
grandparents on both sides of his family. Black Mesa, more specifically
Piñon, Arizona, an area noted for its being off the beaten path and still highly
traditional in its practice of Navajo culture, was their homeland. Trained all
of his life by these practitioners, it was obvious from the start that Perry was
extremely knowledgeable about a wide variety of ceremonies. He had
followed in his family's footsteps and had been a member of the Navajo
Nation Medicine Men Association for many years. The more we talked, the
more I realized that his knowledge and practices went back for generations,
which he readily affirmed. Often he cited the source of his teachings by
stating that his mother or grandfather or some other family member had told
him what he was about to say. Answers to questions often came from
ceremonies or from memorized prayers that he had participated in.

One final point emerged from the interview, something I would see
over and over again. Perry spoke from a seemingly bottomless well of
information from which he drew attaching links to other stories and
ceremonies. In the future during many confirmation interviews, the same
thing happened—he would bring up a new teaching and connect it to a
number of different accounts or practices. At the same time, if he did not
know something that I asked, he would immediately say so. I never found
him to be a "know-it-all" or trying to bluff his way through a question if he
did not have the answer. There would be times when he would reason
through a response or talk about things that he had heard others say, but he
always prefaced that with where he heard it and that he did not have firsthand
knowledge of what he was about to share.

It did not take long for me to realize that even in this initial interview, he was drawing upon a depth of knowledge that is not usually discussed in the literature. Having spent thirty-plus years myself in studying Navajo culture and interviewing Navajo people, I was relatively familiar with what had been shared so that outsiders could understand traditional teachings. What I was learning now was more *why* things were done as opposed to *how* they were done, although there was no skimping on that aspect if requested. Perry was totally open to discuss many different facets of a wide variety of topics; this raised both an issue and an opportunity. On a number of occasions, he would delve into areas that I found extremely interesting but questioned if he was comfortable in discussing them. He did not hedge. One of the main reasons he wanted to talk about some of these things was that, as a medicine man, he had seen and continues to see, the dissolution of Navajo culture. The language is disintegrating with younger people, proper ceremonial etiquette is not followed, family traditions and clan relationships are no longer heeded, the stories and teachings are not being respected or passed on, and no one knows how to counsel children and youth as they did in the old days. While Perry is adept at operating a cell phone, using a computer, posting information online, and in other ways maintaining stride with the younger generation in a technological world, many of the youth are not keeping up with learning age-old wisdom and traditional practices. Perry hoped that his sharing of information would at least, in part, reverse some of this current trend.

My concern went in a similar direction. Since I started doing research on and off the reservation, there has been a dramatic increase in requirements for permission to interview people. The Navajo Nation Historic Preservation Department requires an application-and-fee process to control the flow of information and to protect Navajo people from exploitation and cultural misappropriation. While this is entirely understandable and should be applauded, it has also hampered Navajo people from learning and understanding certain aspects of their culture. Having taught classes both on and off the reservation to a demographic composition ranging from 50 to 100 percent Navajo and from young to old, I had a fairly clear impression of where many Navajos were operating in terms of traditional culture. While there are those who enthusiastically embrace learning the Navajo language and practicing aspects of the teachings, there were far too many who either did not care about or were not in a position to learn either. The standard reply when asked a question about some aspect of this was "I'll have to check with my grandmother." Although not necessarily true of all, there are far too many who just do not know. This is very troubling for Perry, and he is anxious to do what he can to educate about and instill pride in Navajo culture.

As we discussed the problem in the early stages of interviewing, it became apparent that we shared similar goals. As today's elders—those raised before or during livestock reduction of the 1930s, who lived the traditional life in a hogan, who attended ceremonies including their own kinaaldá, whose main transportation was by wagon or horseback, and whose life revolved around livestock—pass away, much of their experience is lost. There are a number of problems that arise from this natural succession. One of these is the growing dependency on what has been already recorded in the form of books, articles, studies, and now online. Much of this is helpful, and so what follows is not criticism, but only recognizes what exists. A quick introduction to sources puts Perry's contribution in perspective.

Anglo and Navajo Contributors

Starting on the Anglo academic side, there are the "deans" of Navajo studies, many of whom will be cited for specific information throughout this trilogy. These are well-known individuals made famous for their intense study of Navajo culture. Many were anthropologists, some religious leaders, others teachers, and one a military man, but all were knowledgeable and invested in the culture. To provide a complete list of their publications here is unwieldy, but as specific texts are cited in this trilogy, a full bibliographic entry is provided. Among the "deans" are Washington Matthews, Berard Haile, Gladys Reichard, Leland Wyman, Clyde Kluckhohn, Karl Luckert, and Charlotte Frisbie. All have done substantial work in accurately recording Navajo life and ceremonies while classifying and analyzing them in an anthropological sense. Each has lived and worked among the Navajo and had good facility with the language. Extensive and important publications followed. Generally, their studies were topically driven. Matthews was the first to work in this arena during the late 1800s, recording mythology and associated ceremonies. Haile, with other members of the Franciscan brotherhood, was encyclopedic in his approach, compiling important information on religious beliefs and helping with an ethnologic dictionary. Anthropologist Reichard also wrote a hefty tome on Navajo religion as well as a number of books about her life experience on the reservation and studies on different social aspects. Kluckhohn studied intensely the fabric of Navajo society; Wyman classified the different types of Navajo ceremonies and recorded various chants; Luckert, concerned about disappearing religious practices, wrote a half dozen books, each one detailing songs, prayers, and procedures; and Frisbie, as an anthropologist, published information on the girl's puberty ceremony, medicine bundles, traditional food, and two lengthy Navajo autobiographies.

In addition to the "deans," there were others who contributed significantly to recording general Navajo practices, history, and culture. Scholars such as Walter and Ruth Dyk, Frank McNitt, Louise Lamphere, Richard Van Valkenburgh, David Brugge, J. Lee Correll, Peter Iverson, and Maureen Trudelle Schwarz, have all made important additions to our understanding. Inasmuch as there has been more written about the Navajo than any other North American tribe, there are many other contributors who have added to the literature. One nonacademic group who has helped with understanding is the traders who ran their posts across the reservation during the early to mid-1900s—Louisa Wetherill, Hilda Faunce (Wetherill), Elizabeth C. Hegemann, Gladwell Richardson, William Y. Adams, Will Evans, Alberta Hannum, and Franc Newcomb. Their day-to-day experience with the Navajo people—although sometimes criticized for its romantic view and exaggeration—gives an important feel for life at their time and often shares helpful observations of cultural practices.

Navajos have had their own spokespeople who provide perspective. Their stories, although often published under Anglo names, are invaluable. In addition to a number of works written by some of the academicians mentioned above, there are individual accounts and compilations provided by Navajo Community College Press. For instance, there are entire books on traditional life and culture, one on the Long Walk, a third on Livestock Reduction, and two on biography. Navajo informants also shared their life history or experiences with anthropologists and linguists like Edward Sapir (*Navaho Texts*), Pliny E. Goddard (*Navajo Texts*), and Robert W. Young and William Morgan (*Navajo Historical Selections*). Other works by Ruth Roessel, and Sandoval (Aileen O'Bryan), Tiana Bighorse (Noel Bennett), and Lucky (Alexander and Dorothea Leighton), as well as John Holiday, Jim Dandy, and Navajo Oshley (all three Robert McPherson) are also life history accounts.

Entering the Sweat Lodge

Yet as Perry and I became comfortable with our recording routine, I became increasingly aware of a difference between what and how he was saying things when compared with much of what is in the literature. There was more vitality coupled with a full explanation of why things in Navajo culture take the form that they do. A few of the authors mentioned above included in their discussion of ceremonies and practices brief explanations of why things were done in a certain way and offered a synopsis of the story that lay at the base of a practice, but Perry laid out in detail Navajo thought in respect to the topic. I have often heard Navajo people who have read a book on their beliefs point out that the detailed account under discussion might be accurate, but somehow the author still "missed it." Somehow the feeling, the understanding, the reasoning was absent. In other words, a real insider perspective had been drained out of what had been recorded. Perhaps it was the information that was shared or not shared, the interpreter, the rules and focus of an academic discipline, or how it was presented in written form—but the native explanation and insight had lost much of its feeling. Perry, who speaks English fluently, was able to maintain that connection.

Even in the first interview, Perry ranged across a variety of topics from the four directions and the separation of the sexes to White Shell Woman and fire pokers. He was obviously giving an overview of a variety of complex topics and tying them in to his discussion of depression; it became apparent to me that he had a depth of knowledge that far surpassed the subject at hand. I started asking confirmation questions that helped him to understand what I knew and the level that he could go without losing me. More questions, more answers as the time flew by for both of us. He had counseling appointments scheduled that day, and so after an hour and a half we called it quits and set another time to meet. By the end of the second session, Perry asked me to put together a list of topics for us to work on during each visit. By now it was clear that he was open and anxious to talk about any subject I raised, holding back only some of the words and prayers that were most sacred and could be harmful if misused. Otherwise, I had full access to the thoughts and teachings of a very experienced medicine man, something that many Navajo practitioners are not willing to do. Again, this was totally in keeping with what he wanted to accomplish by making this material available.

The amount of information was at times torrential. While I might have it recorded digitally, only a fraction of it would make it onto the UNHS website. From the outset, I had made mention of the possibility of putting some of it in book form if he was interested and if there was sufficient substance. By April 2018, it was clear that there was a huge body of information and that what we had initially thought might be a book had turned into what would eventually be three—a trilogy. More specifically, there were well over seven hundred typed single-spaced pages resulting from twenty-five interviews, not to mention further clarification and unrecorded discussions. Once this text had been boiled down by removing my comments and questions, the normal "uhms and ahs" of the interview process, and some repetition, then compiling the information topically, there were still five hundred pages of straight interview material. After I added introductory information, we were back to over seven hundred pages of text, not counting photographs and sketches.

Perry and I discussed what should be done next and concluded that the fruits of the project should be published. After outlining possible directions and responsibilities—i.e., academic press where much of the control of the books' production would be under their purview, or sharing all costs of self-publication with equally split expenses and royalties, or my shouldering the total expense with Perry being able to obtain as many copies as he would like at wholesale value—he chose to go with the latter. His duties in the process would be to proofread and approve all chapters, assist with obtaining photographs, and provide any additional information needed for clarity. My responsibility was organizing the text into topics, editing Perry's information for clarity and readability while he checked for accuracy, providing introductory material for each chapter, preparing the manuscript for publication including editing, obtaining pictures and a map, and paying for the printing of the books. We both felt we had the energy to perform our various tasks and so signed an agreement. This collaborative process is important to understand so that readers grasp that Perry made all decisions about the extent of his involvement in the direction and cost of the project. On a number of occasions, he mentioned how he wanted to have the widest possible distribution and get this knowledge into the hands of teachers and families to increase their ability to share it with the younger generation. We both felt that rather than going with an academic press, self-publishing allowed us to maintain control of the material and its presentation.

Perry's Thoughts

I asked Perry to make a statement as to his feelings about this process. Following some personal history about those days in the past when he struggled with alcohol and understanding who he was, he responded:

> Through that process I learned what it meant to be a good person and what it would take to be a better one, to know what is right and what is wrong. I had been raised all of my life with ceremonies, but many of the teachings had not sunk in, and I never thought of them as being sacred. Listening to my father, mother, and grandfather was just a natural part of life and not necessarily connected to something helpful. When I was struggling with recovery, I started to understand more fully the importance of them and what these teachings offered. They began to answer real questions. I started to feel like the two hermaphrodites during the time of the separation of sexes, who were told to sit by a pond, observe the water running into it, and if necessary, prevent it from overflowing. They were treated by others as useless and so could not hunt or participate in normal activities. They knew nothing, could do nothing, and were worthless. Sometimes I felt like

that, not worthy of anything. As I thought about this story, I pictured them listening to the wind, rain, and the other sounds of nature. Knowledge and answers came, teaching lessons of life. So I started paying attention to my grandfather and other elders, trying to understand the things they were talking about. I began to see some important lessons for daily survival, while in the ceremonies there was never-ending education. Grandfather was an expert in the rituals, and so I questioned him a lot about them. This is where I found my true self; they made me want to live and to help others through teaching their meanings. I began to notice many people just like me struggling through different phases of life; they had no idea where to go for help or whom to ask. I decided to really study traditional teachings and later go to school to learn what western education had to offer about counseling and helping people.

Now by this point in my life, I have learned that this information should be written down to help others understand and add their own teachings. Most of my elders are gone now, traveling the old people's road to the spirit world. Sometimes I still feel like a child in learning, but age-wise I'm getting older and older and know that I need to pass this information on to my grandchildren and other people who want to learn. Navajos are walking away from their language and the essence of what it means to be Diné—what is proper behavior, how should we dress, how and when should we speak, and what are all of the ethical beliefs in our culture? Too much is dying out. Now the schools, instead of families, do much of the teaching, and so perhaps these books from this project will bring some of the language and beliefs to the young people. I want to pass it on to the next person so that they can understand.

There may be some traditional people who think that this information should not be made public. In the old days, when we asked questions of our elders, they would answer, "Don't say that. Hold off. You're not worthy to talk about that," so we never heard or understood the answer to our question; then the elder would die. This is why a lot of my clan people on the Edgewater side never shared. My grandfather had five knowledgeable medicine people in his family, and none of their stories, songs, and family prayers were handed down. I could have really learned from them, but they refused to teach and pass it along. On my mother's side the only songs I know from the Edgewater People are either from my mom or my uncles living in different areas; there could have been a lot more given. Most of the ceremonial songs and teachings come from my father (Naakaii Dine'é—Mexican Clan) and grandfather named Many Beads (Tłizíłání—Many Goats Clan). They never held back. They were always teaching and believed this information had to be discussed, learned, and passed on. We cannot hold off and keep it inside of us. As for those who think differently—you're not supposed to talk about it, write it down, share it, or use it with outsiders—they are the reason that so many of our teachings are lost.

Perry Juan Robinson is from the highly traditional area of Piñon, Black Mesa, Arizona, with a strong family heritage of practicing medicine people. He has been a member of the Navajo Nation Medicine Men Association for over twenty years and continues to work as a hataałii.

I have been in the Navajo Nation's Medicine Men Association for a long time and the tribe's Behavioral Health System for almost thirty years. Over this period, I have noticed that many of the medicine people are much more anxious to share their knowledge now because they also see the need to train people in the ceremonies and to understand our teachings. We took young people and did our best to help them learn specific practices. Almost everyone that I worked with had the same view, which was to share. We taught ceremonies, hoping that others would learn so that we will not be dependent upon just a few practitioners who know them. Medicine people are much more open-minded now than they used to be. I hope this continues and that they are able to use some of the teachings in this book.

Working with Oral History

Anthropologists, oral historians, folklorists, and others who take the spoken word and turn it into text approach the task in three possible ways. The first, the purist, transcribes the interview and puts on the page everything that is said, just the way it is said, and even supplements with additional information as found in vocal cues, body language, and other forms of nonverbal communication. While this technique is highly accurate, almost to a fault, when read, it can sometimes make a person sound less intelligent. All of the pauses, false starts, and vocal segregates or those "umm, uh" words, when faithfully reproduced in a text, can be distracting at best.

A second approach is to maintain most of what is said, but to smooth out the manuscript by ridding it of repetition, perhaps joining some of the sentences, removing for clarity distracting words or phrases, and generally creating a more polished version of the transcript. The third approach is to take what is said and put it in the writer's words with only an occasional quote from the original interview. What Perry and I agreed upon was something between choices two and three. What that meant on paper is that I took his comments, keeping as much of the original wording as possible, but also creating a more readable style; introducing additional vocabulary for clarity and variety; and, in a few instances, adding small bits of information, with his approval, to expand meaning. To ensure that I had not changed the meaning or muddied his thoughts, we sat down together and read every chapter, making alterations by adding, deleting, and clarifying. I provided the introductory material, roughly five pages at the beginning of each chapter, before presenting Perry's thoughts. He now read each chapter, making any changes he felt appropriate. In the meantime, photographs by the author and sketches by artist Kelly Pugh joined the text, Navajo language specialists Clayton Long and Charlotta Lacy checked spelling, and I prepared the manuscript for publication.

A few housekeeping comments will explain why certain words and thoughts were used, but first a caveat. Throughout the text, words such as "Navajo people," "Navajos," and "traditional teachings" or other terms of generalization suggest that all people in this culture share a common belief or practice. Nothing could be further from the truth. To hint that the 350,000 people of this ethnic group hold this information in common is ludicrous. Their knowledge and practices vary along a wide spectrum from the person who knows little or nothing at all about their culture and language to the highly taught and educated medicine man or woman who has spent their lives perfecting their studies and language. Even then, no medicine person knows everything any more than an Anglo person knows everything in white society. When generalized terms are used here, it is with the understanding that they apply to those who have lived according to older cultural values along the upper end of the traditional spectrum, as identified previously.

I tried to keep the vocabulary that Perry spoke, although it sometimes differed from what academicians or the politically correct might use. For instance, he often referred to his people as the Navajo as opposed to the Diné, his being a medicine man instead of a hataałii, the Enemyway ceremony as a squaw dance, and Ancestral Puebloans as Anasazi. I maintained his usage. For the most part, I have skirted the use of the emotionally charged word "myth," but when I do use it, it is in the sense that it is a narrative that is sacred and true as opposed to a fabricated story to entertain children. Indeed, these are powerful teachings that embody the essence of a culture. Along the same lines in English, the use of "he" as a pronoun that could just as easily be "she" can turn awkward if trying to use both and so I elected just to use "he." I meant no slight to females, but Perry tended to talk more about males and male roles when describing a situation. The reader may at times be uncomfortable with the move back and forth between the first person voice (I) of Perry, the second person (you), which he often used, or the third person voice (he, she, they, etc.) found when narrating. Part of the problem occurs in using oral interviews, trying to maintain the speaker's voice while also providing a more general framework. My approach was to maintain as much of Perry's original dialogue and the way he presented it, maintaining the "you" when he is explaining something.

There were times when Perry used parts of a prayer or his sacred name during an interview. I asked if these words should not be removed, but he insisted on leaving them in to serve as a reference point for other medicine people who might read these books. At other times, he thought it better to delete some of the things he shared. It is fair to say that what is in here is with his full approval. We both avoided presenting lengthy prayers or songs, although there are many books that have translations of them. Words are power and so need to be spoken with reverence and presented in the appropriate context. Again, our focus has been more on how and why things operate in the Navajo world as opposed to a detailed exposé of sacred language and practices.

Scholars who have interviewed Navajo elders about stories and ceremonies have most likely encountered the problem of determining to what or whom a pronoun is referring. English speakers are also guilty of what is called an "unclear antecedent" or reference. In Navajo discourse this problem seems to arise more often. I wondered why and arrived at a plausible explanation that goes back to the songs and stories. In some instances, the repetition of names and actions found in Navajo ceremonialism, to the Anglo ear, is unnecessary and could be greatly reduced. Repetition for the Navajo increases the power of the action and creates a stronger mental image that builds and solidifies what is being performed. By saying something four or more times through songs and prayers, there is more power because this is the pattern established by the holy people when they first created an object, spoke the words, or performed the ritual. Just as the number three is an important element in Christian beliefs, manifesting itself in architecture, literature, and liturgy, so too is the number four for the Navajo.

At the other end of the spectrum, there are times when either the "actor" is unclear because of intermixing with other deity or the identity of the individual is not mentioned but assumed to be known. In both instances, the reason goes back to the song or prayer. As in much ritual, what a person hears is not a well-developed story but flashes of scenes calling upon a powerful spiritual essence to heal or protect. A long, detailed narrative as found in the Bible is not provided, but rather short phrases and power-invoking images that summon the holy people and provide a picture of what is healing the patient or participant. The story from which it derives is known but not told. In Christianity, everything is done in the name of Jesus Christ; for the Navajo there is a pantheon of holy people interacting, participating, and lending their powers to the curative process. When that healing is specific to a key individual, such as Talking God or another deity, then their presence is recognized and assistance requested. At other times, the exact identity of the god is not given, because the name is not necessary even though their assistance is required. While the medicine people performing the ceremony are aware of the spiritual being they are working with because of their familiarity with the events and teachings being called upon, the name of the god is not always mentioned. This sometimes carries over when discussing a ceremony, analyzing a song, or interpreting a prayer. It may be unclear as to who is performing the action. We have attempted to clarify who these holy people are.

In working with all of this material, there was also the question of how to group things. Navajo teachings and stories are intertwined with all types of phenomena—plants, animals, holy people, physical locations, other stories—the list goes on. These linkages are often difficult to separate into a single category or topic, which meant that in editing, I had to choose where, in three books' worth of material, certain information should be placed. For example, in the chapter on divination, there are teachings about the moon, stars, Gila monsters, birth processes, offerings, deity, mountains, and protectors—all of which are found in one or more other chapters. Obviously it was important to mention these aspects here, even though most would be dealt with in more detail elsewhere. Thus I chose to have some repetition and to remind the reader that a longer version of a story or ceremony or topic is covered elsewhere. At the same time, enough information is provided to identify the appropriate linkage.

A final point that each reader will have to deal with individually, is the sensitive question of how this all works. Anglo people, depending upon where they fall on the scale of spiritual beliefs, may struggle with some of the things that Perry talks about. Raised in a scientific world of factual analysis, there no doubt will be a search for explanations that goes beyond the existence and efficacy of holy people, the ability to communicate and draw upon the power of an animate or inanimate being, and the miraculous cures and experiences of the faithful. People may cast about for a provable situation, be it faith healing, physical explanations, human intercession, or any number of reasons that fit the skeptic's worldview. Each person frames their world according to how they understand its workings. Perry, as a practitioner in both the physical and spiritual realms, has no doubt as to how they both operate. Through his faith and understanding both are real and "work" once one comprehends the laws in which they are based. I follow suit, realizing that I do not have the same understanding or belief systems that he does, but do not deny that he has experienced deeply moving occurrences derived through those powers.

Thinking through the Text

Each chapter has two parts. First is the chapter introduction that I have written, followed by the bulk of the chapter by Perry, which I have transcribed from interviews, organized, and edited. The change in author voice is noticeable, but we have placed a divider to visually separate the two texts. The purpose of the introductory material is threefold. As an aid for those who are not familiar with the literature about a specific subject, it provides a number of accessible sources for further reading. Teachers and other professionals working with or studying the Navajo will find the references a good starting point for additional information. While not exhaustive, the listing of these sources takes a person a lot deeper than the introduction and into some of the topics that Perry discusses. While this introductory material has endnotes, I have avoided placing them in the main body. To do otherwise would open up a process that would probably double the size of the text and still be incomplete, given the voluminous amount of reference material available on the Navajo. At the same time, a second reason for the introductory material is to provide supplementary information for the chapter itself. Perry knowingly touched lightly on many of the stories and teachings that he considered well known so that he could focus on less frequently discussed concerns. For instance, the story of White Shell/Changing Woman along with the Navajo Twins' journey to visit Sun Bearer are the basis for the Blessingway and Enemyway ceremonies and have well over two dozen versions available. While this is a foundational series of events, Perry delves into only parts of them in detail, then skips over much of the rest of the narrative; I outlined parts of them in some of the introductions. From this main stalk, there are other myths that branch off to different ceremonies. The final reason for the introduction is to make mention of differing views from Perry's. Anyone who has studied the Navajo oral tradition understands that there may be a wide variety of teachings that may be at odds with information shared in other accounts. Chapter introductions provide material for further exploration into these differences.

This last point requires more explanation. No doubt there will be questions raised about some of the information that Perry shared. As we held our interviews, I would ask about a number of things he said that were different from what I had encountered elsewhere. He would respond with chapter and verse from one of the songs, prayers, or ceremonial teachings as to why he believed as he did. This was comparable to a college professor citing his or her sources when explaining a point. For Anglos this may be disconcerting since they are brought up putting faith in the written word and the ability to compare and contrast what is said with other accounts, reaching the final destination of an ultimate answer. Skepticism grows when something is contrary and so research, proof based on fact, and judgment based in the written word ends the argument or quiets the claim. Because traditional Navajo teachings are derived from a wide variety of oral stories, prayers, and songs serving as the basis for a host of ceremonies, there may be differing details, explanations, or versions. There is no ultimate truth when disputing a narrative; Navajos are perfectly comfortable with this understanding that so enriches the spoken word. Anglos are not.

I learned this point in 1990 in Monument Valley. I had been working on a book that would soon be published as *Sacred Land, Sacred View: Navajo Perceptions of the Four Corners Region*. It was a study in Navajo sacred geography, partly based in interviews and partly on the literature. Since there was a community school group comprised of elders meeting at the high school one day and I knew many of them, I went there armed with a Navajo translation on an hour-long cassette tape to see how they felt about it. I wanted to know if it was accurate and acceptable. After playing part of the tape, one medicine man, serving as spokesman, indicated that it seemed good, but that I should not be concerned with what the gathering said. He went on, "That is how you were taught, then that is correct." There was no final judgment, no specific truth or way of understanding, but rather room for thought and meditation. Where Anglos seek the definitive word, Native Americans are comfortable with a variety of options and possibilities.

Still, Perry is quick to point out that there is a way to deal with what is right and wrong. Sometimes during our interviews, he mentioned that his teachings were from his family and so might be at odds with how others were taught.

> The topic is based on what happened according to clan teachings and their interpretation of the story. This is how the clan people understood it. A different clan may look at it another way and have their own way of teaching it. They may have their own little stories and bits of information that vary from those of others. Then they will explain, "This is why it is said this way, this is why we add this into it, and this is why it looks this way." Others may have their way of tweaking it and a good explanation of why they view it in a certain light. But mainly the story is straight, with no variation, yet not all will be the same. Medicine men like to discuss things, see how knowledgeable another individual is, question certain practices, and sometimes even argue back and forth. These are intellectual people, invested in their teachings, and wanting to learn from others. A lot of times, especially at the larger and longer ceremonies, medicine people will attend to see how the person conducting the ceremony does and if there is new information or practices that might be learned. After the completion of the ceremony, they might gather under a shady tree to discuss the things that they know or something new that has just been done.
>
> Sometimes medicine people challenge each other. There are differences in understanding and practice, depending on what part of the reservation—eastern, southern, western, and northern—a person comes from, as well as who has taught that individual. Perhaps it is a matter of how a staff is marked for the Enemyway or how a song was sung with an explanation as to why. Let me share an example of a typical issue—one

that came up about three weeks ago when I was assisting at an Enemyway ceremony. The main question revolved around the markings on the staff. One of the symbols on the stick was of a hair bun that represents Monster Slayer. On the staff that I mark, there should be an opening at the top of the symbol, but on the one that was being used in this ceremony, there was none—it was totally closed. One medicine man had made the symbol while another person was to use it in the ceremony.

When the practitioner received the staff, he noticed that the symbol was closed. The man who had made it was not present, and so the individual conducting this part of the ceremony showed the stick to me and asked what I thought. When something like this happens, the people involved talk about the origin story and what happened in order to understand what should be done. They will talk about why there is an opening at the top, while somebody else might say the opening should be at the bottom, then offer their teaching. The man conducting this ceremony said, "The markings that we carry in our family on this staff have always had an opening; this is the way it is supposed to be, but this stick does not have one, and so I will add it."

I could see how this might lead to an argument with its creator as to why it is or is not necessary to have an opening on the hair bun. The medicine man asked me what I thought he should do, and I encouraged him to leave it as it was, even though my own family—my brother, uncle, grandfather, and people who live within a fifty-mile radius of my home— would all agree that there needed to be an opening at the top. If I had given them a staff with a closed symbol, they would have said I was wrong and have me change it. But this medicine man decided to make an opening at the top without the authorization of the man who gave the instructions as to how it should be made.

As the ceremony progressed, we reached the point where the staff was to be returned to the originator. He looked at it and didn't like it, saying, "Why does this have an opening on top? I didn't give those instructions. You need to take it back, close it up, and then bring it here." The question now became who was correct. Answer: The first medicine man, the one who was to receive the staff. The second man had no right to alter the design by making an opening. That was not his job. The person who created it was working from his own teachings, so although they were different from mine and the other man's, they were still the ones that needed to be carried out. We had agreed to follow him as the leader of the ceremony, and so we went back and closed the opening. He accepted it and the ceremony continued. This illustrates the point that if a person is taught in a certain way and he is in charge, then that is the way it will be.

There is often disagreement among practitioners as to the various ways to handle differences. Let me share another experience I had at a different Enemyway ceremony. In the performance of this ritual, there are thirteen sacred songs sung in a particular order. The four main ones, two on top, and then there are others that go on top of them. The first song belongs to a particular animal, the second to another, and so on. The order of these songs is often used to question if a medicine man is really trained and capable of conducting this ceremony. [Perry asked that I not divulge more specific information.] All seven animal songs should be in order and are followed by a feather song and drum song. They stand this way, and so they cannot be mixed up. That is how it goes, as all songs come together. Nobody can change it; that is the way it is done by the Black Mountain People.

But, when one leaves Black Mountain and travels to the northern side of the reservation, it might be reversed and backwards. Instead of the main last song being sung, they bring it back to the front and add others in different ways. If it was sung that way at Black Mountain, people would stop you just as those on the north would do the same if I sang it my way. They will then explain and show you how they do it by sharing their story and tell you how it goes. The Black Mountain people will tell you, if you have a different story than mine, "I want to know why you are mixing it up. These people do not jump in front of the other ones like that. They stand in line this way and you can't change that."

This happened to me one time when I was participating in the northern part of the reservation. I was asked to assist in an Enemyway ceremony, but as we started to sing, the songs were in an incorrect order. I talked to the lead medicine man and told him that this was not right, but he insisted that it was. I told him that I understood this was the way they did it in his area, but that because I had been trained differently, I could not change the order even though the individual songs were correct. We would, however, remain there and respect the way they had been taught. After the singing stopped and the ceremony ended, I asked the medicine leaders to step inside and share with me the story and events upon which their ceremony was based. As others were eating, we sat in a circle in the hogan and I explained, "The reason I said that the correct order of the songs is this way is that my grandfather from Black Mountain taught the story as follows," then I laid out the sequence and reason for the teachings. [Perry shared the detail order and why.] "Now you tell me why you have your order." They looked at each other but nobody knew. There was no story behind it, just an explanation that this is how they did it. My grandfather had warned that sometime during my practice as a medicine man, someone would challenge me as to how and why something was done, and so I had better learn not just what to do but also the reason for things being done in that certain way.

I knew how these people in this story lined up, and so could not participate in doing it contrary to how I was taught. Now if the medicine man in the other group had a somewhat different order and they had a story or explanation to go with it, then they can perform it their way and I would perform it mine, but not mix the two. This goes back to the idea of "this is how you were taught and so I will respect that." In this instance, I backed off, did not sing, but just listened. The holy ones know who is performing.

If I am singing in a different order, then they ask what I am doing and why I am changing things around. They know that you know your songs that have been learned in a different way. I should get away from there and let the other people sing their songs in their way—this is northern country and so back off, westerner.

This type of insight comes only from an inside perspective and explains not only how a medicine man handles and solves disagreements, but also how he understands and uses the knowledge he has, a major topic of this book.

What, then, can the reader expect in this trilogy? The information is wide-ranging and encyclopedic. The first volume, *Sacred Narratives and Ceremonies*, as the subtitle suggests, is about sacred stories and the ceremonies derived from them. Following the first chapter, which is an autobiographical account of how Perry became a medicine man, there are chapters about interacting with the holy people, the origin story concerning the emergence from the worlds beneath this one, and the role that White Shell Woman/Changing Woman played in establishing the Navajo. All of this is based in the traditional teachings from which the culture was established. Next follows a study devoted entirely to determining how sickness is diagnosed through religious powers; this is followed by an analysis of a ceremony and the equipment needed to perform it. Another chapter looks at medicine structures, from hogans to wedding baskets, used for ritual events. Bears and the Bearway ceremony in chapter 8 takes a detailed look at how land, animals, and the teachings come together in a cohesive explanation of a seldom-discussed ceremony that helps people struggling with emotional issues. The final chapter looks at beliefs and practices surrounding sickness, death, and evil.

Scholars have long recognized that the Navajo subscribe to a land-based religion, emphasizing what is often referred to as "sacred geography." The second volume, *The Natural World*, provides a broad understanding of how these people are connected physically and spiritually to the land. While much has been written about the Four and Six Sacred Mountains, there is much more to include with other various land formations; elements found in the air—the moon, sun, stars, wind, and weather; rivers, springs and other sources of water; and trees and plants—information which has not been studied in detail from a religious perspective. But there is more to add to this discussion about the landscape. An entire chapter is devoted to animals with antlers, another to birds and reptiles, one to the teachings about smaller creatures, and another concerning domesticated animals. Indeed, the entire Navajo universe is a sentient system of relationships in which everything from the stars to the mouse crouched in a burrow underground may be connected. The term "animism," although often misunderstood, in its broadest sense describes the closeness that the Navajo feel toward where they live and who they share that space with.

The third and final volume, *The Earth Surface People*, explores three major topics. The first is the life cycle that starts with conception and birth and ends in death. Everything from naming a newborn and burying its umbilical cord to the elderly walking on the Old People's Road is included in Navajo teachings about the stages of life and how they should be approached. A second aspect is the responsibilities and training necessary for each of those stages to be successful. The coming-of-age ceremonies for both boy and girl, the equipment and knowledge they will need to provide for their families, and their roles and responsibilities as husband and wife are outlined. The teachings of the elders, as reflected in ceremonies like the kinaaldá, wedding, sweat lodge, and hogan blessing, are all part of maintaining a true course. The third topic is that of western medicine as it interfaces with traditional culture. Many new ways of dealing with sickness and preventing future illness have entered into recent healthcare practices, and may be foreign to Navajo elders. Medicine people often discuss how these procedures and remedies should be viewed and either used or discarded, based on traditional beliefs. While flexibility and adaptation are two of the traits that have defined Navajo character in the past, there are still evolving practices that challenge much of what has been historically accepted.

What the reader can expect, then, from the books in this trilogy—each of which can stand alone—is a fascinating glimpse into traditional and contemporary Navajo culture as seen through the eyes of your guide, Perry Robinson. There is no other book in the literature about his people that provides the same kind of depth and breadth from an insider's perspective. Perry, as an accomplished medicine man, shares his family's teachings, which go back for generations, in the hope that upcoming generations will benefit from their wisdom. By receiving these teachings from the past, people will better understand how to prepare for the future.

CHAPTER ONE

The Making of a Medicine Man

E ver since the white man landed on the shores of North America, there has been a literature describing Native Americans and their way of life, but it would take almost two hundred years before an Indian was induced to tell his own story. With the help of a French Canadian/Potawatomi interpreter, Antoine Le Claire, and a sympathetic newspaper man, John B. Patterson, *The Autobiography of Black Hawk* became one of the first book-length accounts of an Indian who shared his own narrative.[1] Black Hawk, a Sauk leader, chose to have this book published in 1833 to counteract misunderstanding about his intentions and the role of his people in a recent conflict, while also sharing some of his beliefs. The book filled in a black hole, where one-sided journalism and literature needed to be countered by a Native American perspective. This work also established a pattern for future Indian "autobiography" that through necessity had to be filtered and produced with the help of a white coauthor.

Not until men like Charles Eastman (Ohiyesa)—a Santee Sioux, active contributor to founding the Boy Scouts of America, and a medical doctor— did true Indian autobiography (i.e., self-written) appear. Of his four major works—*The Soul of the Indian, The Indian Today, Indian Boyhood*, and *From the Deep Woods to Civilization*—the latter two are the best examples of life-writing with a purpose.[2] He unhesitatingly promoted native culture as a counterpoint to the prevailing white attitude that there was little comparative value in Indian beliefs and practices. One of the most popular autobiographical works that has been used and cited probably more than any other is *Black Elk Speaks*, written with the assistance of Nebraska's poet laureate John G. Neihardt.[3] This story of a Lakota holy man, when combined with a companion piece of autobiographical work *The Sacred Pipe* by Joseph Epes Brown, provides real insight into the religious and cultural values of the Sioux during the mid to late 1800s and early 1900s. Few such works compare.

The Navajo have also had their spokespeople. Indeed, members of this tribe have been studied, interviewed, and written about more than any other in North America. Even in the more selective genre of autobiography, the list of books, not to mention shorter works, abounds and would require a lengthy chapter just to list and provide brief annotations. Here, I will mention some of the major works that can serve as background to what follows with Perry's contribution. A number of anthropologists have provided excellent autobiographies in reproducing Navajo life for the outsider. Walter Dyk wrote three lengthy works that examine the daily life of two individuals. *Son of Old Man Hat* and *Left Handed: A Navajo Autobiography* provide over 950 pages about one man's life, while *A Navaho Autobiography* is about another man living during the same era of the late nineteenth and first third of the twentieth century. Both illustrate the daily rhythm of Navajo life, their belief system, and interaction in a changing society affected by a growing white presence. Neither was a medicine man or trying to promote a particular point of view, but rather was content with recalling in detail their lives with both the good and the bad unabashedly present. Dyk provides a real service in capturing the unvarnished truth about two "average" Navajos who lived according to traditional beliefs but gives few explanations as to why they behaved as they did. Perry's teachings provide helpful insight as to what motivates certain types of behavior.

Charlotte Frisbie, like Dyk, has provided two lengthy autobiographies, one about Frank Mitchell and another about his wife, Rose. *Navajo Blessingway Singer: The Autobiography of Frank Mitchell, 1881–1967* and *Tall Woman: The Life Story of Rose Mitchell, a Navajo Woman, c. 1874–1977* give two different perspectives from within the same family—a rarity in itself.[4] A third of the twelve chapters in *Navajo Blessingway Singer* are concerned with explaining the beliefs and practices of this foundational ceremony—at least parts of which are used in many other rituals. Frank's life as both a public servant and knowledgeable medicine man gives the reader understanding about the challenges that many Navajo men face—bouts with alcohol, challenges with social pressure including witchcraft, and blending traditional beliefs with those of an encroaching white society. A short excerpt of Frank's thoughts echo what Perry offers about his own experience when introduced to traditional medicine on a serious level. Speaking of learning the Blessingway, Frank said:

Before I began to learn these things, way back before that, I did not even
think about life as being an important thing. I did not try to remember
things or keep track of what happened at certain times. Nothing seemed to
matter to me; I just didn't care about anything, so long as I kept on living.
But then when I began to learn the Blessingway, it changed my whole life.
I began really thinking about ceremonies. I had heard singing before that,
but now I began to take it more seriously because I began to realize what
life was and the kind of hardships we have to go through. . . . It is just like
going to school: you are being trained and being told what is wrong and
what is right. It was the same way with this ceremony; that is when I began
learning about life.[5]

Tall Woman's story is notable for two reasons. First, there are relatively
few autobiographies of Navajo women, while those that do exist are short
and less analytical. For example, Ella Bedonie, through Emily Benedek,
wrote *Beyond the Four Corners of the World*; Walking Thunder with
Bradford Keeney published *Walking Thunder: Diné Medicine Woman*; and
Kay Bennett produced *Kaibah: Recollection of a Navajo Girlhood*, but none
of them reach deeply into the meaning of events and practices within the
culture.[6] As in *Tall Woman*, these females illustrate much of the lifestyle
explained through Perry's understanding of the role of women and the
differences that exist between them and men, but little is said as to why.
Second is that Rose's life, divided into large sections of forebears and
childhood, young adult and early marriage, middle years and raising
children, grandparent and late adulthood, and finally old age, illustrate not
only the activities and sequences established in Navajo life for women, but
also the changes encountered as the dominant society expressed itself in
traditional culture. Closely involved in Frank's life, she pulls no punches in
illustrating the strengths and weaknesses in their marriage and in his
personality. Her life revolved around the home and family, but he was a far
more public figure as a prominent ceremonial practitioner, community
leader, and later, tribal official. Both were steeped in traditional teachings,
but the more prominent expression of those values is found in Frank's
involvement in ceremonies. While both led interesting lives, his role was far
more dramatic and varied, providing one of the reasons that there are so
many more male biographies and autobiographies than female.

While Frank Mitchell's story is an interesting mix of ceremonial
knowledge and better known events, there is not as much insider explanation
as to why things are done in a certain way. This is true of most Navajo
autobiographies and is even more evident in *Lucky: The Navajo Singer*, a
life history recorded by psychiatrists/ethnographers Alexander H. and
Dorothea C. Leighton and edited by Joyce J. Griffen.[7] Lucky does not
convey his introspective nature as do Mitchell and many other medicine

men. He is interested in narrating events in detail, but forgoes any sustained explanation behind traditional practices and behavior. He at times comes off as a scamp looking to find a quick solution or fill an immediate need as opposed to living a more ethical life. As Frank and Perry point out, that attitude may be common before one starts to practice medicine, but after one begins, life changes, and an individual should be more ethically responsible. On the other hand, some of Lucky's descriptions of ceremonies and everyday life are interesting and helpful.

A more balanced view between the teachings and daily life is found in the story of John Holiday. In spring 1999 while working on the book *The Journey of Navajo Oshley: An Autobiography and Life History*, I had the opportunity to interview John Holiday, a powerful medicine man in Monument Valley, Utah.[8] Oshley's narrative was nearing completion, and although not a medicine man, his explanations concerning divination, witchcraft, and assisting in ceremonies provide insight into religious realms. The recording of his story was an interesting event in itself—he was given a tape recorder and a number of blank cassettes and told to self-record and that in a few weeks the tapes would be picked up. Hardly the way to create an autobiography, but that is what happened. The tapes were retrieved, sent to the Utah State Historical Society, and then sat there for ten years. Once I learned of their existence and began working with them, it became apparent that they held a spontaneous account of a Navajo man's life totally from his perspective. Unfortunately he made many references to people, places, and events that I had no knowledge of. This work started just before his passing, and so his daughter later suggested I see one of his relatives, John Holiday, for further information. I took her advice, visiting John, who eventually inquired about my willingness to record his life. We agreed that it would be a good thing to do and so, with permission from the Navajo Nation, the process began.

John Holiday was a gold mine. As a central figure in Monument Valley since 1919, as an accomplished medicine man, and as a person who saw the old ways fading, he, like Perry, was anxious to share his knowledge. John couched many of his teachings in life experience, but his stories ranged from the beginning to the end of the world, including stories associated with specific cultural values such as the Ancestral Puebloans, women's working tools, introduction of the car and airplane, and ceremonies. He spoke of training to become a medicine man, how he felt as a youth in performing some of his first ceremonies, and how traditional culture either accepted or rejected many of the new ways then being introduced into Navajo culture. On the other hand, he avoided tying much of the mythology into ceremonial practices, did not go into depth as to how the ceremonies worked, and never gave an insider's perspective of what it meant to be a medicine man, nor did he explain their relationship to the gods and healing. Thus, his fascinating life became easily accessible to anyone interested in what it meant to be a medicine person, but he did not go deeply into the underlying philosophy. This is where he and Perry are different, since the latter focuses almost entirely on this aspect.

Another group of people who have provided interesting anecdotal information without the scholarly analysis of the academician are the traders. Two, in particular, Louisa Wade Wetherill and Franc Johnson Newcomb wrote autobiographies of Navajo men who became best of friends with these women, who themselves became accomplished students of the culture. Louisa operated posts in Oljato and Kayenta and grew under the tutelage of Wolfkiller (1855–1926). Fascinated by his life and knowledge gained during the early years of white contact, she wrote *Wolfkiller*, which her great-grandson Harvey Leake published.[9] Unlike most autobiographies, this book is divided into two parts. The first half centers on traditional teachings categorized under qualities such as gratitude, contentment, faith, hope, and courage, some of which are represented by animal characters while others are explained through observation and personal experience. All teach a point, but much of the Navajo voice is filtered out. The second half of the book rests on Wolfkiller's experiences. From a historical perspective, there is a great deal of value contained within.

Franc Newcomb befriended Hosteen Klah (Hastiin Tł'ah) and in 1964 published *Hosteen Klah: Navaho Medicine Man and Sand Painter*, in which she meshes the stories of some of his ancestors and life with contemporary experiences. Klah was a powerful medicine man who let Newcomb copy a large number of sandpaintings, who wove blankets with sacred symbols and god (Yé'ii) designs, and who used his medicine to protect himself and family members from spiritual and physical retribution for performing some of these previously forbidden activities. As an iconoclast secure in the power of his traditional knowledge, he is an example of one who controlled the elements and used his deep knowledge of traditional culture to walk on the edge of acceptability, sometimes going over the line. Newcomb recounts many examples of his performing seemingly impossible feats, using traditional teachings to secure his and other's well-being. For those who insist that Navajo knowledge be contained and controlled, Klah is an example of one who would not falter to share what he knew. The writing in this book is filtered through Newcomb's eyes and vocabulary with a distinctly Anglo flavor and little if any of Klah's own words.

Given the variety of emphasis found in these different autobiographies, the reader will find in Perry's story a contrasting approach. This chapter lays the foundation of the main parts of his life story. In relating it, he could not resist the temptation to share the experience and teachings he has gained throughout the years, much of which he learned through hard times and intense instruction. His life has not been easy, but because of that, he draws upon those difficult times when counseling those who now struggle. Every chapter teaches from those seminal experiences. Yet the thing that makes this different from any other autobiography of a Navajo medicine man is the almost exclusive focus on traditional teachings and their origin, application, and influence on Navajo thought. This insider perspective provides a view that has never before given such an intense, clear explanation of how medicine men understand and use the powers found in traditional teachings. True, there are entire books that deal with a single ceremony wherein portions of it are translated for the reader, but Perry's focus, couched in his own life experience, tells more of the why and the how of it. Through his life and understanding, the reader is able to view the heart of these traditional teachings.

The Early Years

I was born and raised at Black Spot Mountain, ten miles west of Piñon, Arizona. My mother, Alice Nez Robinson, belongs to the Edgewater (Tábąąhí) Clan while my father, Juan Robinson, is from the Water Flowing Together Mexican Branch (Tó Aheedlíinii Naakai dine'é) Clan. My mother's father was of the Rock Gap People (Tsédeeshgiizhnii) and was a very good man whom I got to know well as he shared his teachings and gave me guidance. On my father's side his father, Levi, was from the Red Cheek People (Tł'ááshchí'í). He went to school back east where he received a Christian name from the Bible. Eventually, he went to college in Pennsylvania and became a well-educated person who, when he returned, was the only Navajo in our area that spoke English. My father also went to school out there and became well-educated. My paternal grandmother was Selma Many Beads, but her Navajo name was Woman with a White Horse (Asdzą́ą́ Bilį́į́' Łigai), and she raised my father. Little did I realize that I was being taught and trained by a number of different families, until one day when I was a young boy, I woke up during a ceremony as people were singing. I remember suddenly my eyes opened. I do not know what age I was, but it seemed like I had been raised in ceremonies all my life. Every time one was held, I would sit with my grandmother and she would tell me not to go outside, not to look around, to leave the other children alone, and to remain in the hogan.

*The Healers—objects used in the Blessingway. This ceremony is considered the
"backbone" of all other rites and is used to invoke positive blessings. The elements
in this basket connect and invite the holy beings to enrich and protect the lives of
the People. (Photo by Kay Shumway)*

Until about the age of nine I went to school and learned western ways
and enjoyed being with other children. I lived with grandmother for some
time, then eventually returned to my mother and father. My family and
grandparents all lived in the same camp, with maybe fifty yards between
dwellings. They raised me and my brothers and sisters together as a closely
knit group. As I grew older, I attended boarding school in Piñon, then Chinle
and Many Farms, where I finished eighth grade, then on to Brigham City,
Utah, from 1970 to 1974. Whenever I was home, my father took great care
to teach all of us about the ceremonies. I started singing with him around the
age of thirteen and really learned a lot up to high school when I had to leave.
Dad died in the mid-1970s; I lost a very effective teacher. After finishing my
first year at Utah State University, the military draft called upon me to serve,
so I chose the United States Marines. Boot camp in San Diego launched my
three years in the Corps before returning home. While stationed in
California, I began drinking and smoking, two habits that led to strong
addictions and a downward spiral in life—only the bottle mattered. At the
end of my three-year enlistment, I returned to the reservation and brought

my bad habits with me. For thirteen years I lived as an alcoholic, offending family members and friends, who viewed with sadness the stark changes that now consumed my life. There seemed to be no hope as I lived on the edge of my family circle.

One day, as I staggered down the mile-long dirt road that led to my mother's home, I noticed how all of my brothers and sisters began to leave. I became increasingly angry at their departure so that by the time I reached her hogan, only my mother was there to hear my complaints. I unloaded, accusing family members of feeling they were so much better than me; I knew they were really the problem. Why did they treat me this way? My mother drew in her breath and told me—for the last time—that I was not living up to my destiny. In her words: "We are supposed to be special people on this earth—but look at you—there is nothing special here." She hated my drinking all the time and said, "Look. You are doing this to yourself, but everybody is asking you not to; they don't like you drinking and they don't want to listen to you. That's why they take off."

She was thinking about her experience when she was pregnant with me and was feeling keen disappointment. "Sit down, eat, then go to bed and go to sleep." She was angry about the whole thing and I felt defensive. "Mom," I said, "why did you bring me into this world? Is there a reason?" She replied, "Even if I tell you the reason, you'll never get it. You are playing stupid. I have talked to you for many years and you still don't listen to me. This is the last time I'm going to tell the story. I don't know what you're going to do with it." She told of being a young woman who had given birth to my brother two years previous. Now she was getting ready to deliver me, but she was very sick and had lost a lot of weight. My father had a number of ceremonies performed, but she was dying, a fact she had finally accepted. Mother spoke to my father saying, "The kids are going to grow up with me gone, so divide up all of my animals and give them to the children. You take care of these boys this way."

My father did not like this talk, and although she expected to die and did not want any more ceremonies, he encouraged her to have just one more. She told Perry, "I lay there and could not walk, get up, eat, or do anything. I lost all of my energy and had grown very skinny." Soon my father returned from Kayenta with an old man; my mother was angry and disappointed for wasting her animals and his money for an impossible cure. "I'm ready to die, and so why try after all the others have failed? Nothing works. Just let him go home and leave him alone," but my father refused. "No. I think this is a real medicine man, and this is what I want." The ceremony started that night and went into the morning and then the evening. Around midnight, the medicine man told my mother to sit up and drink some herbs in water. He put corn pollen on top of it and pronounced that she would live. "When you drink this, you will conceive again; vomit into this bowl, but from the medicine you drink you will receive a child. He will be a special young man who will take care of you. He will be a medicine man and will know everything important in this family and about all of the medicine—everything." My mother sat there, looked at the elder and said, "You must be crazy. I'm not going to live. I'm not going to get well. This is just another medicine drink. People have done more than this before; you are just a simple person trying to give me something." Still, she drank it but said she knew the man was lying.

Turning to me she repeated, "I know what I see today. That man talked about somebody special, but look at you. Are you special? You used to be to me, but now you're drunk. You're an alcoholic. You're nobody. You are wasting your life away. This is your story. You're supposed to be a special person and look at you. You're not even that person, so I don't know what you're going to do with the story, but here it is. I knew that medicine man was lying to me back then and I know the lying was about today."

Epiphany

This account really hit me. That night I couldn't sleep. I could hear my grandfather singing all night. That song was in my ears, my father's songs were in my ears, all night long I heard them singing but do not recall how many of these medicine songs I actually listened to. I sat up the whole night. The next morning I felt different and actually stopped using alcohol from that day forward. I never touched it again; I never bothered with it and became serious about our home and the life we were living. Soon I moved out of my mother's house to stay in my own hogan nearby. It was dirty, and she questioned why I would want to move over there. I was undeterred, washed the whole thing down, swept out all of the spider webs, built a fire, and moved my possessions into it. Every night I spent praying the old words my grandfather used to say. I knew the prayers and songs well.

How many nights this went on, I do not know, but many of the teachings and songs began to come back to me. It took about a week for my family to recognize the significant change that was taking place and to inquire as to what was going on with me. "He's not even going to the store, drinking, or anything like that. He's still around here." Now they started worrying that I might be sick—something was wrong with me. My sister even visited and asked, "Are you okay?"

"What do you mean?"

"You're not drinking today. What's wrong with you?"

Then I got mad and scolded, "Can't you let me be sober for a while? How do you guys see me when I am sober?" I realized that people were really looking at me; I got so angry that now I was determined to turn their minds completely around, so that all they could see was a good person.

Understanding traditional teachings and Navajo medicine was the answer. I attended every ceremony held around our community and began assisting in any way possible. I was the first to show up before things started, I helped the medicine men, then I moved on to the next ceremony and the next. Pretty soon I was all over Piñon, helping everybody as people inquired, "What's going on with this man; he is all over the place, singing with everybody." There were four medicine people in particular who really liked the way I helped them, and so every time they held a ceremony, they came by my house, picked me up, and took me with them to perform five-night sings. I was young, my voice deep and loud, and people liked that. Some medicine people just lay back and let me sing all night for them, then shared some of the objects given as pay; I actually started making money doing this.

My understanding of ceremonies and traditional teachings grew rapidly during this time. Grandfather, a master priest, and my father both taught me The Skulls That Came Home Branch of the Evilway. I also learned the Enemyway (Anaa'jí or Naayéé'ee bee bijí—Protectionway), the Blessingway, and the Male Lightningway, which is often attached to the Evilway and combined with it in a ceremony. My mother practiced the Yellow or Chiricahua Windway (Chíshí Biníłch'ijí). I do a portion of that ceremony, the part associated with the herbs, but I cannot do the entire night performance. I also perform the Lifeway (Iináájí K'ehgo) and Knifeway (Béézhee k'ehgo) ceremonies, which help patients in a coma to revive. There are a lot of other smaller ceremonies that are attached to these larger, more complex performances. For instance, I do five different types of smoke ceremony, various kinds of offerings, and four different types of illness diagnosis—hand trembling, crystal/star gazing, listening, and looking into the coals of a fire. So when it was time for me to leave home, I was well prepared, although I continue to learn to this day.

For five years (I was about thirty-five by this time) I practiced traditional medicine and saw a lot of change in my life. One day my grandfather was sitting outside and away from the house all by himself. I walked over to him, sat down, and asked what he was doing. "I'm gathering my thoughts. You sit here, close your eyes, listen to the wind and everything that is around you. The bird calls and other sounds will tell you stories. Try it." I sat down and soon heard hummingbirds flying around me. I opened my eyes and there was one right on my forehead trying to peck on me. I saw its beauty, heard its humming, and felt the high vibration of its feathers and body right in my face. There was another bird near grandfather's face, but it

The Protectors—just as the Blessingway works to restore good things, this Evilway medicine bundle keeps bad influences away. Evil fears arrowheads, dislikes the smell of certain desert plants, departs with the sound of a bullroarer, and hates the power summoned in a buffalo tail rattle. The miscellaneous rocks are put in an herbal solution that the patient drinks. Each ceremony has its own set of equipment to cure specific problems. (Photo by Winston Hurst)

was not moving. He said, "Leave it alone. Don't bother with it; just close your eyes." We sat there and he began singing; the soothing sound really touched me as grandfather chanted, "A beautiful thing hovers over my body (yiską́ą́ danaayééł yiską́ą́ danaayééł yiską́ą́ danaayééł)." My emotions struck me from head to toe and I started to really cry. I wept uncontrollably, until he said, "You're alright now. The gods are ready for you. I want you to go northwest with your pack and belongings. White Shell Woman will be there waiting for you. You will know it when you get there so go, follow your mother."

Walking the Medicine Path

Not knowing for sure where I was to travel, I packed my little knapsack and started hitchhiking north, ending up in Page, Arizona. I got a job as a construction worker at the power plant, but again my life shifted. I met my wife there, as if she had been waiting for me. She changed my world, gave me a home, and I started practicing medicine full time. I began helping alcoholics overcome their addiction. Every time I performed a ceremony, my wife and I did it together with the families, talking and singing and telling stories about how the creators saw some of these things that were happening around these people. The learned negative behavior was addressed through traditional teachings that came together as we met and talked with each other as a family. I wanted to be that person that was supposed to be specially gifted as a medicine man, and sure enough, good things started to happen.

One day I was invited by a detoxification center to attend a sweat lodge meeting with a group of people from the Page community. It was a dome-shaped canvas Plains-Indian-type structure, not a Navajo sweat lodge. This detox center had rounded up people from the previous night and was holding them for twenty-four hours to sober them up before being released. Some of the participants were still drunk; there was no structure for teaching, helping, or controlling them; and many would just come and go as they saw fit. I did not like what I saw. Many of the people, some of whom were white men, were sobering up; others were Navajos drumming and singing Native American Church (NAC) songs. They invited me to join them and appreciated that although I was a medicine man, I had gone through recovery just as they needed to do. I sat by the doorway as the drum went around the circle, but it eventually reached me, which meant it was my turn to sing. I told them that I was not a NAC member and only sang Navajo songs. They still wanted me to sing, and so I put the drum aside and sang some of my traditional songs. Everyone became emotional and asked me to continue. I began to share some of the beliefs that go with these songs, then told them, "Okay, this is not the way you do a sweat lodge. You need to clean some of the blood off your face, wash it, get sober, and respect this." I started talking to them just like a grandfather would, and they really backed off. "There's a teaching behind these songs and we are supposed to be special people on this earth. Born as men, there is a purpose in life and a reason for our existence. We are not supposed to drink, play around, or abuse ourselves. Everything has to be done in a good way. Everybody has to be holy and respectful."

The man in charge of this group liked what I was saying and the direction the meeting had taken, so he asked me to come back the next weekend. That Friday when I returned, the participants were now clean. We started talking about cleanliness and how we could sit straight and act politely. The drumming was too loud and not good for the ears, and so it went outside where people were welcomed to drum all they wanted, but not inside the sweat lodge. I started teaching rules and practices used by the Navajo Nation Medicine Men Association, so that people would not do their own thing. Structure for these meetings started to evolve, which the people appreciated. Soon the director attending the meeting asked me to come and work with him in his organization as an employee of the Medicine Men Association. The people changed their ways. We altered how things happened in the community so that participants felt better about themselves, while the program providers appreciated the structure. Soon I had a job as a traditional spokesperson, which, three years later, turned into a traditional counseling position sponsored by the Navajo Nation Medicine Men Association. This organization issued a license for me to practice.

I developed my own curriculum from the stories and teachings of the old ways of the people long ago—how they talked about depression, feelings about anxiety, and fear of the unknown. Meditation and prayer and making offerings helped them to let go of inner turmoil and begin to recover. The people liked having traditional services, while the program directors saw its effectiveness in healing the effects of alcoholism. The next step for the patients was to recognize who they were and where they had come from. Most of them remembered their grandfathers and grandmothers as they were growing up. These elders had talked about the good way and healing through ceremonies, but as children these men and women had never grasped the ceremonies' power. They had lived too much fast life in this Glittering World and forgotten their old ways. The curriculum addressed these gaps by talking about the old people and how they used to teach, and by reflecting on the patient's younger years when listening to how grandmother and grandfather used to say things. Those attending these sessions really understood what was being offered and liked it.

Next, they took up writing. Topics varied from traditional practices that they had left behind to autobiographical sketches to why they started drinking to things that they wondered about and wanted to learn. I would tell them that now they were in a treatment center and needed to use their life experience and reflect on the fact that today was the crossroads of their life. They had a past, but there was also a future; today was how they feel about and plan for the next day. "Where do I want to go and how is my life going to be? Where are my children? What is my family doing? What do they want me to be like?" This helped the people in the treatment center to realize that they needed to stop drinking and start thinking, observing, and obeying the red stop signs of life. I used things from western society, too, like the red, yellow, and green traffic lights that remind us when it is safe to move forward and when it is important to halt at certain points in life.

Mostly I used elements from nature and Navajo culture. For instance, I compared a person's life to that of a piñon tree. The small seed, one of many, falls to the ground where it is planted. In Navajo we call it "Turn Around White Corn Boy" (Naadą́' Áłgai La'í Náyoo'áłí Ashkii) because it was White Corn Pollen Boy who first arose through the ground and emerged into this new world. With the proper nurturing of soil, sunshine, moisture, and protection, the seed grows. At first it was small and weak, but as it learned to withstand the storms, intense temperatures, and droughts of life, it became tougher and more solid. Now the tree stands in the air straight and tall, and deeply rooted in the ground, looking back, to recognize that all of the challenges it faced allowed it to become what it is today—one that bears fruit, gives shade for others, provides seeds of its own, and is useful for many things—food, shelter, warmth, healing, and beauty. People have similar opportunities to become just as useful in their own way, depending upon where they are planted.

Sometimes I would say, "There's a twisted branch that goes in a circle where my life started to turn" or "two branches went separate ways and everything just died." Somebody would respond, "I had a divorce right there, it seemed like my life was over, and we went our separate ways." But at the end there were still green patches of leaves, sitting on the tip of the branch with a promise of life. A lot of people describe the yucca plant as their way of defending themselves socially. They do not want people to come close and so use their sharp points to keep them at a distance. We often took trips away from the city and into the country to have those healing observe. "Look around. Look around. Look at all of these plants. Look at the trees. Which one resembles your life?" Then they would sit there and write or draw about it before coming together to discuss what they had done and to talk about their lives. We listened to each other. When we finished, they would take their pictures or writings back to their rooms or homes to remind them of their thoughts. A lot of the therapy I did centered around the growth of a tree from the root all the way out to the branches and the leaves, its colors, and use. But whether a tree or yucca plant or stories from life—each had its own way of explaining how we see ourselves.

This was the kind of work I did with the people. We would also go into a sweat lodge, pull the blankets over the doorway, and sit in darkness. This is how a blind man feels. To emphasize this in another way, we sometimes put blindfolds on a person and walked with them for maybe four hours, building in them the trust that they were going to the right place with the right help. These experiences were then tied into the four main elements of life as one enters a sweat lodge. A person sits upon the *earth*, breathes in the *air* heated by *fire*, which causes *water* through sweat. All four of these basic elements combine to direct one's thoughts toward the heat and the darkness that clean the body and purify the mind. Sitting in a dark circle and trying to deal with that heat, darkness, and turmoil within helps one express thoughts about enduring life's problems. They can be as hot as the sweat lodge, and just as dark and scary.

The Navajo sweat lodge, involving the four main elements of life—earth, air, fire, and water—is a primary classroom for teaching traditional knowledge. In the dark, one's eyes are opened; through the heat, one is hardened; and with songs and prayer a person is spiritually lifted.

Although there may be other people present, it is the individual who undergoes the process, who turns the mind toward the sacredness of life. Indeed, the sweat lodge is an example of what life is like. People may feel alone, under tremendous pressure, with some things too hard to bear, and a heat that seems endless. But it soon will conclude, allowing a person to move into the sunlight, drink cool water, examine their experience, and obtain a different view, new thoughts, and focused direction. Now one can see more clearly things in the distance that would never have been visible alone in the dark.

Our eyes are often distracted looking at things. There is too much color, too much light that pulls our thinking away from where we come from without realizing that the darkness is the teacher of the blind man. When you cannot see something, you cannot judge it. But you have a set of ears that will teach you to listen and discover who enters the room. What you hear gives you direction and guides you to safety. This way, we have two different perspectives—one from daylight, the other from night. These are actually two separate ways that do their own teaching—one from darkness, the other from light.

This is how I started working with people and developing curriculum suitable for a young man or woman. These things are not written in a book but instead are about thinking and putting thoughts together in our own manner. In the traditional way we would fall back to our elders, our family— father, mother, grandmother, grandfather—who have these same teachings. I hoped our patients would go home and talk to their elders about where they came from, how they were born, and what purposes they may have in life. We cannot blame our mother and father for our life. One day a young man, complaining about how his parents had put him up for adoption, came in and was crying about how he did not feel loved and had just been passed around from family to family. I explained how we learn from firsthand experience, one of our greatest teachers, and how he could become a good counselor because of his life. After much discussion, the young man understood that he, too, could make a difference and began feeling good about himself. This is what I discovered during my own recovery and how I learned in a traditional manner.

With these thoughts and the help of my supervisor, we put a treatment plan together based solely on traditional teachings, but cross-referenced to practices in the dominant society. For example, I made my own twelve-step treatment plan for Navajos that paralleled a similar Anglo program to combat alcohol and its effects. The ideas came easily and the patients readily understood the concepts offered in traditional thought. The program, offered by the Rainbow Bridge Treatment Center starting in 1997, grew substantially, and the Navajo Nation endorsed our efforts and added different certification programs. The Nation began hiring a lot of medicine people for this and similar programs. The first group of Navajo medicine men was hired into the program, and I was one of the first people on the board of the Department of Human Health Services. There had been a previous group in a different department that was using traditional teachings, so what this new organization did was refine, improve, and enlarge the number of Navajo cultural teachings.

For over fifteen years I worked at the Rainbow Bridge Treatment Center until the money ran out and I was transferred to the Chinle Adolescent Treatment Center for five years. I then filled an opening in Shiprock at an outpatient treatment center for adults where I worked for eight years until I retired from the Navajo Nation in 2016. I like to stay busy, and so I began employment with the Utah Navajo Health System (UNHS) as a mental health worker and practicing medicine man on staff.

Teaching from the Past to Preserve the Future

I am concerned about the future of practicing medicine men on the reservation. For twenty-four years I have belonged to the Navajo Nation Medicine Men Association and have worked with people from a second similar organization, the Diné Hataałii Association. Both of these groups accept young men who want to apprentice as medicine men, assist in specific ceremonies, and eventually become independent practitioners. I volunteered to be a trainer, and money was available for both the teacher and the student, but I never had an applicant. There were relatively few that signed on for the training, and although there is a need for younger practitioners, not many make the effort or take the time to learn what is necessary.

Even Diné College, owned and operated by the tribe in Tsaile, Arizona, has its problems. To me, the teachings there are a collection of different practices and thoughts from a variety of places. Those on staff try to cram a lot of ceremonial knowledge together to make it one thing, to provide a single explanation. When medicine men look at it from their perspective, it does not make sense or fit. Knowledge is mixed between male and female versions of a ceremony, teachings from the eastern side of the reservation are mixed with those from the western, and everything is bunched together. Many years ago, Navajo people were afraid that they were going to lose these ceremonies and so there were a lot of interviews done to preserve practices. The story from one place became mixed with another story from a different area and then was crammed together so that they no longer made sense. The interviewer should have just stuck with one medicine person and kept those teachings separate. What is being taught now and is found in books does not sound right. So I question a lot about what is being done, but stay away from the controversy, sticking to the things I learned from my father and grandfather. One time grandfather told me not to worry about how other people were taught. "Don't waste your time," he said, "because if you are practicing medicine the wrong way, it tends to come back and bite you in the butt and the patient will not be healed."

Three years ago, I was involved in a school-wide counseling issue in Red Mesa High School that illustrates what happens when teachings are mixed and the situation, culture, and people are misunderstood. A high school student with a bright future committed suicide. He was well known and now missed by the students and faculty who were very upset with the loss. The school hired a Native American counselor from another tribe and unfamiliar with traditional Navajo teachings to soothe the situation. He talked about the spirits that have left this world, how they are still present and can be contacted, and other things the students did not understand. The medicine wheel, a Plains Indian object, and four directional colors different from those of the Navajo added to the confusion. As part of the assembly held in the gym, he had students sit in chairs, pretending they were involved in a bus collision that killed them. They fell off their chairs as part of the crash then were pronounced dead. Rather than teaching how to cope with death, the students and parents became deeply disturbed and confused. The role playing caused everyone to react to events and thoughts better left alone. The teaching points were incredibly inappropriate for Navajos given their traditional beliefs about death while also failing to deliver a comforting message about suicide. People started crying and questioning what was being taught. The first day of reconciliation turned into a disaster and the second day was worse. Word spread that the whole experience was counterproductive and so many counselors from the Navajo Nation's Department of Mental Health were called in to stabilize the situation.

I arrived on the second day when there were already a lot of counselors present, but they were having difficulty teaching the parents and students. Everyone was still upset and arguing about the problem. Even the counselors were not agreeing among themselves how to best approach the circumstances, and so they asked me to help out. I sat down with the people and talked to them about the holy ones and how those who live on this earth leave behind teachings and a way of life that we still carry on. Those who have died are not forgotten or totally gone. There are two sets of spirits—those who have left this world and those who are living here now. We cannot put them together as we live here on this earth, but we can still benefit from their having been here. Those who have left this world go to the stars in the heavens but come out at night to guide us. This belief comes from the old people's stories about how the first person died, left this world, and became Big Star or the Morning Star, who gives a lot of guidance and direction. There were others in the constellations—the three wise men sitting and guiding us—In the Mesa Big Path Coming Down (Tsébii'asdáátso), In the Mesa Path Coming Down (Tsébii'adááts'ozí), and Mesa Man (Hastiin Tséłkanii). The story is told of how other stars in the night sky are children who have gone before, and behind them are these three beings watching and guiding the youth as they run ahead. This is how most of the stars are set in this manner. Those people who have left this world share their teaching with the three and assist medicine people who request their help. The children running in front of the three wise ones are stars (sǫ') and represent the spirits of all the young people who have had an early death. They have become holy ones who visit the people on earth in the evening so that they can sleep and receive guidance. I shared a lot of these teachings.

Each person learns to walk by himself. What one makes out of life is up to oneself. Just as this silversmith will melt those silver dollars, then mold, hammer, stamp, smooth, and polish the metal to form an object of beauty, so, too, should each person take great care to create a good life.

Next, we talked about how people are given a full, long life if they live according to the guidance and potential provided by the holy people. There are, however, plenty of things that one can do to shorten it—everything from diet to danger. There are also individuals—parents, counselors, teachers, police—available to help guide someone during troubled times. As one moves through a shattered past to a positive future, we learn and hope through growth and change. Life will be different, constantly shifting—our homes will change, people move from winter camp to summer camp, somebody else is going to put in a cornfield where not expected then say, "This is not how we used to plant, but this is the way we're doing it now." Sometimes the young people do not understand the teachings of the elders, but as they grow older, the ideas become clearer. They put it together. Soon they will have their own stories of how they see things. Change is really a gift given to the people.

Another gift is the two brains we have. One is left and male, the other is right and female. We have two eyeballs, two ears, two nostrils, two sets of teeth, two arms, and two legs, each of which is either male or female. Life was given to us in this manner with a set of each. If these senses and tools are used correctly, you will go far and learn self-control. Your mother and father gave all of these gifts to you. Whether they are here today or gone to the spirit world, we are still enjoying what they have provided. Every time we use any of them, there is a lesson to learn about what to do or not to do to avoid being hurt. Elders would say, "You are the one who is going to walk this earth with nobody to hold your hand, to guide you this way or that, to tell you to wash your face, put on your clothes, and what to wear. You will make the choices. So you choose your own ways with your eyeballs to see what colors you want; you listen to things, smell and taste food. You live on this earth because you are Changing Woman's son or daughter, and you will change every day. Your feelings are going to be different from yesterday to today; you will make up your mind and then reverse the decision. That is because you are Changing Woman's children. When I say, 'It's going to be up to us to make these changes' (t'áá hó ájít'éego), we have to learn to walk by ourselves. You will see your enemies out there, but if you take a hard look at them and figure them out, you will learn from them. You will learn from other people who say, 'This is what's not done; this was how it was said; that's how the song goes.' Listening to that is how we learn, grow, and change."

By the end of the session we talked more about ourselves and our outlook. Navajo people frame such thought within relationships (k'é), which includes everything from shaking hands to being a part of a clan to introducing oneself. When a person dies, that relationship continues through their stories, teachings, and property. For instance, a medicine man will talk about how his grandfather or father taught him by saying, "My grandfather used to be this way and he always taught this" or after singing a song would finish with, "This song was sung by my grandfather a long time ago. He's not here anymore, but I sing his song today." Everything relates back to our lineage and legacy, it is not forgotten. This is how I explained the effects of life and death. The people found it comforting and shared a common perspective that encouraged recalling good memories, thoughts, and the use of objects of those who had died. What they left raises a person to the next level and enriches their life.

The people in the gym that day agreed with and understood these teachings about the connection between life and death. We talked about good things and how we had good days ahead with new ways. As in the ceremonies, we talked about spring, new flowers, and a positive future. New goals, with beautiful songs that go with them, are waiting for us. This is the way to talk about life. We all used the medicine that way and departed with hope. Everything was cooled, and the people liked that.

I always talk about my grandfather and father. Nothing that I have learned to this day comes from my own knowledge, but from my grandfather, grandmother, and father. All of their teachings, tools, and medicine bundles were passed to the next generation. I give them credit by saying, "This is my grandfather's tool, my father's tool, and his father's tool." I remember back only to the fourth generation, but wish I could go further. The memories I have sit there and make me feel good to carry on this medicine. My life is integrated with my relatives from the past. They may be gone, but I carry their life and walk with them through their stories and prayers today.

CHAPTER TWO

Interacting with the Holy People

undamental to Navajo life is interaction with the holy people (haashch'ééh, diné diyinii, and Yé'ii). In this chapter there are four elements introduced in this relationship—the gods, their language, its transmission, and the power derived from it. Each is a complex topic in its own right. Take, for instance, the pantheon of the holy people. There are dozens and dozens of beings that are responsible for many different aspects of life, the functioning of the world, and everything within it. They control the power to heal and the ability to destroy, have their own personal likes and dislikes, share a relationship with other gods both male and female, possess human frailties, and provide wisdom to counsel. Perhaps the best way to understand their wide-ranging abilities and character is to take one, say Talking God (Haashch'ééyáłti'í), who is considered the first and grandfather of the others, and discuss the qualities and responsibilities that he holds.

Talking God is the leader of the holy people. He lives in the east and works with others residing in that direction, controls the dawn, eastern sky, and the growing of corn. As the senior mentor to other holy beings, he is also paired with his brother, Calling God (Haashch'éé'ooghan), who inhabits the west. According to anthropologist Gladys Reichard, Talking God says, "I pity all the people on the earth," and so is considered one of the kinder, more sympathetic holy beings.[1] He is also the only one who can be everywhere; he is invoked in most ceremonies and travels on rainbows or sunbeams. His main rite is the Nightway (Tł'éé'jí), which cures people who are losing their eyesight or hearing, or who have mental disorders or paralysis. He wears a mask made of unwounded buckskin sewn together with the right side holding female power and the left male. The mask is colored with white clay as is the body of its wearer, which along with the green spruce necklace worn below the mask, represent the earth and its forces. Painted on the hide is a stalk of corn that extends from where his nose would be to his forehead; his lips are painted yellow, symbolizing corn pollen and the holy words he speaks. Yet he does not talk while among humans but uses the distinctive call of "wuuhú"; for a person to speak while wearing the mask is comparable to committing suicide. Thus Talking God is a powerful being involved in many aspects of traditional culture as a leader of the diné diyinii.

Language was one of the most important gifts given by the holy people. When Navajos say, "Diyin Dine'é bizaad bee yádeelti'"—"We talk the holy people's language," they mean it. From a fluent speaker's perspective, the language provides a glimpse into a very different worldview and means of expression. Much of what follows is derived from anthropologist Gary Witherspoon's groundbreaking analysis of the Navajo language. One of his basic premises is this: "Knowledge is the awareness of symbol, thought is the organization of symbol, speech is the externalization of symbol, and compulsion is the realization of symbol. Symbol is word, and word is the means by which substance is organized."[2] To understand this complex statement, one must start where all Navajo explanations begin, with the creation.

Navajo teachings say that the People emerged into this, the Fifth or Glittering World, from four worlds beneath this one. Each of the previous spheres had a color—black, blue, yellow, and white—and a name—First, Second, Third, and Fourth Language, each of which had three subdivisions of speech, making a total of twelve language levels in all. Each level had its own forms of communication, each went from a simpler to more complex pattern, as did the forms of the inhabitants in each world—insects, birds, animals, and holy people. Once these beings arrived in today's world, First Man ordered a structure to be built large enough to hold the gods, including First Woman, First Boy, First Girl, and others, to help plan for the future. Coyote, the trickster, remained on the edge by the door and did not participate until much of the thinking was finished and patterns for this world were established. The seasons of the year, phases of plant growth and animal life, forms of precipitation, heavenly bodies, illness and cures, and every other aspect by which the earth surface people (humans) should live were part of this plan.[3]

While specifics vary in different versions of this teaching—colors of the worlds, role of Coyote and other participants, and so on, because of the oral tradition—all agree that there was a definite sequence within the process that moved from awareness to thought to word to reality or creation. The end result was, according to Reichard, a "Navajo dogma [that] connects all things, natural and experienced, from man's skeleton to universal destiny, which encompasses even inconceivable space, in a closely interlocked unity which omits nothing, no matter how small or how stupendous."[4] In simpler terms, everything was connected because the holy people designed it that way, the primary means of which was through language. Song and prayer, preceded by thought, created all.

Navajo language reaches its greatest power in ritual and ceremony. Through prayer and song, thought becomes concrete, the creation of the world and the control of power are exercised, and order achieved. In the Anglo world, with a few exceptions found in Christian dogma, words are merely a means of expression, not a way to control supernatural power. The opposite is true here. "In the Navajo view of the world, language is not a mirror of reality; reality is a mirror of language. . . . It commands, compels, organizes, transforms, and restores. It disperses evil, reverses disorder, neutralizes pain, overcomes fear, eliminates illness, relieves anxiety, and restores order, health, and well-being."[5] Conversely language, when used or directed with evil intent, can create chaos and ugliness.

Power is at the foundation of both good and evil. These two qualities are inseparable, for they are rooted in the same source. Like electricity, this power can be used to bless and protect the lives of others or curse and destroy those targeted for harm. Each person has within a desire for self-protection, but when this ability is taken to extremes, it can become evil and can be used to destroy others.[6] Language becomes the means that directs how the power is to be used. A phrase common in prayer is "the tip of my tongue. [This] symbolizes 'my speech' and means 'may I have the power to speak all necessary words of formula, prayer, and song in proper order.' By implication it means also 'may my speech be so controlled that I will not say anything not needed or use words which may attract evil or danger.'"[7] Through ritual the holy people are compelled to participate, in either good or evil, bound by the sacredness and contractual ties of speech.

In summarizing the role of language in the Navajo universe, Witherspoon returns to the previously mentioned premise of knowledge, thought, speech, and action or realization, when he writes: "The holy people first became aware of things through their symbols and then later went into the sweathouse and organized these symbols through thought processes. Next the organized symbols were spoken in prayer and sung in song. Through these songs and prayers, the inner forms of things were organized and controlled; that is, they were told where to go, how to position themselves, and what functions to fulfill."[8] But the means by which prayers and thoughts are transmitted are through the Holy Wind (Níłch'ih), comparable in many respects to Christian beliefs of the Holy Ghost. This important holy being participates with humans in two different ways. In Navajo thought it can be personified just as the Holy Ghost is, an incorporeal personality who warns, guides, teaches, and protects an individual facing danger. The second belief is that it can serve as a medium to transmit information, similar in some ways to radio waves—an invisible, powerful means of communication. The word itself is interpreted variously as Holy Wind, Little Wind, wind, air, breeze, or spirit.[9] While some people speak of nítch'ih as a very slight breeze, there is no mistaking it for níyol, another name for wind. The former is strongly associated with spiritual communication, while the latter is much more physical and does not transmit messages from the holy people. Thus, níyol is what one feels blowing against one's face, while nítch'ih speaks to a person. Indeed, without this Holy Wind, there would be no life. Teachings describe how, at the time of creation, the first people had no wind in them, so they were weak. Then different colored winds—black, blue, yellow, and white—came from the four directions and entered the bodies of humans and animals, "giving strength to men ever since for this was nature's first food and it put motion and change into everything, even into the mountains and water."[10]

A medicine man utilizes power derived from ritual knowledge. Unlike Christianity, which views the universe as a struggle between two cosmic forces—God versus Satan, good versus evil, light against darkness—power to the Navajo is neutral until one chooses to use it either for good or bad. The results can be both spiritually intangible and physically visible. For practitioners it is as real as any tangible object. The Navajo name for the ability to summon and use spiritual forces—"álílee k'ehgo"—means literally "according to supernatural/magical power." It is the energy by which things are done supernaturally. For instance, Jesus walking on water, withering a fig tree, and raising the dead, or a Navajo skinwalker (witch) running at superhuman speeds or a medicine man performing a miraculous cure are all examples of a divine ability to control this force through words. This power is not discussed or flaunted, while its existence is recognized with reverence.[11]

This is a difficult concept for those coming from a science tradition to accept. Personal experiences of white traders working on the Navajo Reservation are filled with accounts of things that are totally unexplainable from an Anglo worldview. For example, different forms of divination—hand trembling, crystal gazing, wind listening, star gazing—have been used successfully on behalf of white men, even a few anthropologists, who have confirmed their accurate ability to look at events in the past, present, and future. This topic is discussed in detail in another chapter. Perry mentions trying to move a coal through concentration and mental power. Here are two other examples that testify how Navajos use this force, while others are found throughout this trilogy. First, Navajo Oshley told of a time he had a dispute over a woman married to Old Teacher, a potent medicine man. After besting the man physically, Oshley went home still afraid of his opponent's supernatural power and its ability to harm. Oshley recounts, "That evening something hit my toes, and just as I said, 'Paah!' something hit hard against the door. The next morning I went to look for my beautiful spotted horse and found it dead."[12] He went to his mother who used hand trembling to determine that Old Teacher was at the bottom of the problem, trying to even the score. She also told Oshley that he had "felt and heard something, which was true. . . . This event happened."

Trader Gladwell Richardson, living at Inscription House, witnessed a second example of this power. He tells of a Navajo hermaphrodite named Loolo who had been raised to perform witchcraft against those who opposed her. Loolo became known for her abilities, and so others approached her to use them on their behalf. A man who had been witched asked her to destroy the person who had pronounced the curse. She performed the ceremony that Richardson observed, reporting, "During the praying, Loolo placed a miniature strung bow between the feet of the carefully drawn man-figure. On the buckskin string of the bow she dropped a tiny white bead. The chanting and drumming grew into a mighty crescendo then ended abruptly. Had I not been close and gazing directly down at the bead, I would never have believed what followed. The instant that the sound stopped, the tiny white bead jumped from the bowstring and landed on the neck of the man-figure in the sandpainting. Should I live to be a thousand years old, I shall never forget it."[13] Loolo pronounced that the targeted individual who had performed the initial witchcraft would soon die from a broken neck; within a week he had. While these examples are concerned with the use of negative power, there are many others that are positive, including divination, healing, and protection.

The Holy People

Talking God (Haashch'ééyáłti'í) is always the first or main god who is out in front and is considered the grandfather of all of the other gods. He and his brother, Calling God (Haashch'éé'ooghaan), work together. When my grandfather taught in the medicine way, he said that no one really spoke about the Navajo creation, but only about the four sacred worlds through which the people emerged. But he taught about the actual creation and how Talking God became part of this earth. These teachings come from the Coyoteway (Ma'ii ná'ooljilí) and tell of how a god lived in darkness when there was no world but only a black mist. This information from the Coyoteway is now disappearing. The last person that ever really performed this ceremony and taught this information was Yellow Hair Horseman (Bitsiiga' Łigai Hólóní) or Palomino Man from Piñon. He had it recorded in a book called *Coyoteway: A Navajo Holyway Healing Ceremonial*.[14] Since he died, I do not think anybody else practices it.

There is a holy person, Goníłídí (no translation), who created everything, but he was not a humanlike god as were other Navajo deities. One day, he sat in the darkness and thought about what it would be like to put something together and how he could do it. After much meditating, praying, and singing, he suddenly felt very humble and started to cry. His emotions strengthened as two tears flowed from his eyes and down his cheeks, forming an identical pattern on his face. The tears reached the corners of his mouth where they joined his saliva. Together they flowed down to his chin where they merged. Just before the fluid dropped, Goníłídí placed his hand underneath it, catching the liquid in the center of his palm. He saw the wet spot in his hand, tossed the fluid in the air, started singing his song, and blew a little air on it. Slowly he breathed more air into it, causing it to spin and form something solid on top. This was not just the water but also a film that started spinning. He kept blowing and blowing as the object got bigger and bigger until finally, he let it go from his hand to rest in space. He continued to blow and sing about the sphere, which started to spin all by itself. As he watched his creation and sang it into existence, the ball turned blue, while the material on top appeared to be like greasy water, a thin film that grew ever larger.

Goníłídí stepped back and looked at what he had made. The orb expanded then suddenly stopped. Curious, the god said, "I want to go inside and see what this looks like." He entered into the circle of water, then started to notice that there were different types of air layered inside and out. They comprised the atmosphere of that world, beneath which was water and land. Both land and water had their own air and way of talking. The two came together and formed Talking God. Goníłídí charged Talking God to speak to him, and assigned him to be in charge as the god of this world. He was to sit in the east and move to the west each day and report what happened. "Just East to West and you will sit there and talk to me and you shall be known as Talking God as you oversee everything on this earth, to include life itself, new growth, and the things that happen. You will be responsible for what takes place and represent all that is on it, for you are the first god on this earth." He is also considered one of the Water People as well as one of the

Talking God is one of the leading deities in the Navajo pantheon. He is involved in most ceremonies, directs the other holy beings in their tasks, is generally kind to the earth surface people, and blesses those who abide by the laws established during the creation. (Drawing by Kelly Pugh)

Ground People and is able to communicate with all things sitting there. He is the one whose songs are powerful and can make things, explain what is happening, and give life through movement. That is how he sits.

As the first-created and grandfather of the other gods (diné diyinii), he had the responsibility to ratify the decisions that the other holy people made. They would first approach him and then he would say, "Let's sit down and talk about it." He would admit, "I don't know everything. I'm here. I can oversee a lot of things, but I want you to teach me what you are thinking as a god and talk to me. Then we will fix the problem and put a solution together." That is how the whole creation process started. It is not that he didn't know most of the answers, but he wanted the other gods to teach him about their thoughts. He encountered the black body god, the blue body, yellow body, and the white body so asked them, "Where do you come from? What was it like for you to be in those worlds beneath this one? Tell me stories about your experiences. Tell me what the birds are like from that world." Through these discussions, they were actually making plans and putting things together.

One of their major concerns was how to heal a person, asking what caused the sickness, where was it coming from, and was the issue in the physical body or in a person's thoughts or inner feelings. Talking God counseled, "Through a lifetime, this is the way a man will teach another man to heal people, to put things together. This is how it's going to work." The holy people agreed that this was the way it should be. This is part of the reason today that many doctors and medicine men go back into a family's history to talk about what has happened previously to a person as a young child. They talk about it, then put together treatment plans in order for healing to begin. It was the holy people who established this pattern. When they first began to talk about healing, they built a shelter of juniper tree limbs placed in a circle (iłnáshjin hooghan) in a clockwise manner. The ends of the sticks and branches were not dug into the ground, but rested upon it, with the medicine people sitting in the middle to plan, just as when we are born. Then we go outside into the world where we make decisions and cause things to happen. Traditional Navajo planning always takes place in a circle like that.

Another holy person in Navajo beliefs that provides the means of communication throughout the world is called the Holy Wind (Níłch'ih). He acts similar to the Holy Ghost in Christian teachings. Everything communicates through this Holy Wind, who carries back to Talking God, through spiritual means, the sounds made by an object. Everything has a spirit and is able to speak in its own way. For instance, the wind makes sounds, the water has its splash, and the fire crackles and pops. As the fire burns, you not only feel the heat but also hear the thump and hissing as the wood is consumed. The same is true with running water and the blowing wind. Talking God also connects with the Holy Wind through the songs people sing as well as the other noises they make. The Holy Wind and Talking God are like brothers who merged together to make, send, and receive those sounds. Through the Holy Wind, Talking God understands and sits to gather information. When I sing a song from the Windway ceremony, he recognizes what I am saying and that I am looking for answers from the Windway teachings to cure an individual. But it is through the Holy Wind that the answers come.

Everything goes through the Holy Wind, but it can also answer you directly in your ear or in your heart. This being serves as a life force that keeps everything alive and functioning. For instance, the Holy Wind, fire, and water are all relatives. No one is higher than the other, but they live within each other as brothers and sisters. If you take the air out of a fire, what's going to happen? It is going to stop. If you take the air out of water, it will cease to be wet. So they are integrated like brothers and become holy ones together. That is something that a lot of people do not understand. Everything must be united with many elements working in tandem. For instance the Windway songs are not complete until the songs about water are added. You have to put the wind and water together to have the songs and ceremony make sense. That is how it works.

The grandfathers talked about how water came from the thunder. They said the black thunder was made in the north and was loud and boastful. He made himself known as he approached, forcing everyone to hear he was coming. "Watch out. Here I come. Be mindful that you put things away. I'm going to be coming through." That is what he says as he draws nearer, making a big, loud noise. He will run over things if they are not put away; he will take possessions from you as the storm comes in, as the waters flood and carry things away. There is no stopping any of his actions, and he will not wait. He's not afraid and will run over anything in his path. Thunder, with his big powers, has to be respected. The great force of water can do a lot of damage. We hear about hurricanes that do a lot of destruction in people's lives, showing how powerful storms can be. Some Navajos say that water is only good, that we have to survive on it, but it is also powerful and can be deadly. We live with both of these potentials in us, and that is why a lot of people are so mean and angry and misbehave. They are not using their potential for good correctly. In this manner the fire and the water are two brothers that were placed here for the people who have to decide how to use them. One has to be careful and think twice how to use their abilities. Elders say that they are the two most powerful elements and that if they are not stopped they can do a lot of damage. It does not matter whom it walks on; whatever it walks on, it will take.

Now when a storm is coming and the lightning throws itself all around, it may strike something dry and start a fire that could burn down an entire mountain's trees. As it makes its way burning and destroying, it will not stop for anything. This tremendous power is difficult to stop. But fire also cooks our food so we can eat. Before the food is ready, the fire has put its marking on what we swallow. What we do not understand is that we eat the fire itself through the markings left behind. Thus there is a correct way of eating that we should follow. Before you take anything cooked into your mouth there is a prayer offered, asking to give guidance to make you someone who is good and who will live life in a better way. The person praying asks for help, strength, and knowledge that can be used that day. "I'm going to use it this way. I'm going to swallow you and you will be part of my body. Make me strong. Make me a warrior, one who thinks twice about things because I have two eyes, two ears, two of everything including good and bad. Let me use this food for that purpose." That is how people are supposed to sit down and say a blessing on the food. Their prayer is to thank the Creator who put this food on the table. Asking that the food nourish us is a good way to eat and has been practiced for years. But a lot of us don't do that. We take the food for granted because it is right there in front of us, so we just eat it.

If you are angry while preparing or consuming food, you will just cause more of those feelings. Even for the person who provides food or cooks it, she must have a clean mind. This is what the elders used to say. If you are going to feed a lot of people, you have to have good thoughts to do it or else you are going to do a lot of damage. If you are sitting in the kitchen, throwing a fit and making a ruckus while fixing food, it is almost like preparing something that is poison then feeding it to the people. They are going to become like you and pass on the anger.

Talking God and his brother Calling God work with other holy people or Yé'ii. There are twelve other gods in each of four directions, and they are involved in the winter Yé'ii Bicheii dance and ceremony. For instance, the Black Body ones, the Blue Body ones, the Yellow Body, and the White Body, all represent the powers from their respective directions. One story tells of how Talking God lived with the twelve spiritual people in the east, the White Body People, who had a place of their own. There were another twelve that were blue and lived in the south, another twelve yellow gods who lived in the west, and another dozen black gods living to the north. Some from each direction were selected to represent their group and they merged together. All twelve of these holy people represent something and were selected to minister to this earth and oversee the land. For instance, one of these holy people in each of the directions is responsible for gravity, what we call in Navajo Ni' Yiyah Niizíní Yá Yiyah Niizíní. These holy people control the force that holds humans to the earth where the air sits, making sure they remain on the ground and are not flying about. These gods sit in the four directions and are responsible for this.

As we talk of other holy beings, it is important to know what their assignment is in the functioning of this world and where they are located. Thus there are forty-eight gods, twelve from each direction, when there is a Yé'ii Bicheii dance. The physical participants represent the gods from the direction from which they come, but there are always only twelve dancers. Even though these performers are humans, they represent these holy beings that are coming from a particular direction. The ceremony comes in with the holy people from all four directions, with Black God and Talking God always present. Just as dancers from all parts of the reservation are invited to participate, so too are the holy people from different directions. No matter how many come in, only twelve will dance, but the medicine and healing represent the direction and powers from which they come.

The twelve Yé'ii Bicheii dancers, usually associated with the nine-night Nightway ceremony, are the physical form of the holy people as they visit the Navajo. Each of the dancers has its assigned home in one of the cardinal directions, wears unique clothing and mask, and uses specific powers to bless those in need. Their white color represents holiness. (Courtesy Library of Congress—Photo 96721)

During the first night of the ceremony, those who are acting as Yé'ii Bicheii wear a medicine pouch on their left side, just as they do in the Enemyway ceremony. This is done to show that they are medicine people acting as gods. On the second night, when they don masks and cover themselves in white clay, the pouch is moved to the right side, showing that they have arrived at the middle of the ceremony and reached the highest level of spirituality. The dancers remain separate from others in the community, eat together but do not talk, and think about the gods. This is when the holy ones not only recognize them but are working with them during what is called the Finishing of the Ceremony. When people dress as holy beings and have placed the mask on their face, they are not supposed to speak regular language or laugh inside the mask. They can only use the one word or sound associated with the holy person they have become. Once the hood is removed, the holy one leaves. Even before the mask is placed upon the head, there is a short Blessingway performed on it, so that before it or any other paraphernalia or different medicines are used, they have been spiritually prepared. But first, there must be that ceremony.

Sandpaintings and Ceremonies

The holy people have powers and authority that medicine men use to heal the sick. This becomes especially apparent in the use of sandpaintings in ceremonies that might last as little as one day or night or extend for nine days or nights. The teachings behind the etiquette and procedure at one of these ceremonies illustrate how interwoven the activities of humans and the gods become. Even the Navajo word for sandpainting (iikááh) speaks to this point—"They Are Coming," meaning the gods will be present. As in the Yé'ii Bicheii ceremony just discussed, specific holy people with particular powers needed for the curing are invited to participate. Just who these holy people are and how they should be summoned depends on the sacred narrative that describes how their healing power was obtained and first used and what the proper behavior and requirements are to have them assist in helping. Once the proper paraphernalia, prayers, songs, and activities are used and performed, the holy people are obligated to assist. Examples of specific ceremonies will be provided elsewhere, but for now, a general outline of activities illustrates the role of these unseen participants.

The most effective place to hold most ceremonies is in a hogan. To notify the holy people that one is going to take place, a blanket is hung over the doorway as a request that they come, observe, and participate in what is about to happen. The smoke hole in the center of the roof may be where they initially peer in to see what is going on, but if all seems appropriate, they will enter through the door to share their powers. Those humans taking part will sit forward away from the hogan's walls so that the holy people can walk behind them to observe. The patient, if a female, would be in a dress, her hair tied in a bun, and would be aware of the proper procedures. People entering or leaving the hogan move in a clockwise or sunwise direction. The presiding medicine man is seated on the west side of the room, the place of honor facing the door and east, with the patient to his left. Generally, Navajo participants understand what they are supposed to do, but if there is a breach in proper practice, such as a person sitting out of place, it is up to the medicine man to caution them by saying, "Hey, do you know what you're doing there."

When making a sandpainting, the floor is covered with smooth tan sand as the background for the images. On it there are four types of colored bodies that portray the holy people—white (Bits'íís Łigai), blue (Bits'íís Dootł'izh), yellow (Bits'íís Łitsoi), and black (Bits'íís Diłhił). When the medicine man starts singing their songs, they actually start to dress up the way the song describes them. They either put feathers on their head or feathers underneath them; they start holding a particular object needed for healing, then when ready, begin to form in a group to enter the hogan to assist. Often a prayerstick (k'eet'áán) is planted in each of the four corners of the sandpainting. Once emplaced, this is a signal that the holy people are present. Now the patient circles around the completed image that depicts an event from the story about when the holy people first used the power it contains to heal. Next, the patient sits down on the image to absorb its strength, then receives herbs that are ceremonially harvested and identified as having the healing properties found in the story. That person and others attending drink the herbs—an act in which the participants meet the holy ones. This is where the four sacred body people use their powers contained in feathers, plants as held by the squash people and tobacco people, and other physical objects that draw their power into the circle where the patient sits. Most ceremonies are very, very sacred, even to the point that a person is not supposed to have their legs stretched out, an offense to the holy people. A person must carry themselves with appropriate manners so that these gods will want to sit with him or her. In some ceremonies where a human dresses as a god, like in the Yé'ii Bicheii, once they put on the clothing, he or she actually merges and becomes that holy person and must act accordingly. They have moved from being regular people to the holy ones.

What, then, is the role of the medicine man and the patient, because there are three different entities participating in the ceremony? The patient plays a critical part in the healing process. Navajos believe that there are two thought systems in the human body. One is meditation while the other is more visible—what we say, how we talk, and how this is acted out in body language (kinesics). Meditation brings spiritual power into the body and challenges one to help himself. It is as if something has to be part of you again—reintroduced—to start the healing process. A person can make him or herself into a healer. We have to have the faith to do it and accept positive thought. If you keep yourself holy, then the ceremonies and medications can work through you to cure. Thus the patient becomes a holy person within who self-heals, if they have the desire.

The medicine person serves as a director. He provides the guidance, conducts the ceremony, sings the songs and offers the prayers that bring the holy people to cure the patient, provides medicines, and works with the patient to feel and understand what is happening. Still, it is up to the individual to want to be healed. The holy people are the ones who first experienced this process and so, like the medicine man, are there in spirit to return the sick person to a state of health. The sandpainting is theirs and outlines the story, prescribes the steps, and holds the power necessary to help the individual. The holy people are there to guide and provide the power and are in spiritual form to work with the spirit of the patient, who has to accept and have the desire to be well again.

Performing these ceremonies has always been this way. My grandfather taught that the holy people are there and participate. One day we were preparing to perform a ceremony for a woman, but the lady did not show up. Later she notified us that it would be postponed. My grandfather was angry and so I asked, "Why are you upset, Grandfather?" He replied, "She made the date when it was going to happen. When she said that, the holy people listened. The holy people are here, today, waiting for that patient. I am here waiting for her. My medicine is here. She backed off on us." The lady had asked to postpone the ceremony to the next day, but my grandfather said, "No. Go find another medicine man. You lied to me. You lied to my holy people. We showed up and you were not there." He explained to me, "If you say there is going to be a ceremony at a certain time and place, it is going to happen, and if you don't show up, then it's a disappointment. The next time that you say you are going to hold one, they might not want to listen to you. I know that I don't want to do that again."

My grandfather was a stubborn man and felt that if he was treated unfairly, he would not work with that person. He was very upfront about his medicine and that the holy people were there helping and should not be treated lightly. "The holy people are here. Watch your language. Be mindful. Once you come into that doorway, be respectful. Don't stand there. Sit down. The holy people are here." He always taught of the importance of respect and discipline.

Some people saw him as a person who was harsh and alone, but there is a story that explains why he was that way and the power that he held. Many underestimated that power and how close to the ground he was. He had short legs and was like a flat person, but if it came to a fight, he was as good as a dog and could outfight anything. These qualities go back to when the holy people were developing the Enemyway ceremony. The gods talked about the offerings and qualities needed to strengthen behavior and that were necessary to survive in war. Some of the people suggested making an offering from the bears, while others thought that cougars should be used because both were fierce fighters.

A new chief being initiated was not totally satisfied so sent four people out to find the best of all animals that could fight furiously. One of them brought back the badger's way of ceremony, in which they made an offering to this animal. The badger has short legs, is close to the ground, has a flat body, and is a real fighter. If the enemy shoots at him, he ducks down and lies flat on the earth so that the arrows fly overhead. But when he gets involved in a one-on-one fight, he will not be beaten. The new chief felt this was good, accepted the qualities, fought many battles, and led his people through many wars until he became an old man. He attributed his success to the qualities of the animals he chose as protectors. "I am the one who was protected by all kinds. I have the bear in me; I have the cougar in me, but most important, my face and body painting is all about badger. Enemy, come and get me and I will fight to my death in a different way." He tied a rope around his foot and fastened it to a stake in the ground, then challenged his enemies to fight. He drew his knife, ran in a circle, and defeated all that approached him. The enemy lay dead near his circle, but he remained standing. My grandfather was like this, and so people said he stood with the badger.

This attitude of bravery was also connected to pride. Later, other tribes like the Comanche and Cheyenne did a similar thing while the Apache and Utes were also fierce fighters.

The people asked who would fight in a way that would be fair. The Navajos decided to use this way to prove bravery, and so they made a strap out of the yucca plant and colored it red. The fighter fastened it to his ankle, then painted one side of his leg red and the other side black. One of his arms was painted white and one arm yellow, while his face had separate markings. He challenged his enemies to enter his circle one by one, then talked to the sun, saying, "You're the circle up there, you are my father, and I am your son. If you will help me, I will see that these markings that I am using will become a sandpainting one day. I will defeat my enemy within the circle, which will become my sandpainting." Then he drove the stake in. He painted his father on one side and grandfather on the other side—one was yellow representing the sun, the other white, representing the moon. Below were the representations of water and air on each side. This is also how he put his sandpainting together using a stake in the middle.

Almost every sandpainting that is done today is compared to this. That is why the story sits the way it does. Now, nobody really goes deeply into the stories. Why is there red here? Why yellow? Why is it in a round circle? Why are there arrowheads on the back? This young man talked about his enemy, how he was going to defeat them with the help of his father and grandfather using the Lightningway and Windway. He said, "I will be the messenger, the one who is doing the songs and prayers; it won't matter what enemy comes in. I will defeat them." That is how he fought.

Today, when a large sandpainting is being laid out, a peg in the middle with a string attached measures the circumference of the soon-to-be-created image. The same process is used to lay out the diameter of a new hogan. This represents being on the outside making a circle, just as the warrior drove in his stake, stating, "This is where I'm going to sit. This is where I'm going

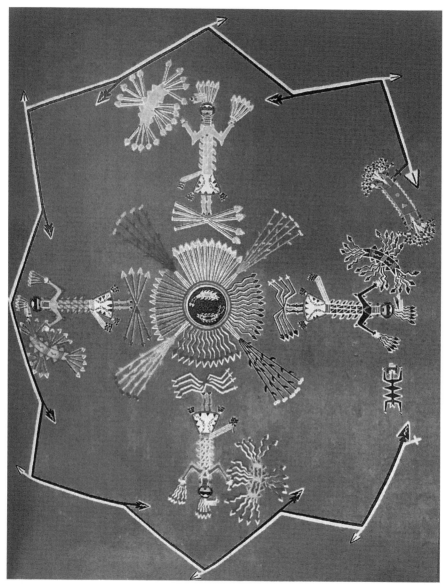

This sandpainting from the Shootingway portrays four holy people dressed in flint (protruding from body), holding and standing upon lightning, both of which act as their weapons and protection. As one of the Holyway ceremonies, this has a number of sandpaintings used in the five- or nine-day performance.

to fight, and my enemy will stay outside of this." Now, we do not think about these things. Sometimes we attribute this way of fighting to other tribes, but the story is already set; we have our own stories right here that pertain to us today.

Ceremonial Language and Thought

Central to any ceremonial healing process is the language that is used. Language is power, and some language is used only by medicine men. The holy people recognize a person who has been taught and "ordained," and who knows the language that the gods use. The words do not work for anybody who has not been initiated. A medicine man has to be "marked"— in the eyes, ears, and mouth—to use this spiritual language. When a person is learning to become a medicine man, this marking is given to him by the holy people. They had their color markings, like the red markings, the black markings, and it was marked all the way down when the ceremony was done. But even after it wears off, you are a marked person, no matter what. Your hand is all marked. So if you should, for some reason, hit something, it would destroy the object with that power. To carry that medicine, you are not supposed to use bad language with people because your tongue was marked and enlightened.

Navajo people try to find out what the magic words for healing are and will pay top money just to hear what words to use. Even the most powerful medicine people, when they are singing their main song, will have in the middle these powerful words. People will not know how to say them or how to put them together, but they are always trying to find out what the words are. For instance, if a person was performing an Enemyway ceremony, then they would sing [words deleted]. This part is very sacred, and only a medicine man would use that because he is initiated and understands how to control the power. Somebody watching from the outside would say, "Okay, this is how it was said; this is the healing part." Not all people can say these words; you have to understand the ceremony and medicine to heal with them. Words can also be used to harm and destroy a person if the speaker knows how to say and control them.

Much of this sacred language and many of the sounds are embedded in the myths and come from birds and animals associated with different directions. They are not those of humans. Talking God used this language to heal. It is the same sound that a dove makes in the language that they use. So the sacred words came from the birds or animals or Talking God or the Dawn God, who put those words together and into that medicine. That is how they were learned and understood by medicine men. They are associated with the creatures in the four directions, but one cannot take just one story from the east and say this is the same medicine as that found in the west. The western people would say, "No. This is ours. This is the way things are," and provide a story to prove it. This is how one can tell who is a real medicine man who is using these things to heal. If I perform a ceremony, I have to share my story first, explain it, and tell which direction it comes from before we even get started. I would also say that this is my story and it comes from Many Beads, the person who held this medicine.

Some of the main songs or prayers in the middle of the ceremony may be different. They may be tweaked this way or that, they may be female or male, so that is why you have to tell your story. This is the female form of the ceremony or the male. This is the white pattern. This is the yellow pattern and this is why it is being taught this way. You tell the person that this story is about fixing the problem they have and that you are trying to get them to come with you, to be part of the healing, and to think about what is going on. The patient and the medicine man heal together and so both have to be in holiness. The story tells them how this is going to work. "Block everything out and be here with me. Even if you can't say the words, listen to me. Be with me. I want you to walk with me this way, so we can get to the healing point together." That is why I always sit down and tell the person the story and where it came from. I try to coach people to stay focused, and so every now and then I will stop my song and say, "Okay, here's a different song that we're going to be singing, so your thoughts will remain." For instance, if I'm doing the underground stone boiling water ceremony, I would tell them, "We're coming to the heat song, which is about the heat that comes from stone. When I put medicine on it, it's going to steam." We are sitting in the steam bath trying to be holy, so I say, "Now, we've got to induce this heat upon me to make it accept me, not as it might burn me but as we accept and inhale it, letting it be part of me and heal me. You have to think this way while I'm singing." It is always about approaching my medicines, walking with this person.

This is the old way of teaching, the way that the people used to do things in a respectful manner. This is about the safety of an individual. The stories and advice relate to you and are respected. They are like your grandmother and grandfather, so you listen to them. You learn from them because they are the elders. As a person, you will grow to that next level with them, and the process helps you to learn more and to become a better person. This is the old people's way of teaching. It is just like preparing food in a respectful manner with clean thoughts in your mind as you meditate. You spiritually prepare together so that people will grow with it through understanding good things. If you have a mind that is not there, then you should just stay away from it. That is what the old people talked about as they looked out for the best interests of others who can learn from these teachings.

Central to all of this is the idea of keeping something holy (yíní dílyinii k'ehgo). This means that we must follow the pattern established by the holy ones and maintain it. Their assistance takes time and is often not a rapid miracle—no quick fix. The moon may set one, two, three, four times, as the healing slowly occurs. It walks, but you don't get in a hurry about things because you feel the holiness is already with you, just keep it holy and it will come to you slowly in a good way and with faith. A lot depends on what type of medicine a healer is working with, but it requires a good sitting down to focus on the message; it is usually the medicine people who have the knowledge and desire to understand the underlying teachings from the stories. They will talk about these narratives and make something out of it. Here is one story about a caterpillar that was slowly going down a tree, traveling an inch at a time, but the world still seemed to be moving on top of him. He couldn't see anything. He felt so badly that the gods had made him so small and that he could not move fast enough to get to his destination. Out of frustration, he just sat on a branch and cried. He tried to pray about it, but nothing happened. Then one night he had a dream about a tree that he was on top of, at the edge of a limb from which he could see far away. Later, when he saw a tree in the distance, he set a goal and started toward it. The caterpillar finally reached the large pine and began moving upward. By the time he got to the top, the season was over, so again, he was disappointed, and he sat there and cried. Even as he spun his web cocoon to hide in, he wailed about his bad fortune. Inside he sat and meditated, wondering why he was alive and what his purpose in life should be. The more he prayed, the more he understood about living in a holy way. Dreams came to him saying, "Keep it holy, keep it holy. There's a purpose for your being here, a reason why you have spun this web, and for the things that are happening today. Just keep sitting there, pray, and meditate about it." That is what he did. Suddenly a thunderstorm blasted the tree, cracked it in half, and broke open the cocoon. Outside it was spring time, and he saw his prayer had been answered. Beautiful flowers grew everywhere, filling his world with bright colors. As he looked about, he had an urge to enter this lovely scene, but as he moved forward, he quickly became stuck. Investigating further, he realized he had grown wings; he really wanted to join in with all of the beauty beyond, which was now possible because he was a butterfly. He launched forth, flying on wings filled with color. His prayer had been answered. Now he could sit on every flower, pick its pollen, and spend the rest of his life in happiness. This is an example of how these stories teach that even though we can be in the hardest place and times, there is a purpose for suffering. By keeping it holy, a person will achieve a good end.

The power of language is the means that summons the holy people, it moves the patient through time to the first event portrayed in the sandpainting, and it connects the healing forces to act upon one's inner being. Here, Talking God joins in with the medicine people to bless this child sprinkled with pollen. (Drawing by Charles Yanito)

Navajo people also have a name for magical, supernatural power through which medicine men work to bring about powerful, often surprising results through unseen forces. This term—álílee k'ehgo—which means literally "according to his supernatural/magical powers," can be used for both good and evil purposes. A person can do or develop something that is powerful, and no one else can do it unless they too control supernatural forces. When the white man brought in the first car, to the Navajo, it was done through supernatural, spiritual powers, as was the airplane. They were a mystery, an impossibility that came into being. In the Indian way, it couldn't be done, but through a mysterious power, there it is sitting before you. "I don't know how an airplane flies, but somebody put it together and there it is in the air. This is magical." Navajo medicine men use this supernatural power all the time to heal people. We know now that the car and plane work on physical laws that the Anglo understand, while healing through medicine works through spiritual laws that Navajos understand and use.

When I was about sixteen years old, my grandfather used to sit me down and put a bunch of hot coals from the fireplace right in front of where I was sitting. He would say, "Sit right there. I want you to really meditate, concentrate, while I sing. I'm going to have you concentrate enough while I do that, for you to move that one coal with your eyes. You look at it, and move it over this way." Then he would start chanting as I really focused on the coal. Sometimes I started to move it, but it did not go as far as I wanted it to. He would stop and say, "You're not doing it correctly. Do it a different way." I had seen him do this a number of times, but that was one of the hardest things I ever did, trying to move something with my thoughts. But that is how álílee k'ehgo works, and that is how one practices to become a medicine man who controls the power. I tried and tried all through the years to master it, but I did not.

One time, I was getting ready to remove an object emplaced by witchcraft by sucking it out of a person. The pipe I was using to prepare the patient suddenly flew out of my hand and across the room, hitting the wall two inches above an observer's head before shattering to dust on impact. This really scared me. It happened a second time and struck a different wall on another side of the hogan. I asked grandfather, "What's going on? What is this?" He told me not to practice it anymore because it was not good and not turning out the way it was supposed to. "Leave it. All of that thing about doctoring," he said, "put it away. We're going to put it away. Let's not practice that anymore. Let's not do it again. Instead of doing these things, we are going to stay with prayers and songs, and just kill it [the sickness] with that because you already have this hoof medicine (akéshgaan—discussed later). You know what to say if needed, and so we are going to just use language and not do any more doctoring, otherwise someone is going to get hurt." And so we did. He put a stop to the use of the negative side of álílee k'ehgo.

This power is often used in group ceremonies, such as the Mountainway, which my grandfather often conducted. On the last night, there are a number of different performances that call upon álílee k'ehgo. One of these is to make feathers stand upright and dance in a woven basket through this power. He was well known for being able to control it. I have seen him do this. Another time, he was presiding over a Mountainway and he told the people to sit down, that no one could stand. "Everybody put your blanket over your head, like this, and sit down," and they did, pulling their blanket partway over their head, but not so much that they could not see things. Three fires burned in the spacious juniper corral (called the Dark Circle of Branches) as the dancers entered. They were painted white, and so are called the "Whities." Once they started dancing in the center, he stood up and blew his whistle. Out of the sky came a whole flock of blue birds that settled in just outside of the corral. Every time he beat on the basket, the birds started to dance. Next they would fly on top of the brush enclosure, then get down. They did this four times before leaving. He knew their songs and so brought them through singing to be part of the ceremony. That is how powerful and magical my grandfather was. This was the first and only time that this was ever seen on the reservation.

CHAPTER THREE

Rooted in Emerging Ways (Hajíínéí)

Central to Navajo beliefs is the creation story, often compared to a cornstalk. The plant's roots are buried in the ground; its main stem supports leaves that branch outward; the ears bring nourishment and life; the pollen on the tassel connects the earth with the sky. In making this comparison, the roots are the stories of what happened below this world during the time of the creation; the stalk is the Blessingway, a primary narrative of the establishment of the holy people and the Navajo on the earth; the branching leaves represent the different ceremonies, each with its own story; and the tassel and its pollen are the connecting links to the heavens and holy people. As with everything in Navajo thought, there are both female and male aspects of the creation, just as an ear of corn has a tassel and pollen, which are male, and an ear with its silk, which are female. This chapter and the next are about the roots and main stalk or the emergence of the people from the four worlds beneath this one and the beginning of Navajo life with the assistance of the holy people on this earth.

The importance of the creation story cannot be overemphasized. If one wants to understand the Navajo worldview, there is only one place to start, at its roots. This is why there are so many recorded accounts about these seminal events.[1] However, as soon as a person reads a second and third version of the same story, it will become apparent that although a general outline is shared, they may each vary markedly in scope, emphasis, and detail. Indeed, no two creation stories of the worlds beneath are the same. Each medicine man will tell his account that he learned from his teacher, yet with every teacher, there will be a different version. Variations abound for other reasons as well: much can depend on what part of the reservation a person comes from, an individual who is knowledgeable about different ceremonies may tie in or emphasize some aspects and ignore others, and the depth of understanding and age of the narrator can affect vocabulary and extent of insight. In Perry's case, he has skipped over much of the well-known and often shared detail to emphasize certain topics he felt important. For that reason, I will provide information held in common with all of the narratives and provide context. Variation from story to story is not a problem for the Navajo people, even when considering fundamental points. Exploring common patterns, as seen in six motifs found in most versions, emphasizes important elements of Navajo daily and ceremonial life.

In every rendition of the creation story, there were either four or five worlds present, the fourth or fifth being the world humans now live in. The size of each of these worlds was much smaller than the one now inhabited. As the holy people passed through each of them, they obtained the creatures, vegetation, and landforms such as mountains, to establish in the next world. By the time they reached this present level, the holy people had gained a lot of experience and the ability to beautify their existence. Placing the Six Sacred Mountains, rivers, and other land formations around the countryside, they were able to blow life into and expand them to their present size. Since everything was created spiritually before it was made physically, each had an inner spirit placed inside. Things like the earth and sky, lightning and thunder, rocks and trees have an inner form roughly glossed as "animate being that lies within" (bii'gistíín), which was present only in spiritual form in the worlds beneath. All of these animate or inanimate objects had their personalities and teachings embedded internally.

The colors of the four worlds are standard and provide a second motif that runs throughout Navajo thought. White, blue, yellow, and black are pervasive whether speaking of the Four Sacred Mountains, the four directions, the materials used in a sandpainting, or the sacred stones provided in an offering, and they are common even in the language used by the people. Just as the different worlds had their powers, so too do these colors when used in a ceremonial context. They not only represent things associated with the realms below but also may be intertwined with every activity that takes place in this world. Everything—from the holy people, birds, and animals, to plants, rivers, and winds—falls into this classification system that calls upon the physical elements present in this world to share their powers. The creatures and plants along with other objects received their power and color when first identified in the world from which they derived. In each of the worlds leading to this one, there was conflict among the creatures that led to that place's destruction and the necessity of their bringing along newly introduced elements into the next level.

Perry's discussion about the White and Glittering Worlds is instructive. Some accounts suggest that today's world is the fourth and make no mention of a fifth, while others insist this is the fifth or Glittering World. Perry's explanation clears the confusion and tells how the White World changed into a glittering one following the introduction of the bright, sparkling, and translucent objects brought with the arrival of the white man. This earmarks an important quality found in Navajo stories by illustrating their flexibility in adapting the creation story to what is still taking place.

Perry also hints at the development of a sixth world, once this one has advanced to a point of chaos, just as it did in those beneath. There are a number of accounts that speak in detail about the end of this and the beginning of the next. Medicine man John Holiday summarized his understanding of what he believed will take place when the time is ripe for change. After the Navajo have lost their language and culture, forgotten their ceremonies and teachings, rejected the sacred for the profane, abused the earth sufficiently, and caused the seasons to reverse, there will be a dramatic shift. "This changeover will signal the end of this life and a new beginning, which will occur without warning. There will be no suffering and it will happen as quickly as lightning. . . . We will once again live like we did before everything took place. Eventually, this will wind down again to repeat this course of events. It is something that has been going on forever and will continue."[2] Thus the events chronicled in the creation story have not ended, suggesting we all may be part of the sequel.

A third motif found in this and almost every other Navajo story is that of the journey or traveling. Just the word "emergence" (Hajíínéí) portrays an action, of rising up through the worlds and into the present level. The narratives that serve as the basis for ceremonies, the teaching tales of Coyote, and the explanations of cultural practices usually revolve around a protagonist traveling and encountering the knowledge or experience that leads to the establishment of some aspect of Navajo culture. Through travel, new things are encountered. Thus, it is not surprising to find the Navajo constantly on the move and ever expanding their horizons. Their language reflects this. Take for instance the word "to go" and how the Navajo language is heavily influenced by this predominant theme. Anthropologist and Navajo linguist Gary Witherspoon writes of "the astonishing degree to which the Navajo language is dominated by verbs . . . [which] also correspond to the Navajo emphasis on a world in motion. . . . I once conservatively estimated that Navajo contained some 356,200 distinct conjugations of the verb 'to go.' These conjugations all apply to the ways in which humans normally 'go.' If we added all the verbs relating 'to move,' as well as 'to go,' such as in walking or running, the number of conjugations would be well into the millions."[3] Traveling started in the worlds beneath and continues to this day.

As the holy beings progressed through the different worlds, they encountered a growing sophistication of creatures. In one sense, the story of the emergence could be viewed as an evolutionary tale, not in the sense of Charles Darwin's theory—for once a creature in the Navajo universe is created, any changes to it are superficial, such as the changes in the color of its coat, or some added appendage like antlers. However, there is also a caveat to this. In the next chapter when Perry discusses animals traveling to the north with Changing Woman, he does refer to aspects of the animals adapting to their environment, à la Darwin. During the emergence, each level has an increasingly larger number of creatures with greater size and complexity. The best way to explain the difference in these spiritual forms is to take a more complete list provided by medicine man Sandoval (Hastiin Tł'oh Ayání—Old Man Buffalo Grass) with Aileen O'Bryan's assistance in 1928. Note that other versions may have different creatures and more or less of them, and so Sandoval's account serves only as a brief example.

In the First World that "was black as black wool," one finds only the "Mist People who had no definite form, but were to change to men, beasts, birds, and reptiles of this world."[4] In this realm there was First Man and First Woman, wasps, a variety of ants, beetles, dragonflies, bats, Spider Man and Woman, Salt Man and Salt Woman, and Coyote. These were all holy people who worked their way through each of the succeeding worlds. The Second or Blue World was filled with all types of birds, many of which had blue feathers. The Third or Yellow World had Six Sacred Mountains that were later transplanted in our present world. Dozens of different holy people lived here, while "on the mountains lived the light and dark squirrels, chipmunks, mice, rats, the turkey people, the deer and cat people and the lizards and snakes."[5] Sandoval concludes by saying, "So far all the people were similar. They had no definite form, but they had been given different names because of different characteristics." Other accounts suggest that these spiritual beings were in human form and that everyone could communicate with one another. That is why men and animals today are closely related, understand each other's needs, and can direct or be directed.

The more one studies the emergence and related events, the more one recognizes the interconnectedness of seemingly unrelated things. This underlying tenet is sometimes difficult for the Anglo reader to understand due to their unfamiliarity with Navajo thought and the dominant principle of relationship (k'é) that ties the entire universe into one big family of affiliation. For example, Perry has already and will elsewhere discuss the four main building blocks of existence in this world—earth, water, air, and fire. Each one of them depends on the other to remain viable. In this chapter he speaks of how fire and water are brothers and how each has its positive and negative characteristics. Both require air and depend on soil and the things it grows in order to survive.

Singling out fire for a closer examination, consider how wide-ranging its influence is here as outlined in just a few paragraphs. First, it is a living being or spirit and has its own emotions and requirements to be treated in certain ways that show respect. Its birth came through powerful agents—thunder, lightning, and storm, which also brought with them water. The sweat lodge is only made possible by heating rocks with fire, which in turn brings forth water (sweat). Appreciation is expressed to the rocks for the work that they do in not just cleansing the body but also teaching and facilitating meditation. There are very few Navajo ceremonies that do not require some form of fire and water; heating and cooking is done on a daily basis with both; and some stars in the sky are viewed as fire. Even the food one eats has the "mark" of the flame and is more nourishing because of it. Viewed as a purifying influence, fire removes evil and carries the prayers to the holy people through smoke and incense, and into an individual through different forms of tobacco, which are inhaled. If a person commits suicide, their "heat" is extinguished and their water goes back to the Water People, who are angered by the disrespect for the water that a person had to maintain life. Even fireflies have their own "fire" and proudly display it at night. In Navajo thought, everything is touched by fire, water, earth, and wind—all of which are connected.

Perry touches on another cardinal point in Navajo thought, that of language with its four levels. He refers to them—starting from the simplest and moving to the most complex—according to the materials that comprise the offering of ntł'iz: white shell, turquoise, abalone shell, and jet. In Navajo ceremonial terms they are linked to different rituals that extend from the most peaceful to the most powerful—those used only by the most experienced medicine men. The white level of language is the Blessingway (Hózhǫ́ǫ́jí hane'), the blue level is the People's language (Diné k'ehjí hane'), yellow is in the realm of ceremonial language (Hatááł hane), and black is Protectionway (Naayéé'jí hane'). Each level builds in complexity and power upon what has been learned previously and added to the basic story (hane').

The most important concept to comprehend about the emergence and its events is that the narrative is filled with teachings and stories that explain why things are the way they are found in this world. Every story is a "teaching packet" that can be used in tandem with other instruction or stand alone. If one wants to learn some aspect of Navajo culture, he or she will have to return to the creation stories. When I first started working with Navajo elders, I did not understand this. I might start an interview with questions about uranium mining or curing an illness or livestock reduction of the 1930s. The interviewee would then start to answer the question by mentioning something in the worlds beneath or an episode from Changing Woman's life or an experience of the Twins. Without really understanding what that person was trying to accomplish, I saw this as a roundabout way of answering a straightforward question. In reality, what I mistook as a side step was really moving toward the heart of how that person viewed the issue. Everything in today's world has its roots in yesteryear. The emergence and other mythical events hold the keys to understanding why and how things are happening today.

What follows here is Perry selectively choosing certain events or "packets" of information that he wishes to use for teaching specific principles. Take for instance his comparison of being blind and the use of the sweat lodge. From this first experience in the underworld came the explanation of the desired attitude of the participants, proper etiquette, and the process by which one becomes physically, mentally, and spiritually clean. A later chapter will go into greater detail of how the sweat lodge is used and why it is part of the preparation for those seeking ceremonial help. Coyote, the trickster, who is so often seen as a charlatan and troublemaker, leads the first sweat ceremony participants through an important aspect of traditional life. This illustrates yet another principle found in Navajo literature in that no one is always bad or always good. Everyone and everything has something to offer in the schooling of mankind. This chapter opens the door to many topics that will be revisited later, but helps the reader grasp the importance and complexity in understanding the centrality of the emergence.

The Underworlds - Establishing Patterns

The Black World was the first, a bottom world where there was no light or colors and everything was blind. There were four different kinds of ant people—black, red, yellow, and some of light color, like white. The different creatures in this world used their feelers or antennae to touch things and to help them move around since they lived in this dark, deep world, where there was a constant beat of the world's heart from the center of the earth. This heartbeat warned them of future change, but the ants and other creatures were restless and kept moving around, groping their way in the dark, feeling each other—often in an inappropriately sexual (ídééchid) way. Anger and conflict overcame them, and each complained, "These people are that way. They touch and feel us and we don't like it." The Black World was a confused place, the bottom of a pit that was filled with hostility and depression, with little choice. It was like an ant hill that is calm with only a few running around, but once someone puts their foot in it and stirs the soil, everything becomes upset. The creatures run in a circle, weave in and out, do not understand what is happening, and are always angry. Frustrated, these inhabitants of the Black World attacked anything that got in their way.

The First or Black World, inhabited by the Ant People and other unsettled creatures, was a place of anger, frustration, and blindness. As with later worlds, improper behavior and conflict forced its abandonment as many of its residents sought a better way of life. (Drawing by Kelly Pugh)

This behavior did not stop but led to even less self-control. Everyone became uncomfortable with the circumstances, lashing out at each other, while at the same time, birds were preying upon them for food. Fighting and destruction eventually forced these creatures to move, but they never seemed to understand what was going on. Self-preservation made it clear that it was time for a change, and so when the holy people asked them to go to the next world, those that survived traveled on. Still, they listened to the heartbeat of the earth.

As the people from the Black World climbed into the next, they wished only for peace. They wondered at the Northern Lights in the sky to the south moving toward the north and hoped that they had come to their journey's end. More sophisticated animals, birds, and fish inhabited this Blue World, each having its own songs. The sky, filled with blue twilight, matched the color of this land's creatures. The birds, many of them blue, were talking and singing their prayers to the holy ones, sending their words deep into the spirit. As they communed with the gods, the words lingered on them, enriching their colors and giving them guidance as to how to do things in the Bird Way. The insects started living with the Bird People, but suddenly they became a main source of food and so feared for their existence. "We can't live here because there are too many people who just want to eat us. We will have to move if we are going to survive."

The Bird Way has many stories and teachings. All of the creatures in this world listened to the birds' songs and enjoyed the blue colors. The blue bird is often referred to as the Sun's Bird because he carries the sun's song, which he enjoys hearing. This is why the blue bird has a light breast but darker feathers on its back. He is associated with the blue twilight that sits to the south. The markings on his stomach came from the sky that he touched and the dark on his back from the earth. He connects the two because he lives between them. There are songs and prayers that go with him that speak about his travels, what he does, and how he heals. Navajos today may bless a little girl or newborn through songs and the smoke that comes from burning bluebird feathers. When she receives the name, the sacredness of all that is held in the feathers will bless her. The one praying says, "Your name shall be Bluebird from here on," then places water on her forehead, shoulders, hands, and legs. As the child grows, she will have enthusiasm and carry herself just as the bluebird does—singing well and talking a lot. This is when her character really starts to develop. This was what the old people say.

Although the creatures from below understood they were experiencing new things, they were still afraid. "We know how the Bird People eat, how they fly, the colors they have, and how they talk about their beaks and claws. These are different people." They learned a lot of things about the birds, who are considered morning people, with songs they sing then and in the evening. They noticed how these songs went from east to west and were very beautiful. The people in this world enjoyed what they listened to as the music made things move and put holiness in them. Still, this world never enjoyed full sunlight and everything had a blue tint, like twilight. It was somewhat like Alaska is now during the summer time—the land of the midnight sun— so that in some places there was light both during the day and night time, but it was never really bright. The air was also cold and everything living was blue—blue birds, blue flowers, blue spruce—they all had different shades of the same color.

Like Alaska, there was also a lot of water and much to learn from the Water People. They live in the water and are called children of the rainbow (tó bite'ashishí) because of colors on their side like rainbow trout. Tééhoołtsódii is described as a mermaid-type individual—a man or woman that looks like a fish. He is the main water monster who is a holy one and the primary chief over water. He is like Talking God presiding over the other gods. There is also a lesser group of water monsters that look like a combination of a cow, horse, and pig and that are called "horse from the ocean" (tééh łį́į́'). They control all of the different species of fish and mammals that live in the water and are spiritual, holy beings. Tééh łį́į́' are found in all large bodies of water, but they originated in the Blue World and represent the fish, frogs, and all other creatures living there. All of these have their own stories about how they came about and why they live in water; it is said they go deep down into the earth to visit where the water monster sits.

Tééhoołtsódii is the one who controls the rain and is the keeper of people's thoughts and feelings. If someone contemplates suicide and no longer wants to live on this earth, this creature, dwelling in the deep within the waters of the earth, captures their mind and thoughts, declaring, "I will hold you to that. I will take your mind and keep it here." That person's mind is taken away, so that as he talks about suicide, his life remains crooked until a medicine man performs a ceremony with water offerings that returns the mind to his system. That is how Navajos talk about the Water ceremony (Tóyee). The Water People can perform this ritual because a person's body is made mostly of water, and the feeling is that if you do not appreciate and take care of it—"I don't want this body anymore"—they will take it back from you, let you suffer with dehydration, and whatever else bad that happens. A person will have those feelings unless he or she says, "I'm sorry. I want my life back. I appreciate my life." Then they will give it back, but there are a lot of procedures that need to be performed through ceremonies. These holy people require things taken from the person to obtain the cure. The Water People in the Blue World are very important and teach a lot to the Navajo. All of the creatures that live in water are holy.

The Water People are also involved in bringing people into this world. They say, "We, the Water People, will come first before your child arrives, and we will guide them out. We are that powerful." When a pregnant woman's water breaks, these holy ones are involved. The water that we have in our rivers and springs is distributed back to our homes where we drink it. That water becomes our body and is part of our holy system. The water within works with us, and when the water breaks in a mother, then the baby comes. Water is always there.

The Water People also helped the creatures in the Blue World to move upward to the next level. As the travelers looked about, all agreed, "Let's keep moving on. We have seen this part of the world." However, they also continued to fight among themselves, ignoring the songs and powerful beings available to help. The migrants looked at the blue twilight and wanted to move on but did not know where to go. They asked the Water People, who told them they could escape through the cumulus and nimbus clouds that stood above them. They were heavy enough to support the creatures like a pair of steps into the heavens while still hiding them, whereas if they were on other types of clouds, they would be seen. These clouds assisted the travelers in connecting with thunderstorms that helped them move to the next world as described in the Lightningway. That's how it was set. When a person is singing in that ceremony and offering those prayers, he is walking with the clouds and says, "I went thru it; I actually walk through it (biyi' yisháál, biníkáníyá). I'm walking on top of it as I walk through it." The lightning serves as a guide. Every time the people needed to see things, the lightning struck in places opposite them. As the rain started to fall, they moved upward and out of the Blue World.

The people arrived at the next level, the Yellow World with its reddish tint, where they joined more creatures that took up their travels. Many of the newcomers were four-legged. This place was a lot lighter in color, as if the sun was behind the clouds, but it was not as bright as the next world and the temperature was not as warm as they wished. The people noticed many of the animals had fur to protect them against the cold and that it reflected the sunlight on top. It shined the light color yellow. As the travelers looked at the four-leggeds with their furs and reflected sunlight, they began to admire the beauty with which these animals were dressed. According to the story in the Mountainway, there were other people coming off the mountains and mesas and over the horizon. The ridges also reflected the yellowish color and so the people called it red and yellow evening twilight (nihootsoi). This color never changed.

As in the other worlds, conflict began to eat away at relationships. The people violated proper behavior, in this case trying to take the animal's fur, but the four-leggeds would have nothing to do with that. The other creatures tried to cozy up to the animals who resented what they were doing. The animals told them that they could not have their furs and did not want to be close to them. Also, some of the travelers were now meat-eaters, which caused them to have different odors. The people asked, "What is that smell?" The animals replied, "We think there's a fire up there. Something yellowish in color is out there." So the travelers went looking for whatever it was that was yellow. Sure enough there was a fire. They saw it from a distance in the evening twilight and commented that it seemed as if something from the dawn was right there.

They visited the fire people as they cooked their supper and were told, "This is something that we call 'fire.' You should not touch it because it will burn you. On the other hand, it will give you the warmth you are looking for. Fire is very powerful. It will not hesitate to do harm. If it is left uncontrolled, it will walk on anything in its path and will not stop or hesitate. It will go through water, through anything." The travelers from the blue twilight went in search of water, the essence of the Blue World, and brought it back to the fire. In this way the Blue World and Yellow World came together. Fireflies (dǫ'tsoh) were there, one of which was their chief. He said, "This is my fire" and then explained how it and water were related as brothers. The main firefly said, "If you have gone back to the Blue World and heard thunder and seen a storm, you know that the water and the lightning come together. When the lightning strikes something, it makes a fire. Fire was born through that thunder and lightning into the water, so fire is related to the Water People as a brother. They say, 'This is how we come together like this.'" One can never underestimate the power of water as explained in the Blue World, for it will not hesitate to do damage. It has no remorse and will run right through whatever is in its way, even if there is a hot fire. Neither one will stop or hesitate; both are equally dangerous and will not hold back. Each has its purpose.

The White and Glittering Worlds—Habitat for Humanity

As the people journeyed through the Black, Blue, and Yellow Worlds, they learned many new things. In each one there was friction, and the Yellow World was no different. The firefly pointed with his wings to the heavens and the horizon and told the people to move on. "There's some kind of lighting that's coming through there. You might want to go in that direction and find out what is causing it." In the meantime Coyote, one of the holy people, had stolen a baby belonging to the water monster, who became so angry that it caused the waters below to start rising. Some squirrels had earlier planted the seeds of a reed on a mountain. The plant grew rapidly toward the heavens, but did not have the power to grow through to the next world. The water continued to push the people toward the reed and to cover the mountain. They had no choice—"Where are we going to go now?"—and so they started singing the water songs and made the sounds of the fire. Suddenly, the reed started to grow again and reached a point where it entered into the Fourth or White World. The people moved up through the reed and emerged into a very bright place (Place of Emergence—Hajíínéí) in what is now Trout Lake near Telluride, Colorado. Coyote returned the water babies, the flood subsided, and the people looked about as they stood on an island in the middle of a large lake.

The animals began walking around in the mud. Their feet, blackened by the earth, kicked up dirt that clung to their fur. Raccoons, like some of the other animals, received stripes on their legs and other parts of their bodies from the mud. Some of the animals told them, "There's mud on your face," and so they tried to brush it away but it remained; that is how raccoons got their markings. They all made fun of one another, commenting on how strange they looked with their newly painted coats. Now that they had reached this place, they did not want to travel any farther. They reasoned: "It was bad enough that we had to come up through three different worlds. Let's learn the behavior of this place and understand the power of the four directions. If we start acting like Coyote and keep bringing in all these different attitudes and behavior, we will become like him," something the people wanted to avoid.

Coyote continued to travel to the four directions and returned with different objects and ways of doing things. The animals cautioned him to stop and not do this, to leave things alone, not make fun of others, settle down, and start talking about things that are important. They wanted to discuss what would be good behavior, but were not sure how to go about it. Coyote, always quick to answer, replied, "Let's make a sweat lodge." The people looked at him. "What's a sweat lodge?" He called it "the water that cleanses," saying "tó-chééh," but that word has now shifted to táchééh. The people asked, "Where did you learn this? What are you talking about?" He answered that he had learned it from the people in the Yellow World and showed his listeners how to put stones together, interlock fork sticks, cover the structure with earth, then heat rocks in a fire. Next he said, "Everybody has to undress; only men do this together or women together, but never at the same time." The people built two of these sweat lodges, one for each sex; one was by the edge of the place of emergence and the other for the ladies a short distance away.

Now that the people had built the first sweat lodge, they asked what its purpose was. Coyote responded, "Oh, we have to go back to when we were in the First World and listen to ourselves. What was it like there?" The people looked at each other and said, "Darkness." He answered, "That's what we have to capture again. We have to enter the sweat lodge, pull the blankets over the doorway, and sit in the dark. Now, as we sit in the dark circle, we can't see anything. That way we do not have to make judgments. Instead, we have to use our ears to listen to things. We will not make fun of

During the creation, Coyote had numerous opportunities to interfere with other people's plans and interject his own ideas. Sometimes good—like introducing the sweat lodge, teaching how to bring rain, and obtaining his own star—and sometimes bad—such as bringing death to the people and performing antisocial acts—he had a large influence on what humans experience. (Drawing by Kelly Pugh)

each other, and whoever talks, talks in the holy way in the darkness, the same way that blind people do. We never really understand what blind people are like. They're very careful people. They will not just jump up and walk or run or do something without thinking about it. Blind people will arise and check to make sure that everything is safe before moving. That is how we have to act. Occasionally we are like a blind person and really use our mind, thinking about something twice and listening to people so that we can put things in order. That is why we go into the sweat lodge and act like a blind person."

The people thought this sounded good and so entered the structure, pulled the blankets down, and turned the space into darkness. Coyote announced, "Now we can sing and talk and counsel about that which

troubles us. What are our problems today? Now we all have to act like a
blind person. We are going to go to the east direction, then south, west, and
north to find solutions. Look at things; don't touch it or grab for it. Excuse
yourself if there are other people there. Say, 'Let me make my way through
here. I'm sorry. You're my elders.' Make sure that you excuse yourself
before you pass into another person's space. This is how we have to act with
our behavior as we learn about each other. This comes back to us as a
teaching that we can use. Our negative behavior must become positive
today." This is what they counseled about, discussing how to improve.

The people were learning the difference between bad and good and how
to put these things in order. They really settled down and connected with the
spirit of the land, mountains, trees, earth, water, air, fire, and light. They
listened to these things and their songs. "We have to listen to the air and how
it sings. We have to close our eyes and be respectful. We have to listen to
the water as it runs down from the waterfall. We have to make songs out of
these things and listen to the crackle of the fire as it burns, and feel its heat,
yet set boundaries to protect us. We cannot just jump in and do things like
we used to. We need to understand the learning process about how
everything works." Thus, spirituality entered in as the people thought more
deeply about what was in their world and how those elements should be
used. These were the teachings of the sweat lodge. This is not just about
improving ourselves, but also the world we live in.

The people that the newcomers were now living among began saying,
"These are very nice people who are polite. We like the idea of them being
here because they have stories about the three different worlds they traveled
through and the guidance that this gave them. They can be our teachers. Here
in the White World everything is sitting out there. You can see the
mountains, the light, the animals, and the water. We have to be polite to all
of these things. We will learn to be a different people as you are nice to us.
Thank you for being this way. Thank you for excusing yourself." Even now,
when we are sitting in the sweat lodge, we always thank the rocks providing
the heat and place herbs on them as an offering. "Thank you, Grandfather,
for being here. Help me be this way." You talk to the rocks, the heat, to the
structure itself, saying, "Thank you for giving me this space and giving me
this time to be here, to be part of this holiness right now. I'm here with all
these problems and I want your help with them. I want to sweat it out, get it
out of my body, and for you to help me find something different."

Teachings about the water say that when one goes into a dry sweat
lodge heated just by rocks and no steam, it is actually your own body
washing itself through perspiration. The water runs off and you begin
rubbing yourself. When the person goes out and rolls in the sand, it removes
any dirt. That was the original way of doing it, but lately, things have

changed so that people pour water on the stones, letting the steam do the work, like a sauna bath, but this is not the old way. You are always excusing yourself to the fire-heated rocks, putting some herbs on them, and saying, "Thank you for helping us today." After you are finished with the sweat lodge, you take the water and pour some on its different parts, cooling down the rocks that were used and the structure itself. Put some water on the blankets, then shake them out and place them in the wind to dry and cool. The rocks are removed and placed to the north, where they cool. Everything is done with respect, and so when the sweat lodge reaches a normal

These three elders have just completed one of four sessions inside the sweat lodge. By rolling in sand, they remove perspiration and become freed from bad elements. In a land where water can be scarce, this practice makes a person physically clean and spiritually invigorated.

temperature, you walk away with a clean house. This is a good place for people who are recovering from something harmful. They can become new people. "This used to be me, but I have changed today. I'm a new person." That is the real story of how the sweat lodge teaches. These are good teachings for young people, too.

The holy beings, animals, and other creatures became increasingly comfortable in the White World as they learned to cooperate. Coyote and some of the elders returned to the sweat lodge and this time they had a vision. Coyote said, "There's a star that talks to me from the east and it comes with the morning star. It is a big star that sits in that place. There is another star that sets with the moon and will always be tailing it. These two stars talk to me and say that all of the stars that we look upon in the sky sparkle. There is a world that is going to come to this White World that will change the world as we know it. Then it will be called the Glittering World. Things are going to come in forms that you can see through but cannot go through." He described it like a crystal and said there was going to be a house made out of crystals that one can see through, but that it would be solid inside and out although it could be broken. He was talking about glass. "This house will be displayed by one of our own children and one of the holy ones who will live in it and will talk about it that way. There will be other things that also glitter, but all of this will be in the future," Coyote said.

This discussion took place in the Fourth or White World but was teaching about the world we live in today—the Fifth or Glittering World. They say that when the Anglo people arrived with other nationalities, that was the beginning of the Glittering World. These people brought mirrors, shiny metal objects, windows of glass, and eventually cars—everything changed. Even at night when the lights are on, it is a glittering world, and so it is considered the Fifth World because everything has changed so much. We lost our voice; we lost our hair buns; we lost our moccasins; we are living in a different way today. We are being mastered by the people that came across the ocean, and we have to live by their rules that control us. We are underneath and dominated and are no longer the Navajos who used to run this land. Now it is "listen to the BLM (Bureau of Land Management) or else go to jail." This world has changed a lot for the people, and that is why they call it Nihodisǫs—the Glittering World.

Later, Changing Woman (Asdzą́ą́ Nádleehé) was born, and after she raised her sons, she went to live in the west with her husband, Sun Bearer (Jóhonaa'éí). There he built a house made of crystal for her to live in. This is part of the story that talks about one of the holy ones living in a crystal home. Through this, people will learn to make their houses out of crystals. All of this has happened. My grandfather taught that "even the lights and the glittering are all going to flash. By the time this world goes to another level, a Sixth World, it will be like changing from the Fourth to Fifth World. It will be all light." Grandfather said that it would be nothing but lights. People will be different, Coyote will be seen only once in a while, and the people will not like him. "I will no longer be that special person. Only the holy ones will know who I am." That is how the story goes.

The Language of the Four Worlds

Emergence through the different worlds also had a large effect on language. In the worlds beneath this one, there were levels of language spoken that changed in sophistication and holiness. As the ants and animals went forth, they progressed and learned more sophisticated speech. The one spoken in the Black World was not as complex—even though there were different levels within—as that spoken in the Blue World, which in turn was not as sophisticated as the levels used in the Yellow World. People define who they are by the way they talk, react, joke, and the role they play with other people. Language has a lot of power. Many of the central beliefs and healing practices of the Navajo are dependent upon the power of the spoken word in prayer and song. In them are sacred names—special ways of talking to holy beings that show the speaker has respect and understands who is being addressed. The holy people are the ones who gave this language and these terms to the Navajo, and it is how they want to be addressed.

The holy people speak of White Shell words (Yoołgai saad), Turquoise words (Dootł'izhii saad), Abalone Shell or Yellow words (Diichiłí saad), and Black Jet words (Báashzhinii saad). Each of them is sacred language that teaches of harmony, an abundancy of things, a positive outlook, and good relations. All of this communication was part of the learning experience of those who traveled through the different worlds to this one. The various levels of speech came at certain places and times to make sure that people grew in their teachings from the four different levels, each with their own color. Navajos can speak four different ways on their tongue if they are trained and respectful. That is what I was told, and it is all part of becoming a medicine man.

As a person begins to learn these different ways of speaking, he starts at the lowest, simplest level of language. He will progress so that his language becomes increasingly complex, then more stories and teachings are added with more sophisticated language, so that eventually he will understand almost all there is to know about a ceremony while using the highest level of language with all of the power those words hold. At the beginning, one uses the simplest, basic language; the ceremony, along with the teachings about it, is also abbreviated. As you move through the different levels, just as with the people emerging through the worlds, much more information, songs, prayers, and powerful words are added. New talk and new language takes place, so that by the time one masters the entire ceremony, his language will be different. When an accomplished medicine man listens to another medicine person, he can determine the amount of

Different levels of language not only summon the holy people but also allow a person to be in tune with the ability and training of those spoken to. Medicine people use various types of language, which for the initiated include sacred words, names, and increasingly sophisticated speech patterns. (Drawing by Charles Yanito)

training and knowledge that speaker has by the vocabulary he uses. The listener will think, "Whoa, this is an ordained person because I hear the language that he speaks." This is all ceremonial language that the two men are using, not the daily speech of most people.

Let me give an example. In everyday language the word for a tree is "tsin," while the ceremonial name is "sadii," which means the representation of all trees and their wood. Only a medicine man would use this word. For a person just beginning, when they hear the term "sadii," they would not understand it, while an individual operating on a higher level would know that it was part of a special sacred language. Ceremonies for a beginning medicine man are going to be short, but as one learns more, it will be a little bit longer; the songs will be different as will the prayers. As you go to the next level, the prayers and songs become even longer so that by the time one is fully trained, the songs are going to be far different than those learned on the beginning level. The ceremony is even more sacred because the sounds and language are far different than the bottom ones. This is why a person cannot just use the top part without understanding and learning everything that it is built upon. There are a lot of Navajo people who are trying to take this shortcut now, but it does not work. They are recording high-level people, then trying to learn what is said. But when they talk about the ceremony, it soon becomes apparent that they do not understand and cannot explain certain elements of it.

If I were to do a ceremony for a person that has a family, children, and so forth, and they are having some type of issue, then I would use the regularly practiced ritual. The next person that I do the ceremony for might be a gay person, so I cannot do the same one that I did for the first person; I have to change the ritual because I was taught in a different way for him. Even the markings on a staff have to be different because his spirit is different. He is one of the two-spirited people, and has both a female and male spirit that are combined together in a reverse way. I have to do my ceremony in a different way to change that. So everything is fixed in one way, but a lot of people don't know how to change it to the other way. If I am doing a ceremony for a young girl that is going through puberty, I would go straight with everything in a simple way. But, if I were doing the same ceremony for two twin girls or boys, I am going to have to change it, which means it will sound different, as will the prayers and part of the ritual. This is another reason that one has to learn from the bottom to the top. There needs to be the flexibility to know how to handle different situations for different people. Medicine men who are just beginning can only perform the basic ceremony or else find someone who can do the next level.

People say, "We walk by our language," but the language changes, not only with the ceremony that is being conducted, but also for what is being overcome and the situation one is in. For instance, if you are using White Shell Talk and are speaking to mostly young people, then you are talking about how to live in good ways, the finer things in life, setting goals, and accomplishing important tasks. White Shell Talk helps one to look into the future at new horizons in a world filled with approaching sunlight—a new day is coming. Turquoise Talk comes from the teachings of the south and is about things that are already on this earth. This is used in solving daily problems; no matter what kind of difficulty we have, there is a blue sky that never ceases. The world is not going to end just because of these issues, which can be overcome. Blue twilight tells stories about problems that are going to be solved. The Yellow World is about discussing the finished product. Perhaps the elders that are growing old have their ceremony done to pray for good things to happen and to give thanks for all the life they have lived. They have accomplished much and have a desire to pass their knowledge and experience on to their grandchildren who will carry these teachings into the future. The north side or Black Talk teaches of the great ones. It tells about great storms, the large amount of water that is going to come, or snow and wind in the future. These elements will put this earth back in order when the seasons change in different areas, and new things are going to spring forth. This is about spiritual things associated with the north that come back to here. Medicine men and elders use this Black Talk to communicate with the sky, wind, water people, sun, and other natural phenomena. They make connection with all of these elements, to control them and improve the situation of the people in this world.

Let me give an example using White Shell Talk. This morning I had a situation with my unhappy daughter. She was all dressed up for school, but she did not want to go, and so my wife said to me, "There's something wrong with my baby. Do you want to talk to her?" I went to her room; as soon as I saw her, I could tell she was sad, and so I asked her what was going on. She handed me a letter from the school. I read it and learned that her grades were down and that she needed to improve if she was going to advance to the next grade level. There was a lot she needed to do to catch up. I told her that I realized she was unhappy and there was work ahead, but that we could get a tutor, and when I came home from my job, I would spend a lot of time helping her. Together we could get her to where she wanted to be. Everything would be alright if we worked together. I said, "Your dad is here. Your mom is here. We will take it upon ourselves to make it happen; there is plenty of time to do it, and there are resources that will help us to get these things done. Don't worry about it—everything will be okay."

To me, I was talking to my child in the language of the White Shell and Blue World ways because of the problem we can fix. The blue light is here today and soon there will be clear skies. That means that we are going to be fine, the sun will be out, her father will be there. Only I knew which world I was talking about, she did not know, but later in life she will understand why Dad was talking that way. She will learn to speak in this same way, too. Medicine men show the path in this manner, making their point, then later saying this is the Turquoise Way of doing things. They know where they are coming from. Usually the levels of language are not identified to people, but when one is saying sacred prayers and talking to the gods, this understanding becomes clear.

The concept of moving through the four worlds is also used when counseling adults with addiction problems. Often I work with people who are deep in despair. They have left the White World and fallen back into the Black World, where they have limited functions, and like the ants and other creatures who lived there, they cannot communicate, cannot understand what is happening around them, and feel a great deal of turmoil inside. When people realize they are in this situation, they need help to reach the Blue World, where there is more light and hope. For the medicine man to assist that person, they need to start their journey from below and move upward into the Yellow World, where there is even greater hope and understanding. This is the place where a healer can assist the person into the White World through ceremony and medicines. Still, that person is not fully recovered because there is always the chance that he or she will slip back into the lower worlds by taking the same path that led them there in the first place. Even after a Blessingway ceremony, each individual has to make the choice as to how their life should be and if they want to remain in the White World. To be in the Glittering World, one needs to recover, learn, teach, and then help others avoid repeating the mistakes that led to their downfall.

I am working with a young man who is getting out of the hospital today. He overdosed on drugs and drinks a lot. He has a wife who left him and took their beautiful child with her. He is about forty years old, has a trade, and can make a lot of money if he works at it. But he is addicted to alcohol and drugs that keep putting him back into the Black World. He is constantly getting thrown out of other people's houses, and even his mother does not want him staying in her house. He is living in the Black World both emotionally and physically. It is going to kill him, just like the fire, just like the water—it will not hold back. That is the way things are. There is a reason that the worlds were fashioned in this way.

CHAPTER FOUR

Changing Woman and Peopling the Earth

Following the emergence, the holy beings and the earth surface people (humans) began a process of adapting to the new elements of life found in the White, later turned Glittering World. It continues to this day. Central to this part of the creation story is White Shell Woman, also known as Changing Woman, who played a major role in establishing life patterns for the Navajo. This formative period shaped the lives of people and personalities through events that are now enshrined in two major ceremonies—the Blessingway (Hózhóójí) and the Enemyway (Anaa'jí). These two rites, however, exist as polar opposites. While the Enemyway and Monsterway (Yé'ii Hastiiník'eh) with their main protagonists Monster Slayer and Born for Water will be discussed in more detail in chapter 9, suffice it to say that although the Twins may be tangentially introduced in the Blessingway because of their relationship to Changing Woman, their fighting, killing, and warrior ways have little to do with the peaceful, nurturing, and helpful life of their mother. Male thinking dominates their narrative while female thought and action drives that of the Blessingway. In this chapter, Perry discusses the events in her story.

Changing Woman is the main personality in the Blessingway, a ceremony that can stand alone or have elements from it used in every other chantway. Leland C. Wyman, an expert in the classification and employment of Navajo ceremonies, notes that the Blessingway is not used to cure an illness, but rather to bring peace, harmony, and good things that bless the life of the individual for whom it is performed. He writes, "In spite of being set apart from the other chantways, the Blessingway rite is said to control all of them." Then quoting Father Berard Haile, who in turn cited an elderly medicine man he had interviewed, he offered:

Blessingway is representative for them [Navajos], it is the spinal column of songs. . . No native ceremonial, therefore, can hope to be effective without this backbone [or main stalk]. It may be said that Blessingway has precedence over chantways and these acknowledge their indebtedness to it. . . . No other ceremonial in the Navajo system can make similar claims of control. At the end of every performance of a chant, the singer lays aside his rattle and sings at least one Blessingway song to justify the chant, to ensure its effectiveness, to correct inadvertent omission of essential song and prayer words, to correct errors in sandpaintings, in cutting and coloring prayersticks, and "just for safety" as natives put it.[1]

This all-purpose blessing may be given in a relatively short prayer or in a ceremony that lasts usually for two days but also up to five.[2] Even the Enemyway rite closes with a twelve-word Blessingway song.

Wyman identifies twenty different parts of the main narrative among which are post-emergence events, the placement of inner forms in material objects, birth of Changing Woman, her puberty ceremony and birth of the Twins, physical creation of domestic and game animals as well as the Navajo people, her travel to the west, clan origin myths, departure of the holy people, and establishment of Blessingway.[3] Perry, who performs the Blessingway in its many forms, touches upon some of these topics here, but also expands upon them in other places including volume 2, chapter 1— mountain blessings and the mountain soil bundle; volume 3, chapter 2—the girl's puberty ceremony (Kinaaldá); and volume 3, chapter 5—migration of the clans. This chapter lays the foundation for that future discussion. Changing Woman, in concert with other holy people, established patterns for everything that takes place on this earth today; there was no god more important in doing so.

What follows is a fascinating story of how the Navajo interacted with the holy people in those early days. As with other narratives, not everyone agrees on some of the specifics. Even the place of emergence is disputed; some medicine men insist it was in the area of Navajo Dam outside of Farmington, New Mexico, while others, including Perry, teach that it was at Fish Lake near Pagosa Springs, Colorado, a distance between the two sites of sixty miles. Regardless of which place it was, both put the Navajo in their Southwest ancestral homeland called Dinétah (Among the People). Many of the initial activities of expanding the land and emplacing geographic forms, the draining of water to the cardinal directions, the introduction to other native people, and interaction with the holy people began here and then spread to the south and west. The Navajo, with divine assistance, settled upon the land in an ever-widening arc.

There is, however, another side to this story. Archaeologists and anthropologists have long embraced the Bering Strait theory as the place of entrance for Native Americans, including the Navajo, onto this continent. Briefly, this theory posits that during the last Ice Age or Pleistocene Epoch, the ocean level dropped by perhaps as much as three hundred feet because of the water deposited on the glaciers that were then spreading across part of North America. The absence of water created a one-thousand-mile land bridge (Beringia) that connected what is now called Siberia to Alaska and the American continent, fostering a migration of Asiatic peoples as they pursued megafauna such as mastodons, mammoths, musk ox, and other Ice Age creatures. This 30,000 year period led to the peopling of America so that by 10,000 BC there were Indians from the tip of South America to the far northern reaches of Canada and Alaska. While this theory fails to recognize or account for the possibility of transoceanic crossings, travelers coming from the east and not just the west, the wide variety of Indian languages, different blood and phenotypes, along with many other factors, it still remains a popular explanation of how Native Americans arrived here.

Language and archaeology have provided whatever proof may exist for this theory. Homing in on the Navajo, who speak the Athabaskan language, they, of all of the linguistic groups, fit snugly into this belief. The largest group of Athabaskan speakers lives in Alaska and northwestern Canada, with smaller clusters along the Pacific coast in Washington, Oregon, and California and an isolate group in Texas. In the American Southwest, there are six broad divisions of Apache and their relatives, plus the Navajo. There are also Athabaskan speakers living today in Siberia. Linguists and archaeologists connect these groups and postulate that the movement of these people had a general southern flow, starting about 600 to 700 years ago, when the northern group separated from the forebears of the Navajo and Apache as they moved south. In turn, these two entities split approximately 500 to 300 years ago.[4] These dates, based on a technique called glottochronology, in which shifts in a base language are assigned a steady rate of change, are the only ways to determine when these divisions occurred.

On a more general level, archaeologists have studied material culture specific to the northern and southern groups and found what they believe to be remnants of adaptation to a cold climate in Navajo objects discovered in the Southwest. For instance, there are similarities in the sinew-backed bow, mountain lion skin quivers, beaver teeth dice, and the male hogan's entryway, said to be a warming antechamber to keep the cold out of the main living space. North of Salt Lake in dry caves near Promontory, Utah, 250 pairs of moccasins of all sizes, similar to those found in the subarctic, have been dated to between 1180 and 1290 AD. Archaeologists and anthropologists have examined other evidence including DNA sampling, oral history accounts, campsites, and cultural holdovers; for those interested in a detailed analysis, see archaeologist Deni J. Seymour's *From the Land of Ever Winter to the American Southwest.*[5]

Perry's contribution to the discussion of emergence versus southern migration adds more fuel to the fire. As he spoke about what he had learned from his father and grandfather, it became apparent that their teachings had a strong northern orientation. Instead of having the movement of Changing Woman and her people start in the north and move south, it was just the opposite. Many other stories concerning her departure from the Navajo have her traveling to the west to her home with Sun Bearer, which agreed with Perry's version. As we talked about this, however, it was apparent that he was thinking more of west-northwest and into the land of the northern Athabaskan. His explanation of the change in the animals, plants, and people marks an adaptation to this environment, a complete reversal of the anthropological theory.

While there is very little discussion of this northern connection in the Navajo literature, medicine men are well aware of "Diné Who Exist Elsewhere" (Diné Náhódlóonii) living in the north. One part of the teachings concerning the end of the world tells of when these two groups—northern and southern Athabaskan speakers—will join together and once again share their cultures and information. John Holiday, a medicine man from Monument Valley, recounts when he was vacationing with some family members in western Canada. They stopped near one of the reservations, and because his back was bothering him, he decided to sit out from some of the touring. He settled down on a nearby bench and waited for his family to return. He said,

> As I sat there, a couple of men from the Diné Who Exist Elsewhere approached. They greeted me with a language I understood. "Hello, my dearest. Where are you from?" "My dearest" is how they greet each other. "I'm a Navajo from the Navajo Reservation, my homeland," I replied. I thought these were some Navajos who were visiting there, too. [After introducing himself through clan relationship, he was told] "Well some of the same clans live back there within those mountains." . . . [Later the two men asked] "Do you know the Blessingway?" "Yes." Then they said, "Our people were separated from your people during the Creation. Why? We don't know. The Holy Beings held us back and kept us here. We heard your people [Navajo] took most of the religious ceremonies like Blessingway and others with them. . . . If a Navajo comes here, he will have to come to our home, perform a ceremony, and tell our people the history of the religion and their beliefs, before he can be released to go."[6]

John was happy to part company once his family arrived.

Equally impressive was the experience of Jim Dandy, a man raised by traditional parents and grandparents. As an employee of the San Juan School District, Utah, and as a teacher of Navajo culture, he was selected to be in a group of people who visited the Yukon Territory in Canada and Siberia in Russia as part of an exchange program between 1996 and 1998. He noted many similarities with all of these Indians—the shared language, belief in the Four Sacred Mountains with identical colors and sacred stones associated with the four directions, and a story about a separation that pushed some people to the south and others into Siberia. Those who remained refer to themselves as the Winter People (Beday Diné). When Jim's group moved into Siberia, he encountered an old Ket medicine man who sang songs very similar to those Jim knew; he learned that their teachings about the thumb were the same, the girl's puberty ceremony shared similar practices, and that the entryway of their old-style tents was similar to the male hogan. Jim fully agreed that these northern Athabaskan speakers were direct relatives of the Navajo.[7]

In this chapter, Perry also discusses the Anasazi or Ancestral Puebloans who inhabited the Four Corners area between 1000 BC and 1300 AD. While he insists that the Anasazi and the Hopi were two separate people, something that most archaeologists and anthropologists deny, Navajo stories about the ancient group explain that they were Native Americans who were at first in tune with the holy people but then forsook their sacred relationship and became a fallen group of Indians who were destroyed because of their evil design. In *Viewing the Ancestors*, there is a full discussion of who the Anasazi were, how they lived (according to traditional teachings), why they were annihilated, and their relationship with those around them—all from the Navajo perspective.[8] At this point, it is enough to say that Perry's understanding of them is very much in keeping with how many Navajos view them and that a more complete discussion will be given in chapter 9.

Changing Woman and Sun Bearer

As the people emerged from the three previous worlds into the White World, they carried mud on their shoes. They began to clean their moccasins, noticing that some pebbles from each of the worlds had stuck to them. The stones were beautiful and so were kept. Once all of the travelers had reached the Fourth World, they stood on a small island in the midst of a huge body of water, wondering how to drain the land for more room to live. As they talked about it, a young man spoke up, saying, "I have a pebble that I brought from the Black World." He held up the rock for all to see. Another person said, "I picked one up from the Blue World," while another chimed in, "I brought one from the Yellow World." Yet another suggested, "Let's pick one up from here," and that was the beginning of the use of the four sacred colored stones (ntł'iz) used as offerings with prayers, songs, and ceremonies. The people sang a song that turned these rocks into spinning stones that cut through the mountains containing the water that now could drain in the four directions. To the east went a white stone, the south turquoise, the west a yellow stone, and to the north jet. These rocks received the name the holy ones.

The people, animals, and gods spread out over the newly formed land and encountered a new set of experiences in the White World. One of the most important ones was the birth of White Shell Woman on Gobernador Knob (Ch'ool'į'í—Fir Mountain), New Mexico. The holy people named her Yikáí Yizhchį, meaning "The Dawn Has Been Given Birth," but call her White Shell Woman, since this shell is associated with the east and a new beginning. As she matured from baby to child to teenager in twelve days, she received a second name—Changing Woman (Asdzą́ą́ Nádleehé). Her maturity increased as her body grew, voice deepened, wisdom broadened, and spirit became more nurturing. The holy people performed the first ceremony, the kinaaldá, which recognized her reaching womanhood, thus establishing a pattern for every Navajo woman in the future. Not until her growing experiences in life ended, would she reclaim her name of White Shell Woman, having passed through the trials of existing in this world and becoming a more perfect god. As deity, she now presides over ceremonies and is referred to by this name since she is now an unchanging individual.

In the meantime, White Shell Woman, then known as Changing Woman, had reached maturity, and had grown into a beautiful young female. As a virgin, she was still quite naive to the practices of men and women so went about carefree and unguarded. Now each day, Sun Bearer (Jóhonaa'éí) crossed the sky, traveling on different trails as the seasons change. He was a handsome warrior who carried the sun as he rode from east to west, stopping at noon to look around for a while before continuing his journey until he finished his task for that day and entered his home. Once he arrived, he removed his armor, taking it off slowly then hanging it up. Next he sat down and ate with his family, an appropriate end for another good day.

One time, however, when he was riding about on his horse doing his work, he saw Changing Woman taking a bath. She enjoyed the feeling of her body beneath the water as it rippled over her. Down from the canyon wall poured more water, streaming in a gentle fall. Changing Woman moved beneath the cascading flow and spread her naked legs as it tumbled down, hitting her private area. Sun Bearer observed this and became aroused. Taking advantage of the situation, he joined with Water, his brother, and had a sexual relationship with the young woman. From this episode, Changing Woman conceived and bore Twins—Monster Slayer (Naayéé'neizghání) and Born for Water (Tóbájíshchíní). Monster Slayer was totally part of his father's doing, but Water also played a part, and so together they created Born for Water, the second Twin. Fire (Sun) and Water made the two boys.

Many people do not talk about this because they are embarrassed. The two brothers—Sun Bearer and Water—had taken each other's wife when they did that. In the past in some families, a brother might meet a woman whom he takes as his wife but then passes her on to another brother who will actually marry her. This was a common practice for Navajos in the old days. Brothers still joke with each other and say, "This is my son," and then the other brother will say, "Your son? That's my son. He looks more like me. He is more handsome like me and not at all like you." When they kid around like that, this is where the practice originated. For example, my father had five brothers, and each one had a family. One of the brothers was really handsome and so my brothers would say, "I think that is one of my dads over there because I look more like him. I carry myself more like him." They are just kidding around, but actually that is the way it used to work. So as these things were happening, Sun Bearer made his own son, Monster Slayer, but also took ownership of Born for Water once the two boys entered the world.

When Sun Bearer had this relationship, he violated his faithfulness with his real family who lived in the east. His wife was sitting there at home and had no idea about what was going on. Once the Twins arrived, they grew up in twelve days and became big, strong young men who were anxious to learn about their father and where he lived. They pestered their mother, asking for his identity and how they could find his home, but Changing Woman was firm and kept telling them that they could not do this. Eventually, they disobeyed their mother and went in search of their father.

The Twins

At this time the world was filled with dangerous monsters and supernatural beings who were evil and did great harm. There were those such as Big God (Yé'iitsoh) and Gray God (Yé'ii Łibá) who roamed about looking for Navajo children to eat. These beings provided enough of an impetus to eventually encourage the Twins to visit their father to obtain weapons for killing. There were also stationary evil beings such as Slashing Reeds, Crushing Rocks,

He-Who-Kicks-People-Off-a-Cliff, and Kills-with-His-Eyes that were positioned throughout the land to stop those who followed the Holy Trail to Sun Bearer's home. These monsters would eventually be tricked and defeated through sacred words, prayers, and wit as the Twins traveled on their way to meet their father. Both types of monsters were considered holy people, but there was a third kind of god (Yé'ii)—such as Talking God, Black God, Holy Wind, and others—who were kind, helpful, and assisted the people as they traveled through the worlds and were with them now. They provided future assistance to the Twins as they faced challenges and defeated the evil beings.

Occasionally as Sun Bearer traveled on his path across the sky, he would stop by Changing Woman's hogan and ask how she was and did she have any children. She told him no because she feared that word would get out and that Big God would show up and demand their lives. Her fears soon turned into reality. Big God noticed what he thought might be footprints around Changing Woman's hogan and other signs of male children in the area. He asked her and others what they had seen, but everybody claimed they knew nothing about it, saying, "No, there's no children here." Big God asked, "Then why are there baby footprints around this home? I see footprints. I need to eat those babies. Where are they?" Changing Woman replied, "Oh, we are lonely for babies, so we are making footprints in the dirt to remind us of them. This is how we do it." She took her hand and balled it into a fist, tucking her thumb into her fingers then using the bottom of her palm to stamp a foot-like impression on the soil. "This is how we do it." "Oh," said Big God, "that makes sense," then went away. Sun Bearer believed the same explanation. Everybody kept the truth to themselves because they did not want either of the boys to get killed; the youth were raised in secret and often hidden underground.

As the Twins grew, their curiosity as to who their father was, where he lived, and how he could help them to rid the earth of these monsters became stronger. Finally and against the wishes of their mother, they set off to find him. The adventures they had along the way are another story, but once they reached his home, they faced new challenges. Sun Bearer had no idea that he had two sons that were now visiting because Changing Woman had not told him. As he learned of their identity, he grew jealous and angry at these two handsome young men claiming relationship. When he entered his home, he took off his armor and threw it across the room, setting the whole house in commotion. His wife said, "Whoa, whoa, whoa. What's going on? What are you doing? You used to hang up your armor really nicely. What is wrong?"

Changing Woman, using the heel of her hand in the sand to create a "footprint" to fool Yé'iitsoh (Big God), thus saving the Twins' lives. The giant's father, Sun Bearer, eventually gave Monster Slayer and Born for Water the tools needed to kill Big God and his brother Gray God. (Courtesy San Juan School District Media Center)

He was mad. "Don't ask me what is wrong. I saw two men coming in here. While I'm working over there in the west, you are seeing other men behind my back." He accused her of having an affair.

Now it was his wife's turn. "I thought you were working out there and not doing anything. Why are there two young men coming around here, saying they are looking for their father?"

"Their father! You know I'm not their father." He immediately denied everything. "They are not my children."

"Well, they are here to see you, not me. They are looking for you." Eventually the whole truth came out and he admitted that he had been involved in an affair. Once he realized that these were his sons, he went to Changing Woman and told her to wait for him in the west, where he would build a home of abalone shell for her to live in. He wanted to meet her over there in the evening when he had finished his journey. This is where the clan people would later find her when they became lonely and depressed because she was not with them. She was there waiting for Sun Bearer.

During today's kinaaldá ceremony, there is a part where some people, when conducting the ritual, react to Sun Bearer's sexual attitude and protect the young girl from any of his advances. Changing Woman had become his wife because of what he had done, but a reoccurrence of that issue is now prevented. When the sun comes out for that ceremony and the pretty young woman has been stretched, dressed in all of her finery, and is most appealing, an elder steps forth in front of the girl, casts a shadow on her, and addresses the sun. He says, "We know what you're doing. Move away. You are not looking at this girl. You did that one time, but that is not going to happen again. Move away." The sun gets pushed away as the elders protect their daughter. They do not want the sun to get involved again. White Shell Woman is on the other side, smiling and telling the sun, "Watch your eyes. Keep your eyeballs moving and stay away." This is also one of the stories about how jealousy first occurred between men and women.

Changing Woman—Mother of the Navajos

Following the defeat of the monsters, Changing Woman continued to live among the people and help them exist in the White World. She understood, however, that she would not remain with them forever and so constantly prepared them for the time that she would leave. One of those teachings was that there would be many things that changed as the earth surface people experienced life. She cautioned, "You will grow through a number of stages and learn something new each time. When you have different challenges or become better in some way, you will grow." Changing Woman instructed them as a mother would a child, explaining why and how humans learn in life. Each day, as the physical world shifted—as homes, behavior, knowledge, lifestyle, and the natural world moved through stages—there would be change. Suddenly, the one who was a boy has white hair, the young man is now an elder, just as Changing Woman went through a maturing process and eventually returned to being White Shell Woman. One follows in her footsteps, walking, growing, and aging. Everyone is the child of White Shell Woman, but lives the life of Changing Woman.

White Shell Woman/Changing Woman is our god and is the holy mother, but in her daily life, just as we also experience, she was changing. She had many tasks and tried to assist her children, the Twins, through their life. This mother with her sons created new ceremonies that now serve as patterns for the Navajo. Just as White Shell Woman or Changing Woman are the same, there are certain times when a person has a holy experience during their life and reverts back to the sacred state of White Shell Woman. The rest of the time, just as this goddess lived a daily life, she is like Changing Woman. They are not two separate people. The day a child is born, the mother and child are holy as is White Shell Woman. When a girl has her

Young women learn at an early age that one of their main roles in life is to follow Changing Woman's example by nurturing and caring for their livestock, gardens, and family members. Nature provides multiple examples to follow.

puberty ceremony, a woman gives birth to a baby, and when one reaches old age and dies—these are the four times that this happens. That woman becomes a holy one through those experiences. At the time of her birth, she is a holy one—a new life is on this earth and so people gather to celebrate, give gifts, and offer prayers as White Shell Woman presents herself. When she reaches puberty, a ceremony is held, and with the blessing of corn pollen and prayers, that day the young teenager becomes White Shell Woman and is able to bless—physically and spiritually—the people around her. Next, when this woman gives birth to a new life, she becomes the holy one and may have a Blessingway ceremony. Finally, when a woman's hair turns white and she shrinks in size as if she is returning to being a baby, she dies, and in that holy moment, she again becomes like White Shell Woman. These are the four times, the four days that she enters into that holy state.

The sacred narratives of the Navajo are filled with stories about how things change. The following is an old traditional story about White Shell Woman and some of her last experiences with the people. Having lived a challenging life in this world, she decided to go with her husband, Sun Bearer, to a home that he built for her in the west. This was the same time that all of the gods moved to their appointed places to remain for the rest of time. In preparation for the long journey to the Pacific Ocean, she selected plants, water, animals, and even some of the people from the Four Sacred Mountains who wanted to remain with her. After gathering an abundance of the things she needed, she began walking to the west and north, where the sun lies down. Some of the animals that accompanied her were wolves, coyotes, ferrets, buffalo, deer, and other smaller creatures. Along the way, some of the travelers dropped off to remain in areas that they liked. By the time she had reached lands to the north, there were only a few animals and people remaining with her.

White Shell Woman with her travelers had reached a place where the climate was really cold and the snow deep. The sunlight became shorter and less intense as the days became darker and colder. The fur on the animals started to modify, many of their coats began to lose their color, their tongues and teeth changed, and their eyes transformed as they looked and hunted for different things. For instance, the coyotes and foxes that are found in our area have different eyes when compared to those located in the north. Ones to the north have blue eyes instead of the yellowish brown of those who stayed behind. Food for these animals also changed. Their songs became different, shifting their behavior and attitude. Now they walked differently and grew bigger or smaller in size, depending on the need and the temperature of the climate. Hunting methods had to be adapted to the new circumstances; the food the animals and people ate was different, changing their diet and eating habits. This new world and way of life offered new challenges.

The Water People adopted some of these animals back. Many of the holy Water People were more numerous than they were in the land of the Four Sacred Mountains. Water was all over the countryside, in rivers, lakes, and in the nearby ocean, so the animals started to eat food from these sources, causing them to swim and dive more and improve their ability to see underwater. For example, some of the bears, like the polar bear, turned into Water People, whereas the bears that live around here are land people. Their body structure got bigger, they depended heavily on fish, their eyes and mouths had changed, even their foot pattern was different. They are now bigger, heavier, and not afraid of anything. The same is true of other animals. Take deer for instance. They are in the same species and family as the caribou, but they each have dissimilar prayers because they have adapted to their own land and act accordingly. Still, they are one and the same animal, but their colors, antlers, feet, and how they walk are different. Caribou are much slower but they swim well, live on land, and travel in herds. Deer, on the other hand, are extremely fast runners and generally do not live in large groups. Change in habitat made a big difference with everything.

At home between the Four Sacred Mountains, the people were becoming lonely and wandering around, missing White Shell Woman and the time that the gods were always present. Now the holy people were scattered to the four directions. The humans had received instructions and answers from them, when suddenly they were left alone with no one to lead. They followed the guidance obtained in the past, but it was hard to live a life without the gods always there to assist. The people became increasingly stressed, looking for something that was no longer available to provide answers. They became very unhappy, did not feel good about themselves, and kept asking, "What is going on? What is going on?" as they spiraled into depression. Tears filled their eyes as they cried for no apparent reason. There was no physical pain, but their mind and thoughts kept returning to the uncertainty of the future and what it would be like to live without the gods. Fear encompassed their world and anxiety shaped their decisions and actions as they convinced themselves that even worse things lay ahead in the future. Even after all they had been through with Monster Slayer ridding the earth of its frightening creatures, there were still storms, lightning, and thunder, reminding them of past struggles. The loud clapping of the thunder gods, remembering the fight against the monsters who killed and ate the children, and the hardships of daily life, wore the people down as anxiety grew. Now that the gods were gone, many of these bad things might return. Even though their world had become safer, their minds and inner feelings were getting the best of them. Black clouds scared them as they anticipated the next thunderstorm and changes in weather. Loneliness, depression, and uncertainty gripped their minds, causing them to trudge about aimlessly and cry all of the time.

Leaders and elders gathered together and said, "There are too many people wandering around unhappy. Something is going on that is not good. We need to get White Shell Woman and talk to her; maybe she can fix what is wrong. This is one part of life that we do not understand." There was a woman who spoke a lot and was boastful, but she also got to the point quickly. Her name was "Woman Who Talks a Lot" (Asdzą́ą́ Lá áníní). Since she was not afraid of speaking up about issues, the leaders selected her to go in search of their elder sister, White Shell Woman, and bring her back to fix these problems. Woman Who Talks a Lot found her and reported on the problems of the people and urged her to return. White Shell Woman was the one who had helped solve problems and make life better in the past and now they needed her assistance more than ever.

White Shell Woman started back with many people following her, while others who had originally left with her remained; still others stopped along the way to settle in different locations. The people who stayed in what is today Canada and Alaska are called by the Navajo the Diné Náhódlóonii (The People Who Exist Elsewhere). They speak our language and share some of our teachings and culture. Those that stopped in other places are also related, but became involved with different tribes through marriage and so lost their ability to speak the Navajo language. Some remained with White Shell Woman and came all the way south to the Havasupai; they speak a language very close to that of Navajo but live in the Grand Canyon area. This splitting off is also seen with the Apache who converse in our language and were at one time part of us. Some of their ceremonies are very similar to what we practice. They used to be Navajos, but they just went farther south. Still, they have preserved a lot of the old ways that we used to practice, including the way they dress.

The medicine men who teach about these things—the ceremonies and traveling—always sing about moving to the west and the people who strayed away and joined other tribes. Their knowledge made them holy ones, and so when they met other people, they brought their medicine and were accepted as part of those groups. We always sing about different people that we encountered, how we talked to them about medicine, and taught them about these things. We became their holy ones by sharing this information. That's my understanding of it.

Other People on the Land

There were other Indian people inhabiting the land during these migrations. The Navajo think of the Anasazi as being here when we arrived, while the Hopi were with us in the worlds beneath and traveled to this land, the White World, at the same time we did. The Anasazi were different people who had been cursed and had a lot of enemies. Their name, Anasazi (Anaasází— Ancestral/Alien Enemies), can be translated as the enemy who used to live here before us. We do not really know where they came from because they were already here. They were short, small people who lived in the rocks, had white feet, and talked differently than we do. The Anasazi were not very smart people, lived as families, but never really grew into communities and kept to themselves in small groups. I have been told that it took them the longest time to figure out how to plant crops and hunt. When the People emerged, they were still around. We tried to kill them because they had some magical things they used against the People. The Anasazi were the enemy, were unhealthy, and were not supposed to be on this earth, and so the Navajo tried to get rid of them. This teaching comes from the Enemyway ceremony, which tells how they were defeated. One of the songs says, "I'm chasing the enemy; the Anasazi I am chasing. His woman is running along the side and this woman is crying and making noise. But some I corner. I corner him. I put a club through his head and I defeat my enemy." That is why I know that the Anasazi were something really bad for us. Even if we just pick up their head or bones or objects that belonged to them, their spirit will jump on us and we will become very sick.

In the Enemyway ceremony we can use their bones. Only a medicine man who understands and can perform the ceremony can obtain one. He will take a yucca stalk and fashion a fork to pick up the bone, but he cannot touch it. He securely wraps bark over it then ties it, but nobody touches it. The person who has been ordained to perform the ceremony must have a sacred name, showing that he is a warrior who has had the ceremony done for him and so is protected. Not just anybody can go out there and pick it up; it has to be a warrior. Toward the end of the ceremony, the Anasazi's bone or whatever else is used from a real life enemy is taken to a medicine place and shot. This kills the enemy or evil spirit afflicting the patient and allows him or her to be healed.

The Anasazi were a very powerful people in controlling spiritual forces, and that is the reason why they are not here today. They thought themselves better and more powerful than the holy ones. These people copied down everything they witnessed, putting sacred images and events on the clay pots they made. As they created these pictures, they drew contemporary views as they watched them happen, but to us they have become only symbols. For instance, Kokopelli is seen walking, playing his flute, and has a large humpback. This is what they actually saw. These humpback people really existed as some of the holy ones back then. The Anasazi started to paint and carve pictures of them, which angered the gods, who caused sickness and death because they were not being respected. The Anasazi did the same thing in portraying the air, sunlight, rain, and Mother Earth. My understanding is that they almost developed a pot that pictured the images of four creators. The holy ones became angry saying, "Don't put me on your pot. I don't want to be on your pot. Don't draw me on there," but they would not listen. For this disrespect, the gods destroyed them by using the Water and Fire people. Still, their medicine was very strong and so are their ghosts, which were left behind. This is why in the Enemyway ceremony, their powers are the first thing to address and why their bones are used.

Navajos must also avoid going into Anasazi ruins. Entering them is forbidden except to pick up bones for the Enemyway. Other than that, a person has no business being in there. Pieces of potsherds and arrowheads can be used when properly blessed. Flint arrowheads are often used in ceremonies because they were their weapon and so you use it that way. Now it is yours because you have taken possession of it. I learned that, nowadays, people are taking small Anasazi clay pots or pieces of pots found on the ground, grinding them into fine powder, adding it to their clay then baking it into their pottery to make it sturdy. In the past, no one would do that and so just left the Anasazi piece alone.

Another thing these people are associated with is gambling. The Great Gambler (Nihwííbjihii—He Who Wins You) was famous for his activities in Chaco Canyon. People use him as an example of what to do or not to do in avoiding the evils of gambling and addiction. It is said that one day, if people are not careful, he will return with all of the vices he controlled. A person will keep going to casinos and become addicted to gambling and lose everything. This story is used to teach about things like drinking, smoking, gambling, and anything else that creates dependency. He is always talked about in this way. Some people believe his ghost still lingers in the form of today's many addictions and that some of them might get a hold of you, so stay away.

Navajos still play a game that is connected to the creation of the world and the Great Gambler. The ruins in Chaco Canyon have stories about when he enslaved the people living there through gambling. After a while a young man approached this leader who wanted to put him in bondage the usual way by playing a series of games that his opponent would lose, thereby placing him under the Great Gambler's control. This particular young man, however, was different. He and the animals and people prayed for success, so the holy

Although Anasazi sites, artifacts, and rock art cover much of Navajo land, remnants of these ancient people are often avoided. Touching a bone, placing one's hand in a pictograph, or living near an abandoned ruin could put that person in contact with the individual who made it, with dire results. (Drawing by Charles Yanito)

beings assisted him. One of the games, tsidił or Navajo stick game, was set up with forty small stones arranged in groups of ten around a larger stone in the middle. The three sticks that were bounced off the central rock were painted white (day) on one side and black (night) on the other. Through the powers of those playing with the young man, they were able to control the colors on the sticks, so he won the game and freed the people.

There is much more to this activity beyond the story of the Great Gambler. The central stone represents the holy ground of life or the place of emergence. When the people entered into the Fourth World, they spoke three languages—white, blue, and yellow, but not yet black. The small island they were on was surrounded by water that needed to be drained so that there would be more land. A different colored rock from each direction—white (east), blue (south), yellow (west), and black (north)—cut through the surrounding mountains and landscape and drained the land, creating the four sacred rivers—to the east the Rio Grande, south Little Colorado, west the Colorado, and north San Juan River. These are represented by the four spaces kept open between the four sets of ten stones.

Before starting the game, a person can place his hand on the central rock to pray and meditate. It is said that the stone can talk and sing answers to the individual praying. This is a form of divination called "listening" (na'íísts'ą'). The one seeking an answer places their hand on it, prays about a problem or situation, closes their eyes, and listens. People pray for a new life or new direction that they might want to visit, and the answer will come to that person in a good way. This is where the ceremony of listening came from with answers provided through that stone. Today, people no longer pray in this manner. I believe back in the 1950s or 1960s, they stopped using it to find answers, and by the 1970s and 1980s stopped using stick games altogether. Only on a rare occasion will one see people playing it. Navajos now know very little about this contest, and if they do use it, the game is only as a pastime while the story and power behind it are forgotten.

The Hopi were with us in the worlds beneath and joined us in the White World after our emergence. There is a place called Hadajiizhnaani near old Oraibi where these people entered near a big mountain called Emergence Mountain. It is said that is where the Hopis built their first home and celebrated their arrival with the kachinas. When we came together in the White World, the Navajos said, "You are the Hopi and we are the Navajo." At that time the turkey was the keeper of corn and other seeds brought up from the third world, and so the two peoples sat down opposite each other and Turkey said, "This is going to be food, so I am going to give both of you a choice as to which end of the cob you will take. There is one end that grows up, but there is also the other end that grows from the inside. I am going to break the ear in half and put it here. Whichever one you take, it will be your story." Instead of the Navajos selecting what they wanted, Coyote took the back end of it, announcing, "We Navajo will take the part closest to the stalk." The Hopis took the top part. To this day, when Navajos plant corn, it grows well if it is watered a lot but will not have many ears on the plant, and those that are there are short. The Hopis, on the other hand, took the tip that grows well, and so they can put a couple of kernels in dry ground and their corn will grow about one foot. Off of that one-foot plant, they will get four cobs, whereas a Navajo cornstalk might grow six feet tall but there will only be two or three ears on it. The Navajos angrily demanded to know why Coyote had made that choice. He explained that the part of the plant that went into the ground would have a better root than the one that sits on top. They replied that might be the case, but the Navajos' corn would be short, and the Hopi would have the more powerful corn pollen for ceremonial use. Navajos now view the Hopi as better farmers, and their corn has better colors, which carries over to more colorful pottery, kachinas, and blankets than those of the Navajo. They also have better stories than us because we only wear one bun on the back of our head, but they actually have a bun in the back, one on the side, and one on the forehead. They have a story to go with each of them—three stories in all.

Navajo people understand that there are other races and each one of them has their own creation story, culture, skin color, and thoughts. The elders long ago foretold this and warned that the Navajo should be careful because one day they may end up living under the rule of these people. There would be black people (Africans), red (Native Americans), yellow (Asians), and white (Caucasians) who would live with the Navajo. Their hair would be different (black, brown, yellow, red), as would their physical shape and practices. For instance, it was said that the White God had a lot of knowledge, could fly, and came from the moon when it was really nice and full. He came from there and visited the people, never landing on the earth, just hovering in the air. Our people were told that this was a white person and they had to be mindful of him because one day he would have a fire in the east, and we had to be careful how we talked to him since his people were able to fly and visit the moon, and they were holy. That is what they were told.

Each of these colors that represent races goes back to the Four Sacred Mountains; they shall all be joined one day. The yellow people that speak Chinese, the white people who speak English, the red or Indian people, and the black people will become one. Each will have a holy being up on their mountain. For instance, the dark-skinned people (Bits'íís Diłhiłii) are associated with the black mountain to the north where Black God lives. At the right time, these people will come together and will be some of the holy ones.

Thus, the colors on a prayerstick (k'eet'áán) represent a number of teachings, one of which is the stages of life of an individual, while another is that they stand for the different types of humans in the rest of the world— black, red, yellow, and white—and how they control their part of the globe through their own songs and prayers. We all live on the same earth and eventually all of us will come together. My father talked about how each group has their own holy people. He said, "It is just one world that we live on with colored people on there, and they will come." And that is how the elders talk about it.

In discussing the entrance of the Navajo and other humans into the land we now know, it is important to remember that the holy beings were and are still very much a part of this world and this life, although they are not seen by the naked eye. They are present, and a few, twelve to be exact, become visible during the winter in the form of the Yé'ii Bicheii dance and ceremony, a part of the nine-day Nightway (Tł'éé'jí) ritual. There are entire books written on this ceremony, but in this context of peopling the world, the gods become manifest in physical form by those who act as masked dancers during the last few days and nights. Only those who are initiated and trained to fill this role can assume the honor of not only appearing but also becoming that holy person when they don the mask of the god they represent and use the "language" or sounds associated with these specific beings. The teachings about the human's role as they become Talking God, Black God, Calling God, Rain God, and others confirm the presence of these holy ones in the physical world today, not just at the time of creation.

When a person—either young man or woman—is initiated to represent a god, they learn of their responsibilities. They receive a short herbal bath and then perform a smudging from herbs placed on two live coals. Once the person conducting the initiation has the coals removed, already endowed members place the face mask on those undergoing the ceremony. As the individual looks through the eye slits and breathes through the mouth of the mask, they not only see the world through the eyes of the god and breathe in its essence, but actually become the deity. This is one of the few times when the holy people become incarnate. The initiation also gives the individual the right to perform as a Yé'ii Bicheii on other occasions. For those who are not trained, they are not to do those things or look at the gods while they dance, sing, or make their special sound. If they do, they will become sick. Once they look through the eyes in the mask and breathe air through it, then they can take it off and walk away. They have secured a right to be at the ceremony and participate, having been initiated into that medicine. Parents are told not to bring their young children to participate in the ceremony, but if they do, they are also introduced to the world of the gods.

Both males and females can be dancers. The female is called Bi'áádii and the male is Bik'ą'ígíí. They are designated this way—female and male—because they appear and represent those qualities. On the last night, when all the dancers are dressed, it is called Bi'áádii ada'niilzhiizh, meaning the dance will be coed. The women stand on the left or north side, the men on the right or south side, and then the lines pass through each other and cross over again. The lines switch places as the people dance from the north to the south then south to the north. At another point in the ceremony, a whip may be used to awaken the participants, reminding them of the seriousness of using the healing power of the gods. This is because many times a person may become relaxed; now they are reawakened and ensured they are aware of all that is going on, underscoring the importance and holiness of the event. This is necessary for the healing to occur.

The Yé'ii Bicheii ceremony is considered a time when gods become visible. You can see them, touch them, and hear them, which makes this ceremony different from most. People wear the mask, dress in buckskin, and don apparel like the gods, and everyone respects the ceremony. During the final night of the ritual, participants wait for the last group of Yé'ii to leave the dance area so that as they go, the spectators' heads can be sprinkled with corn pollen and prayers offered on their behalf. As these holy people walk past, thanks are expressed for the blessing they brought by their being gods that day. The holy people then make their way home after going into the shade house, where they change clothes. Just like the children when they are initiated, the dancers have to be cleansed with herbs, must wash themselves and remove all of the white paint on their bodies, and then must be smudged. Following these procedures, the participants return to everyday life as a normal human being.

CHAPTER FIVE

Determining: Divination, Prayer, and Offerings

T his chapter is concerned primarily with diagnosing what the needs of an individual may be through spiritual or supernatural means.[1] Called divination by anthropologists, the techniques used by the Navajo evoke core beliefs of their religious worldview. There are three major types of divination—wind listening (íists'ą́ą́'); star gazing (sǫ'nil'į́) with its subsidiaries sun and moon gazing and their affiliate crystal gazing (déést'į́į'—literally, to see, understand); and hand trembling or motion-in-the hand (n'dilniih)—all of which are related in that they are spiritually based and serve similar functions. The origin story of hand trembling is different from star gazing and listening, while generally, women may render the former but not the latter. These practices are used to explore the unknown, to find lost people or objects, to identify a thief or witch, to locate water or other desirable resources, to prevent danger or evil, and, most important, to diagnose the cause of an illness in order to provide a remedy.[2] Unlike medicine men who heal through chantway ceremonies lasting from one to nine days or nights and who have spent hundreds of hours to learn their accompanying prayers, songs, and rituals, the diagnostician may spend only a few hours learning the rite, will compose some of his own songs and prayers, and will require little ceremonial equipment. Chantways are normally performed by men who have a sacred body of lore based on complex mythology, whereas diviners may be either male or female (often after menopause) who received this gift at birth and have had its potential later revealed to them.[3]

The holy people play an important part in identifying future practitioners. For instance, a holder of this power may realize their ability during a ceremony when its latent force is activated. Apprenticeship follows to develop the skill. A person may have a dream to help point the way, or there may be strange supernatural occurrences hinting at the gift's presence. Unlike hand trembling, where supernatural beings make a person aware that "the ceremony wants you . . . and that you are known," star gazing is a learned rite that may be acquired as quickly as a day or two. Medicine man John Holiday said he performed star gazing for ten years, but it scared him because he used the sun, which hurt his eyes. In his words, however, "This was a natural gift bestowed on me; it was not something I had to learn or ask for. It is totally impossible to look at the sun with the naked eye, but I used to do that."[4] He described the experience as his sight darkening before a "stream of bright light bounced to the earth. The earth, in turn, changed its form to fit the shape of the sun. . . . When the white stream descended, it drew an image of the earth and all the things on it . . . showing just a little section of it, magnifying it even more to indicate what the patient was suffering from . . . but I still had to guess."[5] Each person who uses any form of divination may have a different experience from other practitioners.

Answers in star gazing and crystal gazing take a variety of forms. One woman explained that she hired a diviner and an assistant, who stared at Big Star until a beam of light shone down on the patient. If the ailment was serious, the star appeared to separate, one part turning red and moving downward, the other part remaining stationary. When this woman had the ceremony performed, two practitioners left her inside the hogan and went out to watch. They "saw" her sitting surrounded by a bright light with a black shadow in the form of a porcupine approaching her. The men could not interpret this latter symbol. One saw a great white object in the distance and felt that good awaited her in the future. Five months later, a movie outfit from Hollywood employed her and her husband for the next six years as caretakers of its sets and equipment in Monument Valley. Good fortune did lie in her future.[6]

Other people give slightly different explanations. One man believed the diviner looked at the star continuously until a thin strand of light started to vibrate, spread, then shine directly on the ailment. For instance, if a person were injured internally, the light from Big Star showed on the spot as a red blood vessel. Diagnosis for a remedy followed, some people visualizing the medicine man who would perform the healing rite.[7] George Tom tells of an uncle, Spotted Shirt, who with some other men stood atop a hill crystal gazing. A nearby mesa appeared to have a "fire" on top, the glowing spot proving to be the location of a future uranium mine.[8] Harvey Oliver from Aneth tells of his grandfather using crystal gazing to view events in World War I in which his son was involved. The grandfather "would tell how it looked underneath the world where his son was fighting the war. He would say, 'our soldiers are going to win again.' It seemed like he could see it clearly."[9]

When a person attempts to learn if he has this gift, regular corn pollen or "live" corn pollen, which has been placed on a Gila monster and then collected, is spread on his freshly washed arms and hands. The teacher offers a special prayer to the lizard, confirming whether this person is to be given an opportunity to learn. A song is sung, then the ceremony "decides if it wants you." A diviner told John Holiday he was to be a hand trembler, but when he tried, nothing happened. Still another man tried both hands with no results. The practitioner used hand trembling and "vigorously tore at my hands and arms," but nothing. Finally, he said, "You were once bitten by a jackrabbit on this hand and a prairie dog on the other; therefore, it is useless; it will definitely not work for you."[10] If any animal has bitten the hand or arm, the appendage cannot be used for divining.

Susie Yazzie from Monument Valley is a good example of a person who had the "gift" but did not want it. Her detailed account provides an "inside view" of what the experience meant to her. Often it is older people who have the maturity to recognize the signals and answers that receive the power. Susie was young when she had this "strange experience" that seemed as if she were going through a trance. "It's a feeling of anxiety—as if you are in fear of something and you are trying to run from it, but you can't find a safe place. It feels like you levitate off the ground. It is emotionally tiring and a strain. It's like remembering something of your childhood and you become very emotional about it."[11]

The first time she hand trembled, a medicine man sang a song and she started. The power entered her body and moved her from one side of the hogan to the other, where her mother sat by the door. She had not yet learned to "think for it" and control her thoughts to seek answers, so the power took over and "literally threw me around all over the place." The "stream" of power surged throughout her body—"It made my heart seem big and enlarged and moved it around to a point where it weakened me. I was afraid of it and so told the medicine man, Mr. Rock Ridge, to take the special gift away from me for good."[12] He tapped corn pollen on the soles of her feet, the palms of her hands, top of the head, then all over her body, and the power stopped. For some time after it had been removed, Susie continued to "question" and "think" in that way and felt that she could regain the gift if she had tried, but there was no desire. She now muses, "It's probably because

I gave up that special gift that I am suffering from so many health problems today."[13]

Don Mose from Monument Valley shares his views based on a long line of hand tremblers within his family.[14] From his grandfather he learned the male form of hand trembling with the zigzag lightning and the sign of the Gila monster, a method that is harshly powerful and can be used to detect evil or wrongdoing. His mother taught him a gentler way with a straight line of pollen that goes down the arm and ends with the four points of the arrowhead. A second method combined crystal gazing with a sand reproduction of the Six Sacred Mountains. These are blessed with corn pollen and have a crystal in their midst. All of this is accompanied with hand trembling. To Don, all three ways are rooted in spirituality that allows the diviner to get in tune with the holy people to receive their impressions. The basis for this began when Sun Bearer tested the Twins by switching the places of various mountains and other land forms on the earth to see if the boys could spiritually recognize where the land forms should be. Born for Water, more religiously oriented and contemplative when compared with holy being of action Monster Slayer, proved most skilled in listening to the spirit to answer the questions. He began pointing out where the mountains were as the two sang the first of five songs entitled "That One Over There" (Níléí át'é) in answer to "which one is it," implying "you are going to figure it out or solve the problem." The Twins were successful, received the necessary impressions, identified the proper locations, and eventually returned to earth with what they had sought. These songs are now used with hand trembling by those seeking answers.

Today, some outsiders—both Anglo and Navajo—remain doubtful about these various forms of divination. Anthropologists, doctors, and sociologists try to explain away the mystical side of it, suggesting tremblers have prior knowledge of events, ask questions to arrive at a "general" answer, play on typical Navajo fears, use soothing psychological techniques, or just plain fake it. Leland C. Wyman, in his investigation of this practice in the 1930s, approached this attitude head-on. In cases where he observed the practice and in one where he had the rite performed for him, there was no prior discussion with either patient or family members. "All my informants insisted that the diagnostician need not know anything about the case before beginning, and that he always goes to work without preliminary gathering of information. They seemed surprised when I suggested such a thing, saying that he 'does not need to' since the information is supposed to come from supernatural means."[15]

Perhaps the best documented and consistent reporting of hand trembling is that of Hastiin Beaal and his work with Franc Newcomb. She and her husband Arthur were running the Blue Mesa Trading Post when they started to lose items to theft. One day they could not find three horses, so Franc called on Hastiin Beaal for help. The medicine man laid out a blanket, covered it with fresh sand, went into a trance, pointed, and drew lines with his finger; when the tremors in his body ceased, he gave a clear, blow-by-blow description of where the horses were, who had taken them (without giving names), and how they were then winning a race. Later, every detail was substantiated. Arthur was skeptical, Franc a more willing believer, but when some merchandise disappeared off a freight wagon, they again called in the ninety-five-year-old Beaal. He repeated the procedure and arrived at a very detailed explanation of where the stolen saddle and other items could be found. Arthur went to a distant post the next day, found what the diviner said was true, and retrieved the goods.

Beaal became a powerful deterrent to crime in the area. He successfully identified a Navajo who clubbed a trader's wife; helped the police capture two men who decapitated a trader and stole merchandise from his store; pinpointed for the authorities a Mexican who had been stealing sheep; and found $3,000 worth of turquoise and silver pawn taken from a post, as well as a wad of bills dropped by accident in the sand. Each of these incidents he reconstructed verbally, in great detail, almost as if he were watching the plot unfold in a movie.[16] The powers of divination were a reality, even to the most skeptical.

Power of the Gila Monster

Before a ceremony of healing is held, the sickness or problem that is afflicting the patient must be identified. The Navajo have a number of ways to diagnose the issue, which include hand trembling, star/crystal gazing, and wind listening. I have used all of these practices. Hand trembling is the most common means to find out things that have happened in the past, are going on in the present, or will occur in the future. They all work through spiritual impressions and power that answer questions and direct a medicine man or woman as to what ceremony is needed to remove the problem or heal the person. The one performing the divination is the conduit through which the holy people teach what is needed. Once the situation is defined, the proper cure, usually a ceremony, is prescribed.

Hand trembling depends on the power of the Gila monster, which hearkens back to the time when all of the plants held a meeting in the mountain called the Holy Hogan (Táálee Hooghan on Black Mesa) near today's Dilkon, Arizona. They were there to discuss their healing qualities and what they could do to help the earth surface people. Two circles of these holy people filled the hogan. Each plant person had to introduce itself, talk about its qualities, what it had to offer, and how its cure would work. There were many, many medicine people there, and so two Gila monsters—one with yellow spots and one that was solid black—were asked to be in attendance. They sat in the middle of the hogan, acknowledging each plant's sacredness and power and telling them how they were to be identified through divination. They had knowledge about all of the medicines. In the future when medicine people started performing hand trembling, they would diagnose the illness and understand the cure. One of the Gila monsters said, "If you call my name, put corn pollen on your arms, and tell me the symptoms; I will tell you what medicine is needed for the patient." The Gila monsters were the keepers of all of that and would direct the medicine people.

Sun Bearer (Jóhonaa'éí) is a powerful deity who lives above the earth, who carries the sun across the sky on 102 different trails, and who is all-knowing because he sees everything that happens. His knowledge is of the past, and so he answers questions about events that have already occurred and controls the things from the heavens such as air, snow, rain, thunder, and lightning. Black Gila monster and the spotted Gila monster are his representatives who live on the earth, and who control and share the power and ability to see into the past in regard to things that have happened on the ground. These creatures are hand tremblers themselves. This can be seen when one of them gets riled because it plants its fingernails in the ground, stands upright, exhales, and starts his front hands moving about and trembling. There are also stars at night that witness and have powers to communicate—thus there are four powers involved—the sun, stars, earth, and the Gila monster—that are available to answer questions.

The Gila monster, like the horned toad, has markings and points on its body that allow for reception of messages from the other three powers. There are certain things that the sun will observe and know about—those that have to do with the heavens, like sickness caused by lightning or the winds. There are other things that the stars will have witnessed at night. The Gila monster is aware of events that have happened on the earth because it is connected directly with the earth when it digs its claws and feet into the ground. It receives impressions for things associated with that realm of either the surface or below. The Gila monster stays on top of the ground, but from there he reflects his horn back into the stars, and it connects with the horns that the stars have. This is like communicating between two antennas. The person doing the hand trembling asks all four, "Which one of you knows what is going on? What is happening?" Jóhonaa'éí might respond, "Okay. It

The Gila monster can divine what has happened in the past because of its connection to the ground while also communicating with the heavens to identify present and future events. There are as many as fifteen songs used to appeal to this holy being, and there are both male and female methods to call upon its power. (Courtesy Smithsonian's National Zoo)

is something concerning lightning," and so he will be talking more or less about the atmosphere and things involving the heavens, like tornadoes, the winds, and storms.

The Gila monster understands things that are deeper in the ground. He talks about roots that heal or about issues with water that might require a Waterway (Tóee) ceremony. Now the horned toad, who has antenna-like points and the ability to communicate, also gets involved and talks about the people who walk on this earth. He says, "Today I perceive glitter. I see glitter in my eyes and see that this is the Glittering World. People are driving vehicles that have lights. They have all these material objects. I foresee that one person living there is doing something to an individual, and I will see it on the earth's surface." When these impressions are not too clear, the medicine person may say, "Let me talk to the stars." The stars will tell a person at night things they want to know because that is when the holy one comes out, and he will know what the future is going to be. These powers counsel that if things are not taken care of correctly, then the problem will persist and something bad will happen. "This might happen, so you better take care of it now." These are the impressions that a hand trembler receives.

When the Gila Monsterway is performed, all the prayers and the songs go to the people being sung over. This is not an everyday ceremony, it is rarely performed, and nobody knows much about it. The old medicine people used to bring their children and grandchildren into the ritual. There the medicine man would paint each one of them—maybe fifteen or twenty of them—then start singing. Other hand tremblers would enter the hogan, and each would go to the children and hit their hand as powerful songs were being sung. If one of the initiates starts to shake his or her hand and recognizes that they were gifted, the adult hand tremblers would remove them from the room. They were the ones who had the gift and would continue in the ceremony. But if they did not have it—even if someone really wanted to practice it—then it is not going to happen. Not everyone has this gift.

Of Stars and Crystals

While three of these powers can deal with issues that have already occurred, the stars have a special ability to see into the future. They are the holy ones, people who used to live on this earth and died, then went back to the heavens and became stars. These beings know what the past was about because they lived in it, but they also know about the future and what will happen tomorrow, because they have lived through so much from the past that they can understand what is going to take place in the future. They talk about it and tell people on earth what they can expect. If it is going to snow or rain, they will show you through the trail of stars attached to the Milky Way. The moon, which is male and controls all of the stars, also tells what to expect by how it sits in the night sky. When a new moon develops so that its points face downward or upward like a cup, it forecasts upcoming moisture or the lack thereof and how cold it is going to be. The moon is the future teller of all of the stars and works with them.

The gods associated with the constellations hear the prayers and answer them. Talking God (Haashch'ééyáłti'í), Dawn God (Hayoołkááł), and White Shell Boy (Yoołgai Ashkii') are all mentioned in these petitions, but most of the prayers about the constellations are found in the Gila Monsterway (Tiníléíjí) ceremony, which is dying out. This was done for people involved in hand trembling as well. The individual is painted in polka dots in the same pattern that the stars are in. The Big and Little Dippers and other formations are painted on the body as a way of either renewing a person's powers or identifying those who are given this special gift by the holy people. It is not performed to give the gift to those who are not chosen to be hand tremblers.

A Gila monster found crawling on the ground is decorated entirely in patterns of stars in the sky. These creatures are also thought of as the beaded people because their skin, hands, and fingernails appear to be made out of beads. When a person looks at the reptile's hand, he will see bead colors all over it as well as on their bodies. Thus the Gila monster is universal in the sense that he represents and can control both the earth and the sky. It is said that his black body stands for that space even beyond the stars, making him very powerful and dangerous. If he bites a person, he or she will die.

Every time there is a new moon, there will be a star that goes with him [note: the moon is considered male]. They sit together and discuss the future. If it is in the east, there will be one star, and when it moves to the west, there will be another one. So there is always one star that he travels with, which talks about when and how much snow is going to fall, how abundant future harvests will be, and how hot the summer will get. This pair, when the new moon comes, will also tell you when a baby is going to be born as well as when a life might end. An old man will start on his spiritual journey because of the new moon and the change it brings. A life will end and a new life will begin that same day. The moon and stars talk about these kinds of future events and are willing to share this information with people who understand how to read and respect it.

Stars are also involved in crystal gazing, which is within the larger practice of star gazing. Big Star (Sǫ Tsoh—Venus, the Morning Star) is particularly effective for crystal gazing, but it is not always available. When a ceremony depends on having answers from crystal gazing or star gazing but Big Star is not visible, you have to fall back on a "volunteer." You go outside and ask the stars, "Which one of you want to represent Big Star tonight? Then show yourself to me so that I can concentrate on you." That is all that is said, then the person walks back into the hogan to perform the ceremony. This way there is someone inside and another outside participating. Later, the medicine person brings an eagle feather and whistle outside, and sure enough, there will be a star flashing at them. This is the one that is talked to as the person stands there, then he blows the whistle to it and says, "I'm asking you some questions today, and you need to tell me how this is going to go." It does not matter what star one works with because that helper makes itself known. It is right there as one talks and prays to it. Once the link between the person and star is established, the medicine person walks back inside, sits down, puts the crystal in front of him, and begins to star gaze by touching the stone with the feather. His eyes are already in tune with the crystal, and only he will see the things that are happening in it.

About thirty years ago, three friends and I went to Hesperus Peak, Colorado, to give an offering on top of that mountain. The climb was very difficult with loose rocks sliding down, making the footing unsure, but it was important that we reach the top. The journey took almost six hours, and as we walked, it seemed like the summit was getting close, but we were actually only halfway there. Even though we were young men at the time, it was difficult, but we just kept climbing because it did not matter to us. All four of us were medicine men, but one of us was an older and more powerful healer who used to carry a hoof rattle for the Hoofway ceremony (Akéshgaanjí). He was like a high priest. When we reached the top, he directed us to sit in different places, saying, "Something very special is going to happen to us today. We are going to sit here while I sing, and two of you are going to say your prayers. After you finish praying, I want you to sing your song, not my song, but your own songs, which fit this mountain today. That is what you should sing. Do not stop until something happens, just continue singing." He was from the southern part of the reservation and was a practitioner of the Lifeway (Iináájí, also called Bééshee). His song, his medicine, came from that area, and so that is what he used. Each of us had our own area of specialty in ceremonial practice and each was from a different part of the reservation—one from eastern, one central, and I was from western—so we sang songs from our own medicine. We all sat in a little flat area with grass, slightly soggy from melted snow, but everyone was comfortable. My seat was farthest to the north. I sat down cross-legged where it was just flat ground, held nothing in my hands, and began singing and praying. My words were about the mountains and how they were put together; how I had a family back home and wanted them to be good. I sang about my job and how beautiful the creation of this earth was and that this was a fine day, with the sun rising to give us its blessing, and how we appreciated it.

Once I had finished my prayer, I started singing my song, but became very uncomfortable where I sat. A rock or something was poking into my right leg. I reached underneath, touched the ground, and tried to smooth it, but felt nothing out of the ordinary, and so remained in that spot, continuing to sing. There was still that irritating feeling on my leg and so I tried to turn and push myself away, but it kept poking me in the same place. I had a thought that something was coming to me from the bottom of the earth to my leg. I did not bother it and tried to ignore the feeling. When we began singing again, I swept my hand underneath my leg and touched something pointed. Slowly I started removing the dirt around it without looking, as I closed my eyes and continued to sing. I unearthed part of it, when suddenly I felt it had a nice, slick body, with distinct edges. I continued to dig, touching all four sides, singing while I worked it loose from the ground by pushing it from side to side and wiggling it around. I just kept playing with it, and before long it was out of the ground. The stone was a big crystal about four inches long with a nicely pointed top and square, knife-like edges.

I held it in my hand and just sat there saying, "Oh, my gosh. The thing that was supposed to happen to me has happened, right here." I began to clean it while singing, and watched the other two men start pulling something out of their areas, too. The medicine man directing us said, "Ah, stop. You men have received things that needed to come from here." I said, "Well, I got a stone," while another spoke up, "I got something, too, over here." We all had very nice crystals that were long with straight edges like they had been cut; as we looked at each other, we knew that they were the gift given to us that day and that it would be the medicine that we will see things with. Our leader started singing with us again and later directed that we should go back down. There were rocks that had broken and fallen off the slope so he said, "I want you to pick one rock from the side of this mountain that will be a connection to what you have." So as we descended, we found rocks that were shaped like a triangle, flat on all three sides, looking almost like the crystal I had just gotten. I took one and carried it down. That evening after we got back to our motel room in Durango, we went to our leader's room. He asked to see what we had found, took one set of crystal and stone, and showed us what to do with them. Taking the stone in one hand and the crystal in the other, he turned the lights off and rubbed the two together, which lit the room up like a flashlight with the sparks they created. I was overwhelmed by this, having never seen anything like it. He gave them back to me, saying, "This is your medicine. This is what we talked about. Today we collected good medicine, and that is the last time I ever want to go on that mountain." These rocks were not something I was looking for, but they found me. They came to me in that manner, which was amazing. I still have them.

These are special stones that I use often. One is crystal and the other is like a piece of granite, and when you rub it over the crystal, sparks fly off. When in a dark room the sparks will light up your feet, arms, and especially your eyes, but it smells awful, like burning sulfur.[17] When one starts singing, one can see visions through it as a part of star gazing. One night I was crystal gazing and a man mentioned that he had a stone similar to the one I was using. He thought that perhaps he could use it in the same way, but when he tried, nothing happened. He said, "Maybe I could use that." I asked, "What kind of a stone do you have?" and he replied, "I don't know, but it came out of the water." He tried to use it as I had used mine but nothing happened. My stone was sacred, but his was just a normal one. It did not work the same way.

The crystal (single terminated quartz) and rock (igneous intrusive andesite with feldspar) that Perry obtained on Mount Hesperus are used to spiritually answer questions. Crystal and star gazing depend upon impressions sent from the heavens, where all is seen. (Photo by Kay Shumway)

Sensing Impressions

When I am hand trembling or crystal gazing, I have to concentrate on the patient and ask them questions such as what their name is, their clan people, age, and where they are coming from. The person is most likely from a place where their umbilical cord is buried, often by a spring near the site where they lived and where an offering had been made to that water. That is a very important thing for me as a hand trembler to know. Then I am ready to talk to Tiníléí, the Gila monster who presides over hand trembling. I name a site called Nidahaaséí tiníléí diłhił t'áá shá bik'eh dasínítį—a place of things of the dark colored Gila monster that lies in the direction of the sun. I ask him a question, saying that one day in the Holy Hogan he had said that if corn pollen was given to him, if his name was called, and if the right person sang his song, that he would tell the story of this person. The patient that I next introduce to him becomes his grandson. He is the one seeking help or some kind of answer that will benefit him. As I pray, I start with the ground saying that this is where we walk, and then from there to the air that sits on the ground, and then another level of air that goes higher and higher and becomes thinner and thinner as one moves upward. We talk about the air, the thickness of the air, and the sunlight as it comes through it. I start mentally walking with that person, as the sun and Gila monster tell me if there is any violation performed through the air level and the wind. I keep asking if there was any kind of wrongdoing to Mother Earth or somewhere that an offering needed to be made on the land, and then were any animals harmed or something inappropriate done.

I walk with them all the way toward the lightning, then talk to the black lightning, the blue lightning, the yellow one, and white one. I see if any of them have anything to do with the sickness and if there was some kind of violation. Next I go into the highest level in the heavens and talk about something that may be incurable—cancer and things like that. Those ailments that are ready to take a life or allow it to continue are things that we have to understand as hand tremblers. All through this, I am walking with the patient, singing and talking through the power, so that somewhere I will receive an answer that tells me what is wrong. This is where we are in the problem. By this I learn what needs to be done.

When starting with the patient, you touch their legs, hand, heart, head, and then back, as you introduce them to the holy people to let them know who is sitting here sick. Next you start with the ground, which has a lot of people living on it: bears, deer, snakes, the list goes on. The ground will tell you a lot of stories not only about the living things that are four-legged people who live on top, but also the two-legged people that may be doing something bad to you. They are also walking on this earth. There are sandpaintings done within the Lightningway or the Windway, each with different medicine that was provided when it was set on earth. So you visit with the living people here first, and then you move to the sandpaintings to see if something had been done wrong. I design the earth on the surface as a circle. My hand goes in a circle and then I go on top of that. If there is any sandpainting that has been done incorrectly, I ask the spirit to show me what it might be so that I will recognize the god that stands there by how many earrings it may have, how many feathers it wears, and what kind of objects it carries or are associated with it. I may be looking at the Lightningway (Na'at'oyee Biką'jí [male branch] or Na'at'oyee Bi'áádjí [female branch]), Windway (Nílch'ijí) with its male form (Diné Binílch'ijí), Blessingway (Hózhǫǫjí), or the Evilway (Hóchxǫ'íjí). I say which one of these fit into that area and the power would tell me, this is why and how it is happening. This is how it usually tells me.

It is a kind of exploring that I have to do by asking questions about the problem. Where do I go? Is it Evil? Is it the Black Body Person that stands within that circle, or is it the Blue Body Person? Is it the Yellow Body Person, or is it the White Body Person? Who are you? Which one? Which one will heal, and what medicine do I need? What prayer do I need? What songs do I need to sing? And what herbs do I need to use? With all of these questions, I really have to talk to them. The answer is never straightforward unless I talk about it, and so I have to ask questions. This is why I am hired to do hand trembling. The hand trembler does not just get answers out of nowhere, but has to ask questions and talk about some of these areas. Who are you? Where are you? How can I help? Is it the Lightning People? Did this sickness come from you? What happened? What was the violation? What was done? I have to talk to the holy people in four or five different major ceremonies; I have to ask each one of them which one is responsible for this sickness. Then how do we fix it? That is the way I talk to them, and they respond by telling me what to do. I think each hand trembler may have a different experience, but for me, I really have to ask questions and talk to them.

While you are questioning the elements in a sandpainting, they will indicate to you the answer by a reflection coming off of the animal pictured in it. The sandpainting will tell you a lot about it as you make different figures. Your hand will draw a picture of that being, then you will question, is it this person? If it says, no, not that one, your hand will erase it and you will feel that you have to go on to another. You continue to do this until you get the right one, then you know. So a hand trembler has to know sandpaintings well. They have to know the inner workings of every medicine that is out there. If it is, for instance, a young hand trembler, say coming from a border town that doesn't know much about how this ceremony works—even though the hand trembling gift may have been given to him or her—he will not be able to use it. That person will not understand what the holy people are trying to show him, and the gift of hand trembling might even hurt its owner for not being aware of the teachings. Well-trained medicine people can see and feel things that a beginner cannot. They know and understand the ceremonies and what needs to be done. Their hand tells them what figures to draw and which ones are right and wrong. The edge of the sandpainting will also speak. If there are four spots, then you know some of these ceremonies will help. If it shows a sunbeam in the picture, you know it has something to do with the sky and the sun. A lot of it, even though you are concentrating on things in a lower level, still depends on help from the heavens. Moving to various levels while talking and praying about them, as well as going through the steps, leads to identification of the right answer. "Yes, it's the sun. He is the main person. He is the one who had an eclipse. That is what he is showing you here." Now, you know what to do.

The person who does hand trembling starts the gesture of trembling down at the patient's feet and then goes up the body, without touching it, to the head. This is a matter of passing through the levels and then centering on the place that is a problem. The hand trembler may have to run his hand above the body more than once to detect the exact trouble spot. For example, if a person has a stomach problem, the medicine person returns to that place where the illness occurs; the spirit will indicate where the issue is located and may direct the hand to touch the stomach and then go back to the source that is showing what is wrong. All of this is performed by the hand, its movement, and where it wants to go; it moves automatically. Sometimes it will tell you there's another problem behind the back, and it will touch there. Following the ceremony, the hand trembler might ask if the patient's back hurts or how he or she feels. Asking questions continues. "What did you do this year and what time did it happen? How did it happen?" The sick person tells the truth, then the medicine person can explain what they saw and what happened to the patient. The patient will already know the story, but this is the beginning of the healing. "I know I'm telling you and you already know the story. So we both know that this is what needs to be done."

Divination is performed by both men and women. In this picture, a medicine person uses hand trembling to receive impressions as to why this woman is sick. The answer: she had come in contact with a lightning-struck tree, later requiring the Holyway ceremony called Lightning or Shootingway. The patient—sitting upright with legs extended—is using required ceremonial posture.

Usually the medicine person's hand remains two to three inches above the patient's body, but at other times, it may touch the person. Once the hand starts moving and indicating, there is no real control over what the power is doing. It just tells you that here's the problem and here is where we're going, and this is where it's coming from and here's the main issue. During this process as you pray through the Gila monster to the power, you ask it to become your protector. You say to that power, "I will be your grandson and I will be behind your shield and stand there with my patient, depending upon your protection." Let's say it is the Lightningway that needs to be called upon for help because lightning struck a tree nearby and some of the smoke from the resulting fire was inhaled. Suddenly that person becomes sick and people believe the illness is caused by this incident. The medicine man needs to talk with the Lightning Person and say, "I am your grandchild, but this thing happened with me. Today, I want your help to take this thing off of me. When you remove it, I will become your grandson. I'll stand behind you, and you will stand in front of me. You will be my protector because we have been introduced to each other due to this sickness. We now know each other, so you are going to be my healer and shield and I will be your grandson." They call this, in the Navajo way, Ách'ą́ąh Ná'iilzį'—The Sickness That Stands in Front as a Protector—meaning that the one who caused the sickness now prevents the patient from being harmed. At this point, the cause is protecting the one he made sick; he is the grandfather, and the patient is the grandson. The Lightning Person faces away from the patient and healer in order to keep evil and harm at a distance.

There is one other aspect of hand trembling that my grandmother and mother used that had specific powers called upon by women in delivering babies. I was told by my father and grandfather to stay away from this practice because it belonged to women and not men, so I do not know a lot about it. Men were usually not involved with the birthing process unless the women invited them. Females have their rules that they follow and allow only their own to be there. My grandmother was famous for using these powers and was called a "baby chaser," which is the name they have given this practice. These ladies and others took that ceremony around to those in need. I asked for more information about this, but my mother just nodded and told me to leave it alone, emphasizing that I did not need to know, and that it is something that I should not concentrate on.

Prescribing Ritual

Once the hand trembler has diagnosed what is causing the sickness or problem, he will understand what type of ceremony is needed to cure the patient. Many people involved in divination may have only that power and do not conduct other ceremonies, while other medicine people may have one or more ceremonies that they specialize in. In a way, it is just like in Anglo medicine where a sick person will go to a general practitioner who conducts a series of tests and then sends the patient to a specialist like a heart doctor, podiatrist, or chiropractor for further treatment depending on the symptoms. Regardless of how specialized a doctor may be, there are fundamental practices and procedures followed in the clinical process based on the germ theory of disease, understanding of the physical body, and social beliefs. Navajo medicine is no different. It is based on an understanding of how the world functions, what type of illness is afflicting the patient, and what type of cure is necessary for a specific problem. Even though there is a wide variety of illness, long and short ceremonies to cure them, herbal medicine to treat physical symptoms, and traditional teachings that explain what is wrong, there are also some overarching ways of thinking about ceremonies and cures in general.

Let me share three personal experiences with hand trembling. I first received this power when I was working in Apache Junction just outside of Phoenix. This was in my early years while I was heavily involved in alcohol before I started practicing Navajo medicine. One night I had been drinking heavily and knew I needed to rest. I pulled over to the side of the road where two big rocks with a narrow opening between them appeared to me to be a comfortable bed. I crawled up on top of one and went to sleep. Well into the morning I awoke, lying on my back, facing the sun. The hand on my outstretched arm began to shake uncontrollably, just as I had seen happen with hand tremblers. I wondered what was causing this and how I could control it, so I got up and started walking around the rock. In the crack between the two boulders there sat a large two-foot-long, from nose to tail, Gila monster, black in color with yellow spots, mouth wide open, with five babies. As it stared at me, I realized what was happening to my hand. I found a sunflower, cleaned out its center, put corn pollen from my medicine pouch in it, then stuck it on a stick. Extending the offering to the Gila monster, I watched her eat the pollen then I prayed to her, swearing that I would be true to her and asking that she be true in directing me. Later, I went home and told my mother and father—both of whom said this was proof that I was to be a medicine person and that I had better give up my foolish ways to concentrate on learning my responsibilities. Shortly thereafter, I stopped drinking and became immersed in learning songs, prayers, and ceremonies.

The first time I used the power of hand trembling was when a wealthy woman approached me and asked if I could help her find her lost diamond ring. After questioning me at some length as to my ability, she became convinced that I could. The ring was large and expensive and so we settled on a price—if she got it back, she would pay me $1,000. I accepted, did the hand trembling ceremony, and then told her I would go with her to retrieve it—but I did not tell her where it was so that I would get paid. We drove to her house, I went into her bathroom and reached down in the bend of the toilet bowl beyond sight and got the ring, which was too heavy and big to go farther down the drain. I received my pay—the first large sum of money for conducting a ceremony.

My last story is about when I was living in Page, Arizona, working construction. I had a woman come to my house seeking relief from symptoms of low blood pressure, fainting spells, and feelings of panic. She had been to Anglo doctors and received medication, but there was no relief, so now she sought help from a medicine man. I was not involved in counseling at the time and was still learning ceremonies, but I did know hand trembling and agreed to diagnose what was causing the problem. The Gila monster and I had an agreement, and so I was confident I would learn what had happened. The impressions were clear and strong, but when I asked her if they were true, she denied them. I asked again and received the same response. Finally I told her that she was very much aware of what had occurred, but that if she wanted to deny it, I could do nothing for her. This was in the afternoon. By evening she was back, tears in her eyes, admitting that a year ago, she had an Enemyway ceremony performed for her and had made a number of big mistakes. On the second night, with her face blackened to keep evil away, she and a man had sex, and even worse, it had happened in the medicine lodge. Not only did she break the rule of four-day celibacy during and after a ceremony, but she defiled a sacred place, and had knowingly upset the holy people. The only thing she could do was to have another Enemyway ceremony to correct the problems—very expensive and time-consuming, but that is what it took. The holy people were well aware of what had happened and knew what needed to be done to correct it.

There are additional ways that the holy people become involved in healing the sick and in ceremonial performance. Medicine men often use prayersticks (k'eet'áán) placed around sandpaintings to summon the holy ones from the four cardinal directions. Each stick is painted or beaded with their direction's color. These sticks are about a foot long with an eagle feather tied on top, meeting the beaded part wrapped around it that extends all the way to the bottom. Medicine men consider that the lower portion, up to the beads circling the wood, sticks into the ground to make the earth move. It stands there, talking about the core of the ceremony and the healing that will take place. The prayerstick has built into it the root (sticking in the ground) and the starting place of the ceremony (beads), then the holiness and healing elements found in this world, with the feathers on top through which the prayers go into the heavens. The four cardinal directions have to be recognized and established as boundaries outside of the sandpainting and are also drawn in the inner circle where the patient is going to sit.

The person sitting in the midst of these prayersticks has the shafts talking with the powers from the east, south, west, and north that accumulate in that person's thoughts, feelings, and internal processes. The feathers act like smoke, bringing information and healing from the heavens. They move around picking up these messages from the Holy Wind, but it is very hard to measure because they just float about. This is just like a person's mind, moving in many directions, nothing concrete, but open to impressions. Just like the Gila monster is rooted in the ground, sensations from this world and the holy people in the heavens, these prayersticks are also part of the healing from the different levels. They are like a tree whose roots go down, main body on the earth surface, and whose branch tips reach into the sky. A human can be thought of as a tree dependent upon this earth being alive and stable. Like an oak tree, people need to be strong and tough. The feather on a prayerstick is thought to be in the clouds and flutters about as if it were moving with the wind. Thus the patient is always considered as having his foot on the earth he walks upon with his body moving over the ground, but his mind and thoughts are in the heavens or the upper level. This same idea continues with the growth of the hair. If it is respected and wrapped correctly with the bun strings attached to a small ceremonial object that is folded into the hair, then that person's thoughts will be on a high level.

Anatomy of a Ceremony

One term used by medicine men to describe where a particular ceremony is located in relation to others is the word "sit," as in "it sits over there with this ceremony" but is "outside of" another. The reason for this is that a ceremony is viewed as being alive and interactive with the patient and person performing it. The ritual is put together in a spiritual way, but also has a body, with a skin or outer part, just as people have skin, but inside there is the muscle and meat, the blood stream, and the nervous system. This is how it sits with the healing moment, and that is how the medicine man sings about this as a whole, as a body, including mental illness such as depression and distress.

Sometimes a healer will have to bring in another ceremony to filter out competing symptoms and match the illness to the remedy. When speaking of this, one says that the additional ceremony "sits on the outside" of the main one. For instance in the Evilway ceremony, the main focus of the primary ceremony is strengthened, not diminished, by having the secondary one added. When medicine men do this, they say, "Let's take this one and add this to it, and call it biza'a'nííł—medicine to the mouth. The sickness is one that is going to give in to medicine to the mouth." So the bowl is set on the outside of how the patient is sitting and on the outside of the sandpainting, and both will be given different herbs as part of the ritual. This is an example of how the sickness will be cured using more than one type of healing. The herbs are added on. Take for instance, a person who has been in a very serious automobile accident. She has broken bones and fractures all over, and so a ceremony is performed to deal with that aspect. But that is not all. She has also suffered traumatizing mental anguish, and her fear is still there. This becomes compounded with frustration, so that even seemingly simple things become difficult and overwhelming. She just cannot let go. This is why the outside medicine sits on the outside, to add to the other ones, and in this case, to help with the mental trauma.

The image of working from the outside into the center or "heart" of the ceremony is important, because that is the way healing takes place. With the ceremony sitting there, the medicine man starts on the outside with the stories and teachings, then moves the actual ritual into the center, where the songs and prayers take him into the middle of pure holiness. By the third or fourth night, the healer enters the main, most important part of the ceremony, called in Navajo átsáleeh—entering the core of a ceremony. Whenever the medicine man sings that part, no one can go in or out during the performance. Everybody has to stay put until this is done, and there can be no type of interference. The holy ones are right there participating at the core of everything. In the innermost part of that circle, all must be holy. There can be no moving about; children are not allowed, only adults; and there is no sleeping because if a person has a bad dream, it will ruin everything. This is the core of the circle, the central part of the sickness being healed, in a pattern as to how the sacredness of the medicine was set. On the outside of the illness, sit the additives or tangential parts that also need to be cured like the accompanying depression. This may be done with the herbs already mentioned or with a smoke ceremony that is discussed later.

An example of working from the outside in is found in the Blessingway ceremony. First come songs about the hogan—The House of the Hogan Song—identifying where the ceremony is being held. That begins the sacredness of the outer layer. The doorway is blessed, and then the singer sets up all the sacred mountains that sit upon the land; eventually the songs and prayers lead into the center of the ceremony with all of its holiness and magic. Once this is completed, there are other songs that return the patient to the outer edge and the everyday world. The morning dawn song may be added to make things better, and finally, the doors are opened and the ceremony ended. This is the standard form and thought for most Navajo rituals, especially the long ones.

Navajo people in general, and medicine men in particular, often provide offerings with their prayers and in ceremonies. I want to talk about those before discussing specific rituals. There are four "sacred stones" (ntł'iz) comprised of white shell, turquoise, abalone shell, and jet, that represent the four elements, colors, and holy people found in the four directions. These stones are crushed to a small size, mixed together, and used to bless a prayer or a place through an offering to the gods.

Most prayers use ground corn and its pollen as another type of offering. In Navajo thought, almost everything in the universe is either male or female, and these corn and corn pollen offerings are no exception. In a Blessingway song, when you say corn pollen, it belongs to the boy, and the ground corn belongs to the girl. The word "tádídíín" literally means "sun shining on its son," thus recognizing the male aspect and separating it from the female yellow ground corn. White corn and white corn pollen are male, and the yellow corn with blue corn pollen (tádídíín dootł'izh) is female. They both work together but are never physically combined. The female side of the ground corn and pollen is considered the grower (aniłt'ánii at'ééd) of the crop and of life in general. When saying a prayer in the morning, one uses white corn and faces the east; in the evening, one employs yellow ground corn and faces west. One might sing the song for the corn and then explain why he or she is standing there. This is a time of thanksgiving, of hope for the future, and of asking for assistance through prayer. The male part of an individual talks to White Corn Boy, who stands in the east. A second song identifying the individual singing, explains that he or she has half of a male person standing within who wishes to discuss their situation. The prayer is closed with white corn pollen. In the evening, when facing west, the petitioner says that there is a female part to him or her, even if it is a male person, and prays to Yellow Corn Girl, thanking her for the day, and asking to have a good night's sleep. Half of everyone comes from their mother's side, which is explained during both the morning and evening prayers. By using ground yellow corn and then blue corn pollen, the individual praying recognizes this male/female dichotomy within as he or she addresses the male and female deity. The white and blue pollen are never combined. They are two different things and are thought of as two separate individuals. You do not want to mix them up and get them fighting each other. Keep them separate because they have attitudes and want to be kept apart.

CHAPTER SIX

Ceremonial Etiquette, Tools, and Performance

A s the title of this chapter suggests, there are three main components in organizing most lengthy ceremonies, each of which is introduced here. The account of Perry's conduct of an abbreviated "The Two Skulls That Came Back" (Tsiits'iin Nát'áázhjí) ritual makes clear the importance of the patient being prepared and properly coached, having the necessary equipment available, and organizing it to provide the correct message behind the cure. With dozens of different kinds of ceremonies and ritual performances, the following is a more generalized explanation of what occurs under ideal circumstances. Two subsequent chapters will look at three separate types of ceremonies and their categorization based on use. Here, a broader approach is taken, introducing Navajo expectations for the preparation and implementation of a ceremony. While there were obviously some modifications to this event due to place and circumstance, the core of the ritual Perry performed illustrates the procedure of healing a battered and depressed woman, seeking help from the holy people.

In a normal situation, the process for a ceremony starts when the patient learns what is wrong and what is necessary for a cure. This is accomplished through divination. Once the problem is identified, the head of the family contacts a medicine person to see if he is available to perform it while also establishing a price for his services. On the medicine man's part, he should not deny anyone his help, but he also (in the old days) did not establish a fee. The family requesting his services would suggest the payment based on what they were able to afford. There is no "bargain shopping" since the holy people, who do the actual healing, are very much aware of the attitudes, value, and sincerity that are part of the transaction. To prepare for the occasion, the hogan and other areas the holy beings will visit are cleaned (hooghan yilzį́įh); a blanket is hung in the doorway on the morning of the event, inviting them to participate; food preparation and collection of ritual materials prescribed by the medicine man are underway; helpers are obtained to run errands; knowledgeable ceremonialists are appointed to assist in making larger sandpaintings; and the patient is dressed appropriately based on the necessary activities of the rite. The family will present a Navajo wedding basket and tobacco to the medicine man upon his arrival. Neighbors, extended family, and friends invited to the event will usually bring food and materials such as firewood, cloth, or money; will help with cooking and other tasks; and will lend their voice in prayer and song to encourage the holy people in curing.

Everyone is expected to practice responsible behavior, as specified by the role they play. Rules may change as circumstances shift, but the guiding principle is to show respect and reverence while in the presence of the gods. For instance, today, using cell phones and taking "selfies" during a ceremony are considered sacrilegious. Franc Newcomb created a list of rules of what was and what was not appropriate during the 1940s, which included the following.[1] Before or during a ceremony, if a relative or close neighbor died, the curing event was postponed. All food used in the ritual had to be cooked in traditional ways and not with the pots, pans, and utensils of the white man. No basket or pot with a broken edge should be used because good luck and power would slip out. Women especially should not wear hats in the hogan during the rite because they would not receive a blessing on their head. Those menstruating should not be present. No one should step over a fire, lean against the back wall, or leave the hogan when the songs and prayers of healing are being said. There should be total silence at this point in the ceremony. Everyone should move in a sunwise or clockwise direction, avoid tripping, and control children. The medicine man should make no mistakes, use only feathers from live birds and skins from unwounded (not shot or killed violently) animals, and know what herbs will heal. For true efficacy, the patient should not wash off any paint or markings for four days after the event. If necessary, the ceremony may be performed up to four times for full effect. Following the first complete one, the others may be abbreviated, or that person can attend and participate in one held for another individual. All of these actions communicated reverence to the holy beings.

The objects used in healing must be shown similar respect. Perry discusses many of these at different times, but here the medicine bundle (jish), prayersticks (k'eet'áán), and sandpainting (iikááh) will be the primary focus. Charlotte J. Frisbie wrote *Navajo Medicine Bundles or Jish*, the definitive study on this first topic.[2] In this wide-ranging study, she points out that the container holds both materials specific to certain ceremonies and objects used more generally. The bundle and the pouches kept within are made of unwounded buckskin. The collective term for ritual equipment (bee nahadláhii) includes a wide variety of materials, some of which may be in small pouches inside the bundle, but all of which have been individually blessed. Examples of elements used in specific ceremonies are "cranebills of Shootingway and Flintway, the mountain earth bundle of Blessingway, and the hoof rattle of Flintway. . . . Non-specific equipment (chodao'íinii) is ritual paraphernalia used in a number of ceremonials. Examples [may] include most equipment for offerings, bullroarer, flints, club, brush, firedrill, basketdrum, yucca drumsticks, baskets, sandpainting equipment, medicine cup, cornmeal, corn pollen, live pollen, little medicine pouches, mixed salves, mixed meat, fossils, claws, mirage stones, crystals, shells, and skins."[3]

Once a medicine bundle is assembled and blessed, it is considered alive and treated accordingly. Both the jish and the person using it need to be renewed. After overuse or the loss or destruction of part of its elements, or for just a periodic "boost" every couple of years of existence, the bundle is opened. Its contents are washed in emetic plant solution, dried with white cornmeal, and blessed with pollen, and a Blessingway ceremony is performed for it with Chief Hogan songs and special prayers before reassembling it. Occasionally it is also fed corn pollen and prayers to keep it strong and powerful. The owner of the jish, by performing these acts, has his ceremonial ability renewed. The bundle is an extension of his powers, and when he dies, his jish becomes contaminated, so it needs to be cleansed and prepared for a new owner—a family or clan member or an accomplished medicine man. Otherwise it is ceremonially disassembled and returned to Mother Earth.[4]

Equally alive as the jish are the prayersticks used in rites. The base of these may be made from cane reeds, mountain mahogany, wild cherry, juniper, or willow, and cut so that they will be three to four inches long and two inches wide. They are either male or female with eyes and a mouth placed upon them along with turkey, eagle, and other feathers. Their dominant color may be those associated with the four directions, or brown, red, or gray, depending on the particular holy person to be attracted and invited to a ceremony. Additional materials found on them may include "rings about the neck, others with zigzag lines on the body of the stick; some with cords of diverse colors wound about them in the ritual (sunwise) manner . . . while others require an ornament like an arrowhead or something similar."[5] Since there is such a wide variety of them and the details must be correct, some medicine men, after training an apprentice for a ceremony, provide him with what Gladys Reichard called a "kethawn encyclopedia." The experienced chanter takes a yard of cloth and on it arranges an example of every type of prayerstick used in the ritual just mastered. Whenever the new practitioner has a question as to what a certain one looks like, he can refer to this memory aid.[6]

Prayersticks accompany most ceremonies. Often they are emplaced around a sandpainting, while at other times they are put outside in a spot where the desired holy person is most likely to find it. They are both a gift and a request for that being to come and be involved in a ceremony, with the Holy Wind (Níłch'ih) helping to spread the word. Reichard provides an example: "In the Shooting Chant, prayerstick offerings may be made to Big Snake, Arrowsnake, and Blue Lizard at the same time. According to the myth, they should be deposited in the crooked root of a piñon tree; according to another person near animal holes. Those of ordinary snakes (rattler) should be put under greasewood, those of Arrowsnake at the edge of a hill, those of Blue Lizard near a heap of black rock."[7] Another type of prayerstick, the "Talking Prayerstick," has two pieces of wood combined—a male and female—who provide protection for the user and ensure a prayer comes true when held during invocation. Most medicine men have at least one of these and take it everywhere they go for protection.

Sandpaintings, more correctly called drypaintings since there are many ingredients used that are not sand, have been widely studied and are a lengthy topic. The designs, estimated at over a thousand in number, originate in Navajo sacred narratives that are portrayed in well over five hundred different paintings.[8] Sizes may vary from eighteen inches to twenty feet in diameter and are laid out in three main compositions—linear (symbols in a row or rows), radial (symbols cardinally oriented around a central motif), or extended center (a central motif or a group of motifs occupying most of the picture).[9] The background for a sandpainting may be either an unwounded buckskin hide or the floor of a hogan that has had fine windblown sand, tan in color, spread smooth with a weaving batten. On this the medicine man and his apprentices draw stylized images with little variation, made from crushed plant matter, pollen, cornmeal, charcoal, and ground minerals including gypsum and ochre. The person conducting the ceremony directs the creation of the picture that is developed from the center working outward, in a sunwise direction, left to right. Any mistakes in these designs approved by the holy people are not erased, but covered over with the correct color material.

The completed image is taken from events found in a sacred narrative, often compared to a stained glass window in a cathedral. The picture, however, transports the patient who sits on it back in time to when the initial healing took place. Once the image is activated by sprinkled pollen, prayers, and songs, the holy people are there to work their healing powers on behalf of the patient. Parts of the sandpainting are touched to a corresponding part of the sick person's body, which through spiritual osmosis receives the curative power. Variety in the images reflects the variety of healing energy that is summoned—"heroes . . . deities, animals, reptiles, birds, insects, sun, moon, stars, thunder, lightning, storm, hail, winds, clouds, holy mountains . . . fire pokers, bows and arrow, flint weapons"—the list continues.[10] Colors also denote powers from the four directions, associated mountains, and deity, while a rainbow might encase the entire design for protection with the east side of the painting left open so that nothing is trapped inside. Not all ceremonies require a sandpainting, but those that do may have only one or, as in the Night Chant, may require eight over a nine-day period. Each image must be completed between either dawn and sunset or sunset and dawn.

The generalized format for a sandpainting ritual, be it one or nine days, would include first finishing the painting and emplacing prayersticks, preparing herbs in a solution, blessing the painting with pollen, then announcing that the ceremony is about to begin. The patient carries in a basket with cornmeal, which is scattered as food for the painting, after which he or she removes their clothing (down to breechcloth for men and removed top for women) and sits on the painting facing east. As the medicine man sings he uses a rattle and at times presses his jish to the patient, who may also drink an emetic that causes vomiting. The medicine man next puts some of the herb infusion on his hands, touches a part of the image in the sandpainting, then touches the corresponding part of the patient, transferring the power from one to the other. Following the event, the patient and spectators are blessed with smoke, any remaining sand on the patient is brushed off with eagle feathers, and the materials that had comprised the sandpainting are removed and carried to the north of the hogan.[11] The four days following the ceremony should be spent in relative isolation with low activity.

Today, fewer of these ceremonies are practiced, so ritual knowledge is being lost. Some estimate that only half (five hundred) of the images are now used and that the number and variety of ceremonies is decreasing.[12] Mark Bahti, a Navajo art expert, agrees. He points out that there are many external forces that have led to this decline, but there are also internal ones such as the commercialization of these sacred designs. For a brief synopsis of this aspect, see *A Guide to Navajo Sandpaintings* by Bahti, and for a lengthier treatment *Navajo Sandpainting: From Religious Act to Commercial Art* by Nancy J. Parezo.[13]

In this chapter, Perry and I share our discussion about different versions of teachings, the elements that comprise his medicine bundle, and what he sees happening with ceremonial practices and the younger generation. The text is more conversational, and so we have included bylines and occasional asides to indicate which author is speaking. This provides more clarity and a feeling for our interaction.

Performing "The Two Skulls That Came Back"

ROBERT MCPHERSON

Everything was ready. Perry had prepared the dirt floor in the ceremonial hogan beside Blue Mountain Hospital to conduct an abbreviated form of an Evilway (Hóchxǫ'íjí) ceremony called "The Two Skulls That Came Back" (Ha'neełnéehee—Upward Reaching Rite, used for unpredictable sickness). He was dressed in jeans, a black shirt, with a purple kerchief tied around his head so that the holy people would recognize and respect him. His glasses were darkened by indoor light, as he presided on the west side of the hogan, facing east, shaking a rattle, and singing with a firm voice. Beside him, to his left, sat the patient, a young woman in her mid-twenties, the victim of abuse. For the past few months she had lived in protective custody, attempting to heal from her traumatic experience. Hair down, dressed in shorts and a tank top, she was not attired the way most participants are expected to dress, but this is what she had, and there was no other family support to help her with correct procedural details. Only three very young children romping beside their mother and a female Navajo social worker were there for company. Later three Anglo social workers from Salt Lake City and another from Blanding joined the group.

Drawn on the floor with ashes were four lines, approximately a foot and a half apart, representing the Black, Blue, and Yellow Worlds. On each end of the lines were a small group of eagle feathers planted upright in the dirt, while six feet away was a four-foot-diameter circle drawn in ash, designating the fourth, White, and/or Glittering World of today. Following some chanting, the holy people arrived, summoned by blowing an eagle bone whistle four times. More prayers and explanations followed, then the woman was "marked" (ak'ina'asdzoh) with ashes placed on the bottom of her feet, legs, hands, arms, shoulders, back, and face from chin to ear. Perry added lightning patterns to her arms and back, then sprinkled additional ashes on the four worlds pictured on the floor. Seating himself beside the patient, he next sang over a bitter liquid medicine prepared from different plants. After

This picture, taken during a Coyoteway ceremony, illustrates how the medicine man works with the patient, in this case supervising the washing of hair, then the entire body, with strong-smelling herbs. The solution not only cleans but also chases evil away so that goodness can come in.

the woman drank some of this potion, the two arose, and with songs and prayers, and jointly grasping a bundle of eagle feathers, moved forward to the different worlds. The medicine man led her through and into the Glittering World, where she knelt and washed herself with the bitter herbal liquid in the bowl—first her face, then her hair, then the markings and ashes on her arms, back, and legs. Perry, standing by, removed the eagle feathers surrounding the Glittering World and brushed out the ashes outlining this sphere and the woman's footprints. As she returned through the other worlds, he again collected the feathers and swept away the lines of the remaining three worlds and footprints.

The patient resumed her place next to the medicine man, but this time she was totally covered with a blanket and grasping two eagle feather bundles that she held to her forehead next to the hood of the blanket. She prayed along with Perry, repeating the Returning Protection Prayer. He continued to chant until he reached a point when the woman arose and moved in a clockwise circling to the door, where she exited with two feather bundles. Shortly she returned, moved back to her seat, and gave the medicine man the bundles. He next lit a pipe and blew smoke over the patient from foot to head and then to the four directions before giving her the pipe. She also took in and blew out the healing smoke. More songs—this time about changing seasons, about how the smoke, like clouds, often drifts and dissipates just as emotions and problems shift, and how spring brings new life and beauty after the winter. The smoke was compared to a person's mind—people explored with it, and similar to thoughts, it cannot be measured. He reminded the woman that although many bad things had happened, just as she had passed through the different worlds without harm, she could now move through her troubles and leave them in the north, as when she had left the hogan earlier. The smoke carried away the issues.

Next came counseling. Perry taught that no one had the right to harm another person. Fortunately, the man who had been abusive was not in her clan, but he had left children—something that everyone should look forward to having. What she wanted in life for them and herself would be what really mattered. "No one can distort your beauty and good life," he intoned, as he now acted as the girl's grandfather. He cautioned that people protected themselves from evil through law, and so she had to surround herself with this shield. The bitter taste from the liquid she drank came from eighteen different plants collected from both on and off the reservation, while the tobacco she smoked was also a combination of eighteen other plants. Each left a bitter taste, as did her experiences, but they would soon be gone, dissipated like the smoke, which would be replaced by truth and peace. The ceremony ended, leaving the young woman a wiser soul, better understanding how to overcome conflict in life.

This was the framework of an hour-and-a-half-long ritual that occurred on February 1, 2018. In a later discussion with Perry, he noted that there were a number of things that he would have liked to have had different, but that one has to meet the patient in his or her own circumstances and that everything is not always ideal. If this had been performed at a Navajo family's camp under better conditions, there would have been a blanket hung in the doorway, the woman would have been more modestly attired in a dress and not shorts, the family would have collected many of the materials used in the ceremony, and the woman would have been better coached as to proper procedures. Perry assured, "Navajos usually know what they are doing and have been well trained to ceremonial responsibilities, but if something is not right or someone sits out of place, the medicine man will say, 'Hey, you know, you know what you're doing there.' But in this case, things were not really put in order." There were also modifications in how designs were drawn and the ashes applied due to contemporary rules of sexual conduct. For instance, in applying the ashes to the patient, Perry had her put them on herself from the knee to the hip, while the female Navajo social worker applied them from the foot to the knee. In a more traditional setting, the patient would have removed her blouse rather than wearing a sports bra or similar garment. The children would also have been under stricter control if a relative had been present. Still, there was enough flexibility in the practice to meet these less-than-ideal conditions and still assist the patient.

Ceremonial Etiquette

PERRY ROBINSON

Men should sit with their legs crossed because that was the way that Monster Slayer sat, while women should sit on their legs with the feet to the side because that was how Changing Woman sat, or with her legs straight in front if she were about to receive medicine. This is done because all of the medicine applied starts with the feet and legs, which have to be straight for the healing to flow easily through the body to the head. Bent legs or knees interrupt that movement of power by creating corners around which the lightning or other power has to work its way. The old people used to say, "Sit up straight. Sit with your legs out there. Sit like that so this medicine man can put corn pollen on your feet and your legs." A young lady should also not sit cross-legged for reasons of modesty, especially if she is a niece or someone from the same clan. A female should always try to sit with her knees tight together with no opening through the legs because, they say you might have a brother or uncle or relative sitting there. As a lady, one does not open her legs to those people, a bad sexual practice when performing medicine. This is also true at any time or place. "My mother taught this and if she or another elder saw an incorrect position, she would take her stick and hit the offender on the knee and say, 'Don't spread your legs like that. You've got relatives here. Put them together or get out,' and if they did not comply, chased them out of the hogan. This was one of the main things that medicine people taught." Enforcing this type of discipline stressed respect even though it was harsh.

When people attend in a medicine place, they are taught to stay still and listen with respect for the person who is having a ceremony performed as well as for the medicine person conducting it. One tries to be quiet, not constantly getting up and walking out, sitting there with reverence, and participating when appropriate. One is to pay attention to the people who are having it done, because everyone there acts as a holy one. When the doorway was hung with a blanket, it indicated that humans and the holy people were in attendance. An individual, like the holy people, hears about this event and wants to be part of it. Each person is considered one of the holy people and so will not be running in and out. Everyone is there for a purpose and should leave their worldly business outside. Thoughts must be focused in a positive way for healing and not interrupted. Sometimes one may sit with his or her eyes closed and think about the prayers and songs being sung. Closed eyes and concentrating on the words puts one into the ceremony, and he or she becomes part of it. This is why children should not even attend. They do not understand, and they can distract from the activity and disrupt.

Two Stories, One Purpose and Meaning

Robert McPherson

Perry, after discussing this etiquette, returned to speaking about the ceremony he performed for his patient. He mentioned that it provided an ideal example to examine and illustrate information discussed in previous chapters. Here are a number of things to consider. First is the origin of the ceremony—the sacred story from which it derived. Two versions are provided here, one first published in 1948 but no doubt recorded somewhat earlier by a trader, Will Evans, from the Shiprock area, who had a penchant for gathering Navajo lore; the second was provided by Perry when explaining the intricacies of the ritual. While there are obvious differences, the two versions also bolster each other by adding information about the performance. A second point is that Perry has provided a lot of insight that explains the ritual objects he used and how the ceremony healed the patient. Emergence through the worlds, the ceremonial pattern, and involvement with holy people is now familiar territory and was the basis for teaching the patient. How do myth and ceremony apply to everyday life in the Glittering World? What practical advice and counseling was there to inform daily life? Perry shared those lessons.

An abbreviated version, offering the essential elements by Evans, follows.[14] A woman named Chee-Kent Nadle had two twin brothers who went hunting but failed to return. She became increasingly concerned and wanted to know if they were alive or dead, and so she turned to different forms of divination to discover what had happened to them. The grieving sister tried to replicate what she had seen medicine men do—sprinkling corn pollen high in the air and smoking mountain tobacco, but the pollen just fell at her feet and the smoke dissipated with the wind. Neither indicated the location of the brothers; she watched deer urinate on the ground, thinking its flow would hint as to direction, but it just sank in; perhaps bear scat would indicate their whereabouts by the way that it leaned, but she was disappointed again. She decided to try one more thing. During four successive nights, she sang the songs of the Evilway. The last night she heard a song in the distance and felt that her brothers were approaching, although it was not their voices singing. The music was strange, scary, and put fear in her heart; when she went outside, there sat the skulls of her two brothers. Crying softly, she placed their heads on the skin of an unwounded deer inside her hogan and summoned her neighbors to council.

Among those present were Monster Slayer and Born for Water, the Twins of Sun Bearer. They had been the first to receive the Evilway ceremony and so would be of great help in trying to restore these two men, plus their father was extremely powerful and could be called upon to assist. Gopher Man had all the objects needed to conduct the ritual and so offered to preside. Everyone knew this would be a very difficult undertaking. Before starting, Gopher Man took out a small buckskin pouch and removed red powder (chííh—red ochre) to sprinkle on and around the skulls. By the end of that night's singing, flesh had reappeared on the heads, which now looked lifelike. The people smoked mountain tobacco and talked about what should be the next step. There were many different ideas but everyone agreed that the Red Ant People, who knew everything that occurred underground, would be the best ones to assist in finding the rest of the twins' bodies. A messenger brought them to the meeting, and after a lengthy discussion, they agreed to give all of the help they could. Bit by bit and bone by bone, the remains of the brothers returned to their sister's home. Gopher Man continued the ceremony, and by the end of a night of performing the Evilway, the flesh had returned to the bones, the heads attached to the bodies, and they were alive.

Still there were problems—something was missing—the boys could not speak as they used to. The Red Ant People had been thorough but had not totally succeeded. Everyone got in on the discussion and finally decided that the Black Ant People might find something that the Red Ant People had missed. Sure enough, after a diligent search, they discovered the top of the two skulls under a large round rock. With the help of the Red Ants, they removed the bone matter and brought it to the two boys. Following a long chant, their ability to speak had returned. There was yet another problem— the two could not move their limbs. Gopher Man and Monster Slayer were the only ones who knew how to fix this problem through a long, difficult ritual. During this ceremony, Badger Man mixed mountain herbs in water and gave the potion to the boys to drink in a large sea shell. Eagle feathers were wafted over their bodies during the chant by Monster Slayer and Born for Water. Gopher Man used a rattle made of buffalo hide, decorated on top with a small eagle plume, and at the lower end of the handle with hairs from below the chin of a buffalo.

The Twins painted lightning on the body of the firstborn of the stricken twins and then another image [term omitted, but concerns use of the tongue in life and death], on the body of the other. This sacred word is only used by medicine men. Badger Man chanted over the boys while this took place. At the end of the ceremony, Lightning and [sacred term] came in and took the boys away for a little while. When they returned, both brothers were completely restored to life and action, while the whole group, and especially the sister, were very happy. She said, "My prayers have been answered and my loved ones restored to me." Thus ends the story of "The Twins Who Were Raised from the Dead," as recorded by trader Will Evans.

Perry's narrative, with variations, highlights other aspects important to this ceremonial performance of the Evilway. In his version, Monster Slayer and Born for Water were the two killed that had to be brought back to life. He explains that as they returned from some adventures, an avalanche from the side of a nearby mountain slid on top and destroyed them. People began asking where they were, but it was not until the wind uncovered their skulls that the truth became clear. Jealous evil people had seen this as an opportunity to get revenge and so with powerful sacred arrows of lightning, they shot the side of the mountain, causing the rocks and dirt to slough off the slopes and kill the two travelers. Some of the people retrieved the heads and brought them home, giving the name to the ceremony, Tsiits'in Nát'áázhjí—The Two Skulls That Came Back. Talking God summoned the community and began scolding the mountain, telling it that it knew better

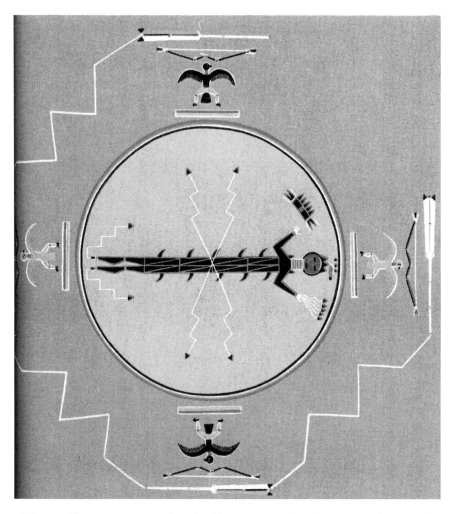

Monster Slayer as portrayed in the Shootingway when he journeyed to visit his father, Sun Bearer, who is represented by the enclosing circle. Monster Slayer is dressed in black flint, holds in his right hand a club with five stone knife blades capable of producing earthquakes and in his left hand five lightning arrows, with lightning also protecting his head, body, and feet. The surrounding birds and bows are also protectors.

but stood by and watched the Twins get overwhelmed and defeated by this evil deed. Talking God commanded that the ground and mountains work together to bring to life and heal the young men. The ground people set to work from the bottom of the feet upward, restoring the heels and the joints of the feet while the mountains put the knees back together and much of the rest of the body. The Water People joined in, as did the sky and thunder beings, until both bodies were made whole.

These holy people worked hard, but even with all of their singing, neither one of the young men moved. Further diagnosis showed that Crow had stolen Monster Slayer's eyes and refused to bring them back. The holy people selected two stars and placed them in his eye sockets and he began to move. Born for Water remained inert. A second diagnosis indicated he had no blood because the Red Ant People had taken it. The holy people commanded the ants to fix the problem and so they lined up in rows, many thousands of them coming out of the ground to put the blood back into Born for Water. The Twins were now completely restored and ready to return to their important duties, thanks to the ceremony created by the holy people. From this story came two other Evilway ceremonies—one was the Ant Evilway and the other the Big Star Evilway.

To understand the depth and meaning of the ritual, there are two elements that need to be discussed. The first is what is represented and taught in participation with the holy people and second, what the physical objects used in the ceremony represent. The patient in Perry's ceremony had undergone a lot of trauma, which needed to be removed. Ordinarily, performance of the Evilway lasts for five nights, and so this was a very abbreviated version. The markings of lightning on her arms, legs, front, and back, as well as three on her face, come from the Lightningway, which represents the pain, anguish, and evil she suffered. The ashes are for protection from further harm, created from desert and mountain plants, such as juniper and spruce, with pungent odors that repel evil. Her walk through the three worlds between the feathers meant that she was moving out of the problems encountered in the worlds below, where fighting and harm were now left behind, as she entered the circle or the Glittering World. This world represented today's life, with all of its danger and challenges, a place where people are hurt but also learn through growth. Man has changed the White World as the gods designed it into their own way of life known as the Glittering World. So here, she rinsed off all that was bothering her, as represented by the Protectionway markings accompanied by the whistle, before she came back out and through the worlds, when her footprints and any traces of this world were erased. Here, also, the feathers were removed. Blowing four times on the eagle bone whistle alerted the holy people of the prayers, adding to the hope that past troubles will be forgotten. Once she returned to where she had been sitting, she covered herself with a blanket without putting her shirt back on. None of her body was showing, just the feathers, as she offered the sacred prayers. She said, "I came out of the circle and I'm not going to go back. Give me a new way of life with new directions." The prayers were also for her children, everyone's well-being, and help in the future. Next, Perry blew smoke on her and she inhaled to gather her thoughts and feelings. The crying and fear were gone; she had returned to a neutral state, and healing had begun.

In summarizing the meaning of this ceremony, the patient was going through a transition from a world of problems and depression to one in which her thoughts and plans became positive. She could now make her own world and a successful future. It was as if spring had come, the earth changed, new life arose, and thunderstorms with rain refreshed the earth. It is the anticipation that new babies will be born, that horses, cows, sheep, and people will arrive. A new beginning now was possible and good things with happy thoughts would be obtained. No matter how much a person was damaged and traumatized, there is always a new way that can lead to fulfillment and a better life. Time itself is like the smoke used in ceremonies. It represents the future and thoughts that constantly shift in direction and meaning. When one tastes the bitterness of tobacco on the tongue, it erases the bad things that had been there, like the unforgiven issues one had or things that were said. Now the tongue will become holy again and will remain so if one is careful with how they talk. If a person curses another, it is not good for either. When an individual has this ceremony performed, they can participate in another one and learn more about it, but unlike some ceremonies that can increase power if done up to four times, once for this ceremony should be enough.

A second ceremony unconnected to the Skullway but that "sits beside it," was the Blessingway, performed in the presence of a young tree, where an offering was made for the woman. This rededicated the life of the patient, noting that all bad things were gone, taken away by the previous ceremony. An offering of four sacred stones to the four directions and the water, air, wind, and the ground that one walks on cleared a path for the future. This was where the woman received her new direction, as she rededicated herself in a new world. Now the ceremony was complete. The prayers offered were different from the ones in the Evilway, as they opened doors to a new path of life and its possibilities. This is where the real healing starts as one approaches opportunities. The Blessingway (Hózhǫ́ǫ́jí) finishes it out.

The physical objects used in the ceremony are tied to traditional teachings and practices specified through the origin stories. For example at the beginning of the ritual and at certain points along the way, an eagle bone whistle was blown to open up the medicine and alert the holy beings in the sky through this bird's ability to serve as a messenger. All of its help for the patient will be needed this day. When the woman held the eagle feather bundles on both sides of her head, they served as a conduit of prayer that strengthened each side of her brain, male and female, with good thoughts and messages from the holy ones. Ashes were also sprinkled on the eagle-feathered bundles, then blown upon the person, who along with saying the word "paah," chased evil away. The drinking and washing with the herbs and the marks of lightning drawn on the woman worked in a similar way. Lightning is one of the most powerful forms of protection, as seen by how the Twins used it to defeat their enemies and clear the earth of monsters. It is sacred, and only those who have been trained know how to use it and can handle objects touched by it.

An overview of part of Perry's jish. Many of these items are discussed and explained individually, but the two sets of eagle feathers on the left and the turtle shell on the right were used in the Evilway ceremony just outlined. This medicine bundle has many objects, gathered from far and wide, that have healing properties for different rituals. (Photo by Kay Shumway)

There are two types of clay pipes used in ceremonies. The first one comes from the Anasazi and is called a cloud blower. It is cone-shaped with a hole in the tapered end through which the smoke is drawn. Navajos use it in two different ceremonies for people having problems with hearing or voice (Windway) and the other for sucking an object out of a witched individual. This pipe is not really made for tobacco and normal smoking. Practitioners call it kǫ' bee áda'diikááh—the fire way of giving medicine— because the fire sits on top of one's mouth. When the patient starts sucking on it, the fire hits them straight in the mouth, the heat of which is not lessened by going around a corner as it is with the second type of pipe that is "L" shaped with a stem and bowl, similar to ones bought in a store. With the first type of pipe, fire gives the medicine. "I don't think people practice this procedure anymore because they have forgotten how to do it," Perry explained.

Understanding the Contents of a Jish

PERRY ROBINSON

A turtle (ch'éédigháhí—Slow Walker or The One Who Looks Tired All the Time) lives on land and in water and is considered one of the holy people that went to the ocean in the south, then returned. He is associated with the Protectionway and the water monster Tééh łį́į́'. A story tells how he had conflict with Horned Toad over controlling certain powers. They both had a protective covering on their backs that held this potency. Horned Toad had eighty-seven different horns or points used for defense, but which also attracted spiritual force. Turtle said, "Well, I didn't count mine, but every square section on my back, with different colors and patterns, will hold many stories. It's going to be set on top of me like this. So one day when I go to the water, I will open one of those doors and see other things in there, each one having a purpose and teaching. I have been to many different places, and each one has left knowledge and experience in those small squares on my shell. There is a door that opens to each one that tells me a lot of stories about how I am."

Turtle became one of the representatives of the Deep Water People who live on the bottom of bodies of water. Their domain is where underwater plants and algae grow. He suggested, "I can go down to the bottom, look around while still breathing, and bring medicine up to the surface. At the same time, I can live on earth and walk with the people." Since he can do both, the holy ones selected him for a special task. He offered to donate his shell so that every time a healer distributes medicine as a liquid, the patient drinks it from the shell. Turtle can also open one of its "doors" on its back and offer a story from his experience related to the illness. Only he knows these stories, and so we pray for his assistance. Turtles are connected with the Waterway (Tóee) because they can visit the green murky part of a lake or the bottom of a river. This is where they gather their medicine. When people drown, they can be brought back to life; if their minds are not straight, they can take the turtle medicine to restore lost capabilities. By using algae from a river bottom, a person who drowned can be revived.

Wooden hoops, made from different types of trees and approximately two feet in diameter, are also used in the Waterway to represent the four worlds a patient passes through. These serve the same purpose as the lines drawn with ashes in the Evilway ceremony while also representing the reed through which the people escaped the floodwaters during the emergence. The patient crawls through them, moving through the four levels in the four directions and leaving their problems behind. All of the sickness remains with the hoops, removing the evil and bad thoughts attached to an individual.

One of my medicine bags has an arrowhead tied to it for protection. Pouches like this are used by prominent people such as community leaders, medicine men, and Navajo tribal officials. The arrowhead attached to the outside of the pouch is made of jet, not obsidian. Its edges have to be sharp with many serrations or "teeth" created when being pressure flaked. These points are very hard to find and are often passed down from father or grandfather to son, although they can be made by the individual. Inside is a holy white mirage stone (hadahoniye' łigai) that represents the morning god. Two animal biles (atł'izh)—one from a cougar, the other from an eagle— are also used. The cougar's bile is bluish in color and very bitter tasting. This is used because he is thought of as a successful hunter and protector and one of the top creatures in the hierarchy of animals. It, like the mirage stone, is very difficult to obtain and has many good stories associated with the cougar's abilities. The eagle also operates at high altitudes, can see long distances, and is hard to catch. Its bile also holds properties of protection. The reason that bile is used from these two animals is that it comes from their center. Medicine people say that the center part of an animal is where all of its qualities and functions are found and distributed. Bile is considered one of these main sources, almost like a heart. Also inside the pouch are two flints—one red, the other bluish black with a red streak. They represent the sky. Everything in the pouch is related to the mountains and provides protection through awareness. There are no life feathers or pollen.

When a person leaves home or a safe place and goes to a meeting or gathering, they take this bundle and pray for safety. The elements inside protect the individual from those who may want to harm or work against them through witchcraft. Prayers for a safe journey and success secure the protection necessary, but the individual should always carry this pouch with them. Evil is kept away by the powerful elements inside. Everyone can have one of these medicine pouches, but they are expensive to buy and difficult to obtain. A person has to look hard to find the correct elements: the skin of an unwounded deer; an arrowhead of just the right size, shape, edges, and stone; eagle and cougar bile; and a medicine man who knows how to put it together with song and prayer. It may take years. When I created mine, I had to go to Utah to a taxidermist and get the bile from a cougar. The taxidermist saved it for me. Other people have to hunt and kill a cougar during the right season. Eagle feathers and bile are also difficult to obtain. The laws are very strict, even if one finds a bird lying on the ground already dead. Most people get these materials now by applying to wildlife refuges, or they go to Canada or Alaska. Still, one has to have a medicine man's license to obtain the bile or feathers for ceremonies or paraphernalia that is going to be put together. Nowadays it is very hard. If you do not pay attention, you will end up in jail.

MCPHERSON'S NOTE: Next Perry picked up his prayersticks. At the base of a prayerstick were two pieces of cottonwood with faces painted on them, forming the handle. The two figures represented the male and female sides of this prayerstick associated with Talking God. Behind them was a feather from a yellow warbler, then a feather from the western bluebird, then two turkey feathers.

The latter represents the north and the darker side of life, while the yellow one comes from the west and represents the yellow sunset, and the blue feather the south and blue twilight. A white plume that sits on the front faces east and represents the dawn and a new beginning. Associated with the feathers and directions are four gods—White Body Person, Blue Body Person, Yellow Body Person, and Black Body Person—each bringing their power to the prayers. Repeating this imagery, the handle was wrapped in four different colored yarns—white, blue, yellow, and black—denoting the four worlds and directions. There was, however, another color, red, added to represent the male and female rainbow. Each of the directions had their own colors and birds. In the east sits the white-winged dove (*Zenaida asiatica*), a white bird; on the south, the western bluebird (*Sialia mexicana*) sits in blue twilight. Yellow sunset sits with the yellow lesser goldfinch (*Spinus psaltria*) in the west, while a red wing blackbird (*Agelaius phoeniceus*) sits to the north.

All of these birds are similar in size and personality, but each has a different song referred to in the ceremony. The birds, as present through their feathers, are important to the healing process. Their songs speak of each feather and the power it represents. During the tobacco ceremony, I sang to the east, about the white mountain that was sitting there as a mother, and how on top rested a white shell with a white tobacco pipe holding white-tipped tobacco inside. The white smoke became the first light of morning dawn, and through that mist came the song of the dove, using the sounds of

Talking God to clear the smoke and point the way. The dove represented the morning god who sat with the bird—the two come as a pair. The same is true of the south. We sang the song of the blue mountain, a mother in this direction with a turquoise shell, turquoise pipe, and turquoise tobacco, which when lit, created a blue twilight smoke that was parted by the bluebird's song and healing power. The same was true of the west with its mountain, abalone shell, abalone tobacco pipe, yellow tipped tobacco, yellow mist, yellow bird, and yellow dawn. To the north was a black jet mountain with a black jet shell and black jet tobacco pipe that burned black-tipped tobacco that created a dark smoke that the red-winged blackbird parted with its song. All of these birds with their powerful voices and chants came from the second world to teach of learning about life, solving problems, and searching for a better way. Thus the prayersticks with their feathers are objects of power that encompass everything associated with the four directions, its gods, and healing powers.

MCPHERSON'S NOTE: Perry next discussed two rattles he had in his jish. The first was from the Hoof or Clawway ceremony (Akéshgaan). This is used in a three-day ritual for people who have concussions, fractured skulls, and broken bones, and need to have strength restored when in recovery. On the sides of the rattle was a cluster of the front tips of buffalo hooves, a handle covered in buffalo hide that came from the rear flanks, and part of a buffalo's "bell" or goatee from below its chin. This animal is believed to have very strong medicinal power and so the hooves and bell are extremely potent for healing. The rattle itself identifies an accomplished medicine man who has mastered a number of important ceremonies and who can direct extensive spiritual power. The story of the medicine buffalo leaving the Navajo is shared later. The second rattle that Perry held was made from a gourd with small pebbles inside.

These little stones may be picked up along a river or small catch basins (tsésjaa') in the rocks, but most are borrowed from the Ant People on their ant hills. These creatures donate their help by providing the pebbles through the Antway version (Wóláchi'íjí Hóch'o̜'íjí) of the Evilway. The ants have their own ceremony, and so we borrow these specially colored pebbles (garnets) from their hills. Small bits of white shell, turquoise, abalone shell, and jet are added to these rocks and are always present in every rattle.

The rattle represents the world; sometimes constellations are carved into the top, representing the heavens, while the inside sound is the voice of the different colored stones. When they are shaken, they say prayers, sing songs, and make noise for the world. Rattles with the constellations sitting on top are used in the Windway (Dichishíjí), while those without the design

Tools for the Lifeway, Evilway, and Enemyway ceremonies. The lion skin brings protection and is worn around the neck of the medicine man, as is the shell necklace. Each shell stands for a prayer and song braided into the cord, while the bamboo whistle represents the reed through which people escaped during the emergence. Its joints are the stages the people traveled through, feeling trapped until finally reaching the entrance into the White World. By blowing the whistle, the evil is pushed away, and the patient is mentally freed and reaches the "surface." (Photo by Kay Shumway)

are all-purpose and used in the Yé'ii Bicheii, Evilway, Mountainway, and other ceremonies. The tumbling about of the pebbles denotes gravity (Ni' Yiyah Niizíní Yá Yiyah Niizíní), the same that pushes down to keep us on this earth. There is also a kinetic energy that comes off the people and animals as the rattle is shaken. So when a person uses the rattle, that energy is turned loose and comes alive to make its song. Every time one shakes a rattle, everything around wakes up. The gravity and the energy inside the rattle work together to sing just as an animal moves something with its noise. Even a dog lying on the ground will react. Shake the rattle and he will wake up and start moving about. They really respect this song. I did not believe this until one day my grandfather took us to the zoo after we had finished a ceremony in Salt Lake City. Grandfather said, "I want to show you something," and taking his little rattle, we approached some cages. He said, "Watch the animals," then shook his rattle. Some of them even ran off while others looked around with their tails up and ears twitching. "This is so holy," he said, "that the animals respect it and will wake up very quickly because there are holy ones in the area." This awakening is through the supernatural or holy way/power (álílee k'ehgo), which starts the process of healing through the help of the holy people. It attracts their attention.

In another pouch I have a collection of eighteen different plants which I use as a healing medicine to induce vomiting. They were part of the cleansing ceremony to remove harmful evil elements that bothered the sick person. This emetic with its blended medicine was accompanied by sets of songs given by the holy ones as they created this medicine. There were twelve holy people, each with their own song. Four of them came from beneath the ground, four from the earth surface, and four from the heavens— the sky, thunder, wind, and sunlight—all of which comes from the four directions. They joined their songs with others, making eighteen holy people present, each represented by a different plant. For instance, the sun has a sunflower that is reddish-yellowish in color and is called azee' nidoot'eezhí, meaning colored medicine coming down. Then there is one that comes from the Lightningway that stands for the rain called The One That Attaches to You (iłhodiitł'iizh). The wind has its own medicine, as do all of the other plants. From the ground there are four sacred plants like the juniper, piñon, and one called Baby Crib (awééts'áál—cliffrose). These are all in that drink. Some of these herbs and plants are very hard to find due to the season and general availability, while others no longer exist. Medicine men often ask each other, "Where do you find that, and will I be able to get some there?"

This is very strong medicine that in the old days caused people to vomit. Now it is different. Some of the harsher tasting plants are substituted by milder ones. The medicine is also placed on a person's body, giving protection at the same time. I think this lessening of the strength and substitution of some of the plants began in the 1970s and 1980s. Medicine men started coming together—my father was part of the group—saying that some of these medicines were very harsh and needed to be brought down to a certain level. Part of the reason was that more people were having surgery, and the induced vomiting was affecting them. There was one story about a woman who had a hysterectomy. She came out of the hospital and was healing just fine, but when she took some of this medicine and started throwing up, some of her internal lining started to open and tear. The doctor went to the medicine people and said that the potion was too harsh and if this woman threw up again, she would pull a lot of muscles and rip more inside. People started saying the old way had to be changed now that surgery and suturing were part of the medical process. "Let's not use it this way," the medicine men said, "only if we have to use it in extreme instances. Perhaps a younger person or somebody who does not have surgery may be able to use it this way, but otherwise we will need a milder form." Still, the songs remained the same. Now it is left up to the medicine person to gauge what level of medicine to use. Both are available.

I had one patient who was really an alcoholic and would not stop drinking. He was very addicted, so I used some of the old medicine on him, and he really vomited a lot. In this instance, the cleansing he had was very beneficial, and it worked. He stopped drinking. There are also a lot of people coming out of prisons today, but often soon return. Their minds and thoughts are not serving them correctly. Some are very young. If they really want to have a cleansing ceremony performed, then we have to go back to the old way with its strong medicine. We enter the sweat lodge, heat it with hot stones, give the person this strong drink, and let him vomit. The more he drinks, the more evil is removed, the greater the cleansing. This is accompanied by teachings that point out how bad his life has been and how he is now free from those issues and should not go back to them. They had made his life unmanageable but now there is the possibility of change. People learn from this, and it is good.

CHAPTER SEVEN

Living Medicine Structures

T he Navajo people throughout their history have made many beautiful and practical objects—from traditional homes to baskets and blankets—and adopted many others—from tepees to cars. Each has been given its own unique identity, prayers, and teachings of respect and use. This chapter highlights the adaptive nature of Navajo culture with a special emphasis on how various items are tied to medicine practices. Certain aspects of these objects have been discussed in other chapters. Here, the goal is to give a more rounded picture of the importance of their spiritual, traditional, and healing roles. Central to this is metaphorical thought, which provides a condensed, intensified view from within the culture. Perception, framed through language, is embedded in a word, phrase, or sentence in which lies entire systems of classification and understanding. Extended metaphors expand that connective meaning. The comparison of two seemingly dissimilar or unconnected objects or thoughts becomes a unified expression that teaches important values for the continuation of society. Rather than becoming immersed in didactic preaching about values and the way one should act (although there are certainly times when discourse is direct, sometimes bordering on brutal), the Navajo use the objects of daily life to teach lessons. Every time they are encountered, thereafter, the lesson is retaught. More than just an intellectual comparison, however, the metaphorical thought is imbued with power from an animate universe that teaches what is right and wrong. Its depth is our topic.

Before getting into the realm of comparative thinking, there is another approach that explains how an object is made, the materials used, and its evolutionary development. This introduction will focus on two iconic items—the hogan and the wedding basket—made famous by the People. For those interested in a scholarly explanation of the hogan's construction, materials used, and variation, see Stephen Jett and Virginia Spencer's *Navajo Architecture* and Cosmos Mindeleff's *Navaho Houses*.[1] Jett's work is wide-ranging with a major emphasis on the home, but also including everything from sweat lodges to corrals to outhouses. This work is thorough. An excellent study on basketry is found in Georgiana Simpson's *Navajo Ceremonial Baskets*, while a detailed analysis of both hogans and baskets appears in Clyde Kluckhohn, W. W. Hill, and Lucy Kluckhohn's *Navajo Material Culture*.[2] The latter takes a sweeping approach toward traditional items that go from hair ties to horse equipment to ritual paraphernalia to children's toys. It is highly recommended for studying aspects of physical culture.

I had the good fortune in 2007 to help a Navajo man named Jim Dandy write his autobiography.[3] Raised in a highly traditional family, surrounded by medicine people including his mother and father, and grandparents on both sides, Jim was a very knowledgeable individual anxious to share their teachings. I have decided to include an extensive part of his understanding of the hogan because it provides both variety in the depth of metaphorical expression while illustrating how Navajo families use it to teach values. Jim has since passed away, but thankfully, he left behind an irreplaceable experience that testifies about the concepts this wood-and-dirt structure evokes in traditional thinking.

As a child my grandparents taught me at an early age about hogans. Grandmother, especially, had extensive knowledge about them that reached into many aspects of my life. These teachings helped me understand the world of my grandparents. The holy people designed the first male hogan (ałch'į' adeez'á) for ceremonial purposes in the beginning of the world, while the female hogan (hooghan nímazí) is mainly for family and daily life. There is a sense of greater power with the male structure than with the female hogan. The sweat lodge has the same shape as the male hogan, with its posts coming to a point, and contains similar power. The female hogan is built by overlapping logs and has a calmer feeling because it is not pointed. When building a female hogan, there are six main posts, while in a male there are five, but in both, the four cardinal directions are represented. These logs are partially buried in the ground with prayers for protection and assistance performed before anything else is added to the structure. This is called "addressing the mountains," where each post represents and is blessed to hold the powers of one of the Four Sacred Mountains. There are two poles for the door that faces east. These posts represent wealth on each side of the entryway and bring all kinds of good things to the people living there. The foundation, or the legs and other logs at the bottom of the structure, are aligned with the four directions, and represent the whole hogan. There are an additional twelve posts in the female hogan, symbolizing the twelve people who compose the main part of the foundation, forming the circumference of the home. They are holy people, the same ones involved in the Yé'ii' Bicheii ceremony and dance, who serve as primary deity, who participated in the creation of the world, and who represent different things such as water, colors, and teachings.

My grandfather was a pretty quiet man and did not get after us unless we really did something wrong. He did not say a lot, but he was very knowledgeable about sacred things to do with ceremonies and healing. My grandmother, on the other hand, was more outgoing in her discipline and taught about things around the home. Whenever we entered the hogan, we had to behave ourselves. She taught us a lot and I miss that. One of her teachings was about how the hogan is compared to the body with the fire being the heart of the home, the floor like one's back, and the opening of the smoke hole symbolizing a person's navel. She also taught about the four directions and how to do things in a respectful way, especially during a ceremony and the blessing of the hogan. Each one of us had our turn to learn.

The hogan represents life. A person comes in from the east with birth, goes to the south, which is life, enters old age to the west, and ends with death and spirit-travel to the north. While life starts in the east, west is where the heart sits. When a person follows a circular direction in a hogan, he follows the path of growth through life. When one enters, he moves clockwise, especially when there is a ceremony being performed. If there is a stove, one always puts the food either on it or in the center of the hogan in front of the medicine man to show that you are going to be feeding the people.

Fire, like a grandparent, is a provider and must be respected. My grandfather started his teaching about the home by saying, "I'm afraid I'm not going to live forever. Your grandmother has taught you that as she cooks, she prays for you as part of your life. By doing this, the fire becomes your grandfather also. When she sings about you, there is a light involved in that process, and the fire, as the great-grandfather, keeps everything alive in the universe inside the hogan. As with the sun, the fire sits where there is moisture and air, and everything that makes you alive is found within the hogan. The fire represents the sun because everything that is cooked for you becomes a part of you. When your own fire dies out you will be just like your grandparents and pass on. It is our job to share these teachings with you to carry on. Keep the light going all the time; that is your responsibility, and as a father you should teach your children."

Every time my great-grandmother cooked, she would stir the coals with her fire poker, pray, then place in the fire any food that was left over so that the fire could eat, too. She thanked it for being a holy person, a great-great-grandfather who provides. When my grandparents prayed, the fire was always addressed as a male in the prayer, thanking it for its help. The fire poker, like the fire, is a help and guide. There should be one in the

hogan at all times; a person should not live without one. There are two
different kinds—one is used for cooking, the other for ceremonies. The fire
poker used for cooking is female, the one for ceremonies, male. They are
shields that protect the home and must be cared for as living beings.

Grandmother started with the ground inside the hogan and likened it
to the Navajo wedding basket. When the hogan is compared to an upside-
down basket, the point of communication and connection is the smoke
hole. The logs in the cribbed roof become smaller as one moves closer to
the top; they become smaller each time, step by step. The rainbow is like
the inside of the roof as it surrounds above and arches over the people
below. One cannot go beyond its sides, but on every sacred mountain, the
rainbow reaches over it, just as the roof inside the hogan does.[4] So the
rainbow for the hogan goes from the floor up to the smoke hole and down
to the floor on the other side.

The stove or fire with its opening is in the center. There are the
mountains, which are the upright logs, the roof like the rainbow, with the
sky and clouds above. The roof beams are similar to a ladder that leads step
by step to heaven. When the sunlight comes in the top through the smoke
hole, it is a part of the heavens entering. The outer rim of the wedding
basket is like the dawn that goes around it, with the two stitches on the rim
that get bigger, the same as when one moves closer to the floor of a hogan.
Beyond that point a person does not really know what is there. When
building a hogan, an opening (smoke hole) is always left, just as in a basket.
It represents the knowledge one receives from the heavens, and so this hole
for learning should never be blocked. The same is true when making a rug;
there should be an opening somewhere in it. One does not just put a rug
together without a string or a pathway to keep the rug open so that one can
learn a lot about what is on the other side, beyond the object.

A person should never write his name on a hogan or make other marks
because it is disrespectful. To do that is similar to writing on one's hand,
which is like putting a curse on oneself. A hogan is also like a person; when
the mud comes off, it is like one's skin peeling. If there is no fire, it is as if
the heart has stopped and the hogan cannot stay alive and functioning. It
should be cared for just like a human.[5]

As with so much in the Navajo universe, Jim Dandy brings the
teachings about the hogan down to a personal level that serves as a
mnemonic device to guide one along the path of life leading to hózhǫ́.
Literally from birth to death and every other important event in between, the
hogan serves as the stage upon which many of life's most important events
are held. Little wonder that Perry provides so much detail about this setting.

Another example of metaphorical thought is associated with the Navajo
wedding basket. There are many different interpretations as to the meaning
of its pattern, but all of them reflect the deep sensitivity with which Navajo
philosophy is imbued. Many speak to an individual depending upon their

stage of life and personal circumstance. The first baskets made available for the People came from Sun Bearer (Jóhonaa'éí), who gave it to the holy people for their ceremonies. Sun Bearer agreed that this was good as long as they were used for worship, and so few ceremonies are performed without the basket. Medicine men place their medicine pouch or a mountain soil bundle in it, pray and sing with it, use it to hold sacred cornmeal mush during a wedding, or an emetic in an Evilway—indeed, all major ceremonies require a basket to be used during some part of the ritual.

Beyond the strictly religious implications of its designs of the earth, place of emergence, mountains, sun's rays, clouds, and so on, found in the creation story, there are other forms of guidance woven into its familiar pattern. In one instance, the entire design is said to represent a person's life. The center of the basket is the point of emergence, where life in this world begins. As the small coils spiral outward and enlarge, so too does a person's world expand, moving from family to playmates to associates in an ever-widening arc. The design in the center is small, representing the small things done as a child. As the coils widen and broaden, they show a parallel growth in the accomplishments of the individual. Once the rectangular points of black are reached on the outer edge, a person's life of achievement starts to dwindle. Things done in the frailty of old age do not have the same consistency or breadth as those done during the prime of life. The red center band or rainbow is the harmony and foundation upon which adult life should be built, while the white line that passes through the entire design from center to edge shows that no matter what happens in life, one can get through it. There is always a way out of problems. The basket thus represents growth and progress, a snapshot of one's life. The care with which it is woven and the tightness of its weave are left to the individual creator, just as each person makes his or her own life and determines the value and beauty within.[6] Once the basket or life is made, it must also be treated with respect. It is said that if a person spins around while holding a wedding basket, he or she will lose his or her mind. This provides a physical, visual meaning to the Anglo thought of how one's life is in a "whirl" or out of control.

The next three teachings about the basket are closely aligned, but share insightful variations in their interpretations. Betty Yazzie tells of how the center of the basket represents the whorl on top of a baby's head with the central white part representing initial growth. The first ring of black is one's brothers and sisters, the red is marriage, and the second ring of black is one's children. If there is red above that, it depicts grandchildren. As the design returns to white, "it represents how you are growing old and how you are reaching full circle in your life."[7]

Another understanding gleaned from this design begins in the center, which is said to be the umbilical cord of a newborn. The start of the black design is when the young child begins to speak, the next white line is when parents step in to teach, and the red section is a protective rainbow that shields the important knowledge that the growing youth wishes to keep. The second black design is when that person shares and teaches others of the things they have learned thus far. As white space becomes interspersed with the black, one becomes more forgetful, and by the time the totally white outer rim is reached (old age—white hair), the individual is returning to the baby stage. "The braided rim is like another seal. If you notice on a ceremonial basket, the ending rim is aligned with the beginning of the basket as if to say, 'Life ends back where it began.' All of your knowledge goes back to the beginning."[8]

A third interpretation ties the stages of life to teaching correct behavior. Medicine man June Blackhorse noted that the basket is used in blessing a newborn. Each ring of the basket is like ten years in a person's life. "It is like little kids are standing in the basket as their place to grow. That is why you don't turn a basket over their heads because that will cause them to stop growing. That is the way of life in the basket. For the rest of your life, you will use the basket. There should be twelve coils in the basket to symbolize one living a long and productive life."[9] In each instance, the basket becomes the individual moving through the challenges of development. This is also why most important events have a basket present—the First Laugh ceremony, kinaaldá ceremony, and wedding ceremony, as well as every healing ceremony up until the time of death. In each, the basket is a very real participant, not just a functional container.

A final note on the use of the sweat lodge will add to Perry's description. The structure is intentionally kept small, usually capable of holding six or seven men or women (but never men and women together). It looks like a pointed male hogan without the smoke hole, and it is perhaps four feet high, made of wooden poles covered with dirt, and usually has some type of plant material (juniper bark, grass, or rabbit brush) on the floor. Heated rocks, capable of maintaining enough heat for four twenty-minute sessions (lengths vary), are placed inside to the right of the doorway that faces east. Blankets or some type of mat or canvas cover the opening to maintain the heat.[10] The holy people prescribed the rules for building the structure—it must be planned at least one day in advance and built within a single day; participants, before entering for the first time, shout an invitation to the holy people to take part; the bathers sing sweathouse songs inside, as well as other songs; and if the sweathouse is used subsequently, additional earth needs to be put on it. As one man noted: "This was commanded by the Sweathouse. 'Unless you throw something on me, you will be a poor fellow; you will never get anything for yourself.'"[11] This structure is used for cleansing and refreshing an individual, curing colds and other forms of sickness, removing contamination from the hunt or warfare, and generally dislodging "ugly things" out of the body. Emetics and purgatives may be added to intensify the purification. Rolling in the sand or plunging in water removes the sweat and ends the process.

Thinking about Hogans

Elements of the hogan have already been outlined—the cutting and placement of the logs, selection of the dirt that is used as an outer coating, the blessing of the structure, and the division of space inside. Site selection is another important aspect as well as the use of alternate materials. When a person is looking for an area in which they wish to build a hogan, they often consider the trees that are located there. These trees, which are usually juniper and piñon in the lower elevations, can do a lot of good things such as providing shade, cutting strong winds, creating cool work areas, and offering storage space, as well as supplying a little wood for tinder and kindling. As many trees as possible are left around the hogan site, while the logs needed to build the structure are hauled in from other areas. An elder often accompanies a younger man when selecting a spot. The experienced person inspects the trees and soil and rocks to determine how to lay out the camp and preserve many of the natural resources nearby for future limited use. He chooses a place, then starts planning: "You can put a corral underneath this tree and cut off some of the lower branches to build a fence. And then in the higher branches store things you want to keep off the ground. Over here you can stack your hay for the animals in the winter. There is always a way that a tree can be used. The hogan will be built among the trees, each of which may have a specific purpose."

Rocks and rock formations are also considered. For instance, my uncle always paid attention to how the ground and stones lay about the land. He tried to live next to a small mesa or rock platform or a little plateau. I asked him why he did that, and he replied that his corral was going to take advantage of the placement of the rock or formation on one side, saving him the effort of building that part of the pen. Sometimes he would not have to do much construction at all, using the natural lay of the land as a fence with just a few parts connected with logs, brush, or wire. This saved a lot of work so that before long, he could chase his animals into the enclosure surrounded by rocks and close the gate. He always thought about these things when he settled into an area. His house and corrals were almost always near a mesa, canyon, rock formation, or some other land feature that he could take advantage of. The reflected sunlight from rock walls also helped to warm the area around a winter camp.

Many Navajo people talk about the wind, especially from the north. Homes are built so that a rock formation or plateau will either break the wind from that direction or cause it to pass over the hogan. Winter camps built out in the open, with no rocks or trees around them, can get very cold. Sites are often put down in the bottom of a canyon or at the base of a mesa, but the trade-off that needs to be balanced is how much sunlight will be available during the winter so that the camp is not in the shade throughout much of the day. Sunlight needs to be abundant with the sun pointing at you, heating your home. In more modern hogans, there will be windows to let in the air during the summer and the sunlight in the winter. Windows on the south side of the home let in more light during the winter when the sun is on lower paths in the sky compared to where it is located in the summertime, high overhead.

In the old days most, if not all, hogans were built entirely out of wood. As time passed, there were some homes made from a combination of wood and rocks, while now, there are many made out of all different kinds of modern building materials, but which maintain their characteristic shape. Hogans built with rocks on the bottom are sturdier than those made totally of wood. Their foundation is solid so that the wind and cold do not go through as easily because of the denser insulation. My mother used to talk about my father's hogan. She really liked it since it was so spacious inside and yet very warm in the winter. There were rocks around the bottom for a foundation, which reflected the heat very well even if there was only a small fire built in the middle of the open space. In the summer, all she had to do was to open the windows, and a breeze could blow through to cool the inside. Whether heating or cooling, the hogan was an efficient and comfortable place to live.

There are two different types of hogan—male and female. The round female structure is associated with Blessingway ceremonies and many others that are dealing with positive, feminine characteristics. The male hogan, on the other hand, is always tied to the Enemyway because it has a "tongue," or the projected entryway, which represents male qualities. Anything that deals with Enemyway or other male ceremonies sits in that structure. Blessingway belongs to the round one and is spoken of as the mother's stomach and womb, while the doorway is viewed as the vagina area. The opening can be entered straight into, while the smoke hole where the chimney comes out is the umbilical cord where the feeding takes place. This hogan is only about healing and protecting, but the male hogan with its long narrow entryway is about destroying evil influences just as the tongue through prayer does. The long entryway is also said to be a penis while the pointed tepee shape of this structure is an arrowhead. Yé'ii Bicheii, Enemyway, and Evilway ceremonies go with the one with the fork sticks forming the roof. That is how these hogans are considered.

Today, there are still many Enemyway ceremonies being held even though there are not many male hogans. In the old days, male hogans were built just for these ceremonies to be performed in, but now people are lazy, and so they use female hogans for male ceremonies. People have mixed up the functions of these structures, but if you go to a gathering of medicine men who understand these teachings, they would say that this mixing should not be done. The people do it anyway, and the medicine men have no control over what they do. The family is the one who either follows the teachings or not, causing the children to walk in the steps of their parents and copy what they see being done. The teachings always sit in the home. In the old days, male ceremonies were in male hogans and female ceremonies in female hogans with no crossover, and if the elders saw that this was not being practiced, they would step in immediately and stop the ceremony. Somebody

The male hogan (above) next to a wooden post corral and a shade house for summer use, illustrates a normal camp set up. This hogan, while significantly smaller than a female structure because of its slanted roof and leaning-log construction, is more powerful for ceremonial purposes. The female hogan (next page) with Navajo Mountain in the background, shows the attempt to maintain the trees as part of the camp and also how living close to family members was desirable.

would say, "No. Do it a different way. We are going to change it for you."
Now people believe, "I have the freedom to do this, and I can walk how I
want, talk as I wish, and practice my religion how I think best." If a person
tries to stop a ceremony, the police will arrest him and take him to court.

The thinking behind which hogan to use is based on the fact that male
ceremonies do not have the Blessingway lyrics at the end of the songs that
say "long life with happiness" (sa'ąh naagháii bik'eh hózhǫ). This is left out.
Instead the person singing just ends with "anything that is bad will die this
way" (yádí dida'achxǫ'í yei la bee ayóónizini yee yee nabiisyįį yee),
meaning that if something evil is left following the ceremony, it will cease
to exist. There is no Blessingway in it, no remorse whatsoever. It stops right
there; this is the Enemyway. If I am performing this ceremony or the
Evilway and there is only a female hogan available, such as at the Utah
Navajo Health Systems Hospital in Blanding, Utah, I do it outside alone and
in a place where there are not a lot of people. It is safer that way when few

people are around. This all falls back to whoever is doing the ceremony and what respect and teachings they have for it.

The cardinal directions associated with these ceremonies inform how the structure should be used. The north, one of the places of power where men are in control, also has the color black that is available for medicine people to utilize. The black markings mentioned previously and the figure of the black meadowlark that is placed on the bottom of the cheek all the way around on the chin, come from this direction. This bird is used because it represents change that will be taking place in the person's life. All of these symbols indicate that this is serious business with no fooling around. A red marking is placed on the top of the forehead. These all show that when this medicine, like the blackening in the Enemyway ceremony, is there, strong male powers are present. No children can be involved; they are not allowed to enter the hogan while this ceremony is taking place. Likewise, young people who are immature and women who are pregnant are warned away because they will get sick and be jolted by the presence of these powers. The direction north was selected for this purpose to be the place for serious things and something not to play or trifle with. The medicine there can overcome the enemy quickly and protect a person when handled correctly. The ceremonies represented by the north are not for women and children, who have their gentler Blessingway. The north belongs to the hunter and the black bow. This is not necessarily indicating that the north is bad, but it is for serious people and powerful medicine, and is no place for beauty and peace and a gentler touch.

When a person has encountered problems with evil spirits, broken strict taboos, or indulged in harmful excess, an Evilway, Enemyway, or Excessway (Ajiłee) ceremony is necessary to remove the problem. Strong heat and cleansing are part of these four-day ceremonies, which may require that a hole is dug in the center of the hogan to hold many heated rocks, which induce sweating. The holy people are there participating. If there has been some sexual misconduct, the medicine man might tell the couple, "I'm not doing this to make it appear that I am higher or more important than anyone here. I want to put this corn pollen down because I want both of you to put your hand on the ground where the basket is with medicine and talk. I want to put corn pollen out here, corn pollen right here; the basket is here, put another one here, put another here in four places. I want you to walk up to the basket and put your foot on this marking here. And I want you to put your foot on this marking of corn pollen here."

The man and woman move to their appointed places facing each other over a basket filled with water and herbs that have been blessed, then they drink from the basket. The medicine man points out that they could not do it standing on the corn pollen markings, but must be down on their hands and knees. "You stand here and you stand there, then both of you bend down and kneel in the sand on which the corn pollen rests. Here's a basket. With your other hand on this side, back off with your foot on this marking, and put your knees on this one, and do it on both sides so that you will have two knees and two hands on the markings. Now you can bend down and drink the water with your face. As you blow on it like the wind, it will separate the herbs floating on top so that you can get to the liquid underneath. After you do this I will tell you a story."

The medicine man has a lot of responsibility to advise and correct wrongdoing just as the gods do. He will use teachings that go back all the way to the time of creation, relating helpful stories and thoughts, sharing different types of medicine, and explaining what and how ceremonies cure. This is why Navajos are always told to go to ceremonies, observe what is happening, and ask questions so that they know what is being done. By the age of fifty, one is supposed to understand a lot about traditional teachings. When a question is asked, one should never be cornered. Grandmothers and grandfathers are supposed to know everything. Everything. They are supposed to talk about the Protectionway, the Four Evils not killed by the Twins, and other stories helpful in life. Elders cannot just sit back and say, "I don't know." They are considered holy ones who, like my grandfather, talked about anything, were counselors and mediators, and knew a lot about traditional medicine. He was known for being that kind of person.

After drinking, the couple will return to their seat and learn why they had to follow these instructions. They are taught, "These hands are now to be used for holiness. These feet and your two knees will take you to the holy place. But it will be the hand that is going to be your healer. I don't care what you touch. I don't care what you have in your hand; you will either heal or kill with it. If you have something in your hand and pray with it, it will become holy. Your answer will be prayer. Anything that you hold with these hands will be holy. If you pick up a baby with this hand and hold him, he will grow up to be a man who will be holy. When someone is grieving or needs help, hold and hug that person so that they will be healed. Your hearts will beat together and the heartbeat will heal. This is how your hands will be used. Do not take your five fingers and use them as a fist." The teachings of the body parallel the teachings of the hogan, illustrating how they can be used to destroy evil, protect life, receive blessings, and establish important goals and processes.

The inside of this female hogan has been compared to everything from a womb to the universe. Site selection, placement of logs, the smoke hole, east-facing door, and use-areas all speak to Navajo traditional teachings. (Photo by Kay Shumway)

Teachings of the Sweat Lodge

Returning to the physical aspects of the hogan and a sweat lodge, these structures are treated as living entities holding spiritual powers. Rocks, whether in a hogan or a sweat lodge, work with the fire to maintain the heated space for the people. In a sweat lodge, rocks are baked in a fire outside of the structure, then brought in and placed to the north. The enclosed space made from cedar logs and covered with dirt holds the heat inside, especially once the four blankets covering the doorway are pulled down. As the limited room becomes extremely hot, the people inside have no control over the heat radiating from the stones—the rocks are the ones in charge and working with you. The high temperature and the air and the rocks are taken care of by the fire; these elements facilitate the cleansing of the individual inside by bringing out their sweat (water). The four basic elements of life— earth, water, air, and fire—are present. The person is in there, but not controlling what is happening.

Today, many Navajos use the type of sweat lodge made famous by Plains Indians where a framework of wooden saplings are lashed together, then covered with skins, blankets, or canvas. In the center a pit holds the heated rocks. A man sitting inside sprinkles water on the hot rocks creating steam. Sometimes he burns himself by accident, which is not good. Meditation in this structure is not as powerful as that which is obtained in the traditional Navajo sweat lodge because the heat is controlled by humans, so people cannot think as deeply. Thoughts created in the wood-and-dirt lodge are stronger because the elements are left alone to do their work. When one sits in a Navajo sweat lodge with all of their clothes off and with the rocks and heat and dirt floor working together, that person becomes more spiritually connected with the holy elements. No individual is trying to control what these four do or say. You are there as a patient, and so you let them work you over. That is the way it is supposed to be. If a person feels like they are getting too hot, they can excuse themselves anytime, but the elements are always there ready to instruct. In the other kind of sweat lodge, the person pouring water does not have respect for the fire or the rocks because he is the one who wants to be in control. He wants to talk, pray, and sing, but to the holy people, they are wondering, "Why are we hearing you? This man is doing all the work and is in charge. He apparently doesn't need us." This is how we are as human beings. We like to take charge and control everything, including the elements. This world was not set up to be this way. There is a big difference between how you think about the things that happen in these two different sweat lodges.

A lot of Navajos are not familiar with the old songs that teach about our early homes and sweat lodges. The first song that talks about them says that they were made out of a fabric or buckskin that was placed on top as a covering—not the dirt that is used now. It says, "I'm putting it on top; I'm putting it together." When one listens to this old, old song, it is really telling about how things were done in the past. The old cloth or skin sweat lodge has now become quite popular. Both this type and the one made from wood and dirt were used long ago. This was also true of the homes used in the past—portable tepee-like structures made out of skins. Navajos have recently come back to this type of dwelling made from fabric. My grandfather said that some of these practices originated with the Papagos, Zunis, and Havasupai, who first had the idea of making willow frames for their homes, then covering them with skins and brush. These tribes today build their sweat lodges this way and pour water on heated stones.

Navajos tell the story about when the Twins—Monster Slayer and Born for Water—came to visit the sun. He was not sure that they were really his sons, and so he gave them a series of tests to prove their worth and claim of relationship. Sun Bearer placed the two young men in a sweat lodge, heated the rocks to a terrific temperature, put them in the structure, then poured water on the stones. The steam was tremendously hot, but the boys, with supernatural help, were able to withstand the heat and prove that they were who they claimed to be. Navajos do the same thing today when they put water on the stones to increase the heat. This practice came from the beginning and is still being performed. Some people think this type of sweating comes from the people of the north, but our stories are already set here. Navajos do not understand that this was already established with them at the very beginning.

The story about Coyote, the trickster, and his desire to remain with the five-fingered beings discussed previously, is another example of the use of this type of sweat lodge. When he asked to remain with them, they refused his request, insisting that he was one of the gods and so needed to be with his own kind. Coyote argued with them, so they put him in a sweat lodge covered with fabric, poured water on the heated stones in the center, and "boiled" him until he cried and passed out. Grabbing his legs, they dragged him from the structure and waited for him to awaken. With the words, "Those humans are going to kill me," he left and returned to the holy people but maintained many of his animal characteristics.

White Cloth, Ashes, and the Fire Dance

The origin of this type of sweat lodge, as well as that of the tepee, comes from the same narrative. The idea for these kinds of structures is found in the stories of the black widow spider and of the caterpillar. Both of these creatures spin their own homes out of white web material that is woven into a form that is wide at the base and pointed at the top. The first sweat lodge songs speak about their weaving this material then creating an entrance that they can walk out of. The songs refer to a white cotton cloth (naak'ą'áłgai) that glistens in the morning sun, then says, "I'm taking a cloth and putting it over. I'm putting a dome together with the cloth on top of it." My father taught that the first tepee and sweat lodge came through copying these insects' methods. Other sweat lodge songs talk about putting hides over a frame before cloth made by Anglo people was ever introduced. This goes back to the time when the Navajo people used to travel a lot as hunters and gatherers. To have that type of mobility when chasing game and moving from summer camp to winter camp was very practical when compared to the stationary hogan and earthen sweat lodge. So the story is set in our songs, about how the spider and caterpillar provided the model for the tepee, something that did not come from other tribes. Now the Navajo have returned to what we used to have made of buckskin, but is made out of woven cloth or canvas like the spider and caterpillar first showed us.

Men entering the sweat lodge will sit on juniper bark across from the heated rocks and sing the sacred songs about water, fire, air, and earth as they pray in this structure first designed by the holy people. It is a place of thought, worship, and discussion.

There are further, deeper teachings about the white cloth found in the Mountainway ceremony that also tie in with things developed in the beginning. This ceremony is a nine-night event, some of which was discussed earlier. On the ninth night a large brush corral comprised of piñon and juniper branches is made for the "fire dance" and other medicine practices. Following ceremonial activities held in a hogan nearby, a dozen or more performers covered in white clay and wearing only a white breechclout enter the enclosure, each holding a two-to-three-foot-long stick with a piece of white cloth tied on the end. These men are called Ones Who Become White (Neigahí) or "whities." These are specially selected individuals, who, as young people, were chosen to assist in different elements of the ceremony. They were blessed with white paint on their face, arms, and the rest of their bodies, and they drank special herbs to cleanse and purify. This is done whenever they participate in this ceremony.

Once they are adults, the medicine man presiding over the Mountainway asks them to dance and perform. They are blessed with white corn pollen and then prepared for the fire dance by creating their own stick from a juniper tree with a piece of white cloth tied to the end. When the dance starts, the cloth is lit on fire, and it burns until completely out. The whities continue to dance, constantly calling upon their sticks to turn white. Soon the white cloth reappears on the burned end, and the dancer exclaims, "I see white; mine has returned," then runs out of the enclosure, returns to the ceremonial hogan, washes off the clay, puts on regular clothing, and returns to the corral to participate with the rest of the people.

The cloth, feathers, and color white have deep significance in this event. The song teaches that they are connected to the time when the first day was born in the east and the first white stone was found. The cloth also represents a woman from that direction who carries the healing powers of the east. The white cloth lives in the east (naak'ą́'ałgai nídiiyaa jiiná éí lá neiyaneiyá hanei) and was first woven by spiders in their webs. With this white cotton comes the dawn (Naak'ą́'ałgai bił hayoołkááł). Both the feather and the cloth in the performance represent life. Anything that has to do with feathers always stands for life and renewal, so they are never destroyed the way the cloth is. They are kept out of the fire. Bringing them back means a healed individual. While the ceremony, dance, and activities are taking place, the holy ones are there visiting and participating right along with the human performers. The beating of the drums, the singing, and the prayers all summon and ask them to participate.

White is also tied in with the purifying qualities of a fire. Every time one is lit, there is a white color, and it is part of the holy ones. Smoke is black, then at the top of the flame the fire is yellow, further down is blue, and at the bottom there is white—each color being part of those established in the four directions. The white part is at the source of the flame, coming from the coals and burning wood—the place where the fire and heat start. Thus the white cloth represents dawn, and the beginning of everything. For the patient who is being healed by this ceremony, there is a fresh start, a new day.

Part of that light is found in a person's eyes. Sometimes when one blacks out, faints, or has a heart attack, they will see nothing but white before passing out. They say that white represents something to do with the eyes and that when one wakes up again after fainting, the eyes start by seeing white. The same is true when involved with divination using sun gazing—the sunbeam comes into the eye so that the only thing that is visible is white. The color white has to do with the holy ones. When something begins to have an effect on a person's eyes, whether dehydration or sickness, the first color is white, then it goes to blue, yellow, and then black.

As the ceremony in the corral continues, another group of men, daubed in white clay and dressed in breechclouts, come into the circle, each carrying a torch of twisted cedar bark. Four selected individuals approach the large fire burning in the center and light their torch on one side of the cardinal directions, then move to the brush fence and throw it over—the first going to the east, the next to the south, then west, and finally north. This is a signal that the other performers can light theirs and can chase each other around with the fire, sometimes burning each other until the torch has burned down to a nub. The ashes from the torch's glowing cedar are collected by the spectators and brought home as a medicine applied to burns for healing. The charred bark is relit, cooled, and the ashes put on first and second degree burns. Those who have used this medicine will not have scars.

Roles of the Wedding Basket

The fire dance officially opens up the last and most spectacular night of the Mountainway ceremony, with its many feats of magic and supernatural power. Everyone in the corral, and even those observing from the outside, is blessed by the sacredness of these events. Two medicine men and more dancers with sticks tied with feathers will perform and then depart, making opportunity for other medicine men to show their powers. There are feats of arrow swallowing, dancing Yé'ii, bullroarers (voice of thunder), dancing animal performers (including a bear for the Bearway), and miraculously sprouting cactus—all of which exhibit supernatural powers. This is also when a group of individual feathers stand upright in the center of a medicine or wedding basket and dance by themselves, motivated by the power of a rattle. Soon two young virgin girls will come and dance to the scraping of a serrated rasp placed on the bottom of an overturned wedding basket that amplifies the sound. The two girls perform, using a distinct step and waving their colorful fans back and forth. They will also dance toward the fire, cover themselves, touch it, and then move back out to the medicine people, continuing to dance to the rhythm of the drumbeat on the bottom of the basket. The patient will sit there and wait for the medicine man to bring a mixture of herbs in water in a dish for him to drink.

The beating on the bottom of a basket is normally considered disrespectful outside of a ceremonial setting. Here, a specially formed drumstick, usually made of juniper that is thinned at one end, then bent around in a loop, is used. The songs that are sung and accompanied by hitting the basket help cure the patient. Every time the basket is rolled over one time, the sickness is put down and the medicine begins its work. Following each turn, there is a sacred song that goes with it. Singing the sacred songs furthers the healing; the opening of the basket or line that extends from the center to the rim faces east during a ceremony, letting that direction's powers in to heal and provide a new beginning.

Another practice that is usually forbidden except in a ceremonial setting is putting a basket on a person's head. However, in the Coyoteway, the patient wears a basket on their head with things placed on top of it with a string tied under the chin. The medicine practices of the Navajo people in this Coyoteway and the Buffaloway are similar, in many respects, to how the Hopi practice them. The dress is almost the same with the only difference being in a sash belt that has different colors and more stars. In these ceremonies, as in many others, it is the sunlight that touches the patient and causes the healing. The sun's rays are what make the connection when the healing starts to take place. This is why a lot of people open their windows if they have them in their hogan, to make sure the sunlight is coming in. This is polite to introduce the light into the circle of the home.

Once the medicine men have completed their part of the Mountainway, they will pick up their basket, put it underneath an arm, and then while shaking rattles, sing Blessingway songs as they leave the corral. This pair has done their part and so now a second pair, representing the south or blue side, enters in to perform. Outside of the corral there are other groups of medicine men waiting to share their practice. Each one brings a different power that represents one of the other ceremonies. Beyond the corral, there are sheep and other forms of wealth awaiting them as gifts for conducting their ritual specialty. This is how the fire dance is performed.

In the Mountainway ceremony, a Navajo wedding basket (ts'aa' bii'ha'noots'ee') is used for both the dancing feathers and as a drum carried by Yé'ii Bicheii dancers and medicine men. This type of basket is used in

A finished wedding basket woven "clockwise." Starting where the "bump" begins on the outer coil and tracing it to the center, it follows a clockwise spiral. If it went in the other direction, it would be used in an "unraveling ceremony." Regardless, the bump alerts the medicine man, if in poor lighting, which direction the basket should point to have the "entrance" face east. (Photo by Kay Shumway)

almost every lengthy traditional Navajo ceremony to hold medicine, medicine bundles, and all types of ritual paraphernalia. It is also central to the wedding ceremony, kinaaldá, and corn grinding practices, while in the past, women used it for daily food preparation. The basket is considered an important object (habeedí) for women in their home. There are many significant teachings about the wedding basket, only a few of which are discussed here, and a number of taboos for handling it that should be avoided. Indeed, actions taken in the Mountainway ceremony and other rituals—turning it upside down, drumming on it, and so forth—are considered disrespectful outside of the medicine context.

The design in the basket has many interpretations. One tells of mountains and dark clouds with the red ribbon of sunset or a rainbow, while the center is seen as the place of emergence. Many people use different stories to teach about proper behavior, the stages of life, and aspects of the Blessingway. These are all good ways of showing respect for the basket while teaching important concepts of life. From the time when the men and women separated and the two nádleeh created the first baskets, this object became holy because of the way it was put together. The wedding basket took on responsibilities and roles in medicine that cannot be substituted by any other object. It is different, say, than the plaited water jug made out of the same sumac material, but has no religious function. Once it is created and heated, pine pitch is poured over the jug to seal the vessel; its use is purely functional. The wedding basket, on the other hand, is made with a lot of thoughts and feelings, which like a rug, are stitched into its circular form. While it is being created, the earth has time to look at its development and be a part of the process. Woven into this creation is the spirit of the basket, making it one of the holiest objects that medicine people can use to heal the sick. This is especially true if the person making it knows the individual for whom it is being made and the type of ceremony in which it will be used. The thoughts and prayers are then woven into the basket, making it a spiritual object filled with power, showing the holy beings how much the maker wants the sick person to be healed. The basket maker is using her powers on behalf of the sick, which shows respect for their use.

In making a wedding basket, there are a lot of stitches that go into each row. The split sumac is wound around the rods that determine its shape and size. Each stitch that is placed into the next row is a thought, something the maker is contemplating, or a song she may be singing that is put into it. It is carefully stitched into the hole and then comes back out as it makes a circle. Some people say that each hole represents a day in the use of the basket, so that 365 would mean a year. The larger the basket, the longer its use, and the greater number of years it will serve. This does not mean that the owner has to stop using it when the number of stitches is equal to the days since it was finished. Still, one might think of it as a two-year or four-year basket.

Today, ceremonial baskets are made to sell to anyone who would like one, but they have become increasingly expensive. There are also a lot fewer people who remember how to make them or who take the time to gather all of the materials, prepare and dye them, then form them into a tightly woven basket. A lot of times following a ceremony, people say they are just going to put money in front of it (pay) and keep it for themselves. This is wrong. The basket is part of the healing side of the ceremony, which during the ritual, absorbs the illness that is being treated. Traditionally, the medicine man performing the ritual takes the basket with him, partly as payment and

Basketmaking is an art that requires patience—from harvesting the sumac, peeling and splitting it into thirds with teeth and fingers, soaking and dyeing the strips, forming a three-branch foundation, and then wrapping the strips around it—little wonder there are not many women who continue the practice today.

partly to remove the sickness that has been bothering the patient. If one keeps the basket, they also keep the problem. The basket's job is not yet done. Instead of letting the medicine man walk away with it, the family holds on to what they tried to get rid of and keep it in their house. A lot of people nowadays say, "I don't have the money, I can't afford a basket. I'm going to borrow one, and so instead of giving the basket to the [medicine man], I will give him the money and just keep the basket." It does not work that way. If the healing is going to take place, the medicine man has to walk with the basket. That is what it was made for.

Wedding baskets often hold liquids filled with medicine. In order to prevent them from leaking, they have to be soaked in water overnight, causing the stitches to swell and fill in any spaces. It tightens right up. Put in some cornmeal on top of the water, and when through, rinse it out. Nowadays people line their basket with aluminum foil or put on a plastic shower cap inside. This is a lazy way that uneducated people who do not understand the principles of Navajo medicine take to save their basket. When this is done, it is the aluminum foil or plastic that is doing the ceremony, which just does not work. They have no power. Let the basket do its job.

When a basket becomes old and no longer serviceable, there is a respectful way to dispose of it. Around the rim, there is a special kind of stitch that seals the basket's edge. Cut into this stitch in the four different directions, then loosen the top rows or bands and sprinkle corn pollen on the remaining part of the bowl. Bring it to a young tree that is out and away from any kind of activity where it will not be disturbed, then place it face down underneath the tree's branches. When the rain falls upon it and the sunshine hits the outside, it will dry up and untangle itself. After a number of years, only spiral rings that were inside of it remain.

CHAPTER EIGHT

Land, Animals, and Ceremony: A Case Study—Bearway

S erendipitous—making fortunate and unexpected discoveries by accident—is the only way I could describe it. Some time ago, I had received a partially translated interview recorded in the 1970s in which a hand trembler, David Kindle, shared part of a narrative called "Killer Bear" (Shash Agháanii). There was sufficient information to get the general drift of the story, but too much was sketchy. I contacted a good friend and translator, Marilyn Holiday in Monument Valley, and asked if she would be willing to give a more complete rendering, which she agreed to do. What I thought would be a relatively easy process of reading transcribed Navajo, turned into much more of a chore, to the point that she first read it, then recorded it on tape before translating. Even with this effort in hand, I still had too many questions.

I turned to Perry for help and played Marilyn's twenty-five-minute rendering in Navajo to see what he thought. I sat there curious, he sat there unflinching. When the recorder clicked off, I asked if it connected with anything he was familiar with. His passivity melted as he became animated, having encountered an old friend consigned to the mists of the past. He talked about a ceremony—the Bearway—which is rarely practiced and is now bordering on extinction. The literature about it is sparse, and no mention is made by Leland Wyman in his summary classification of Navajo ceremonials, although he analyzes an entire subgroup of the Mountainway of which the Bearway "sits inside."[1] What follows is the explanation that came from that tape and a prime example of the extensive teachings derived from animals found in chantways. Other creatures play a similar role in the Coyoteway, Dogway, Eagleway, Red Antway, and others—all of which have as much detailed information and interpretation behind them as the Bearway. They also describe a world of relationship with many of nature's creatures.

Addressing an animal with both common and sacred names not only has the ability to communicate respect, but can also summon that animal whether wanted or not. The more important and powerful the creature, the more names it has. For example, in daily conversation a bear is referred to as "shash," which may have a number of descriptors that identify what type. In addition to its color (black, white speckled, and silvertip), there are also anatomical characteristics: "whose feet are spread" (black bear); "long back" (grizzly); "yellow chin" (cinnamon); and "whose legs stand up" (unidentified).[2] Add to this the sacred names used in ceremonies that show deep respect when a bear may be listening: "Reared in the Mountains," "Roaming in the Mountains," "Roaming in the Forests," "Who Lies in a Den," and "The Fine Young Chief."

Tall Woman explained how her father impressed upon her and her sister just how important this type of respect was. As young girls, they herded sheep high on Black Mountain (Mesa) in the summer and often encountered situations that upset their dogs. Frightened, the girls asked their father what was causing the problems to which he replied "That Thing That Roams the Mountain," avoiding the word "shash." The girls did not understand and kept asking what it was until finally he broke down and told them it was a bear, adding they should not be scared of them, but under no circumstances when they were in his area should they use the word shash.[3] This type of respect, however, can also be used to show disrespect, when an angry person accuses another of being "from the bear's den," a male or female bear, or "bear's children."[4] Reason: in traditional teachings, the bear can be both a helper and protector or a powerfully destructive enemy. It is all a matter of words in context.

As Perry points out, the bear, like everything else in the Navajo universe, has an "inner form that stands within" (spirit) that is human in shape. Anglos may struggle with this concept, but for traditionalists like Navajo Oshley, it is real. He told of a time in the 1930s when he was herding sheep in the Abajo or Blue Mountain in southeastern Utah. His camp was near a cluster of berry bushes, which attracted bears and encouraged them to snoop around and take freshly butchered meat that he had hung in a tree. Perturbed, Oshley:

told the bears not to eat on this side of the mountain, and they listened to
what I said to them. They stayed where I told them they could. Now I am
not frightened of bears. I just tell them to leave me alone, and they do. My
maternal grandmother told me that if a bear blocks my way and does not
move that I should take my shoes off and throw them to the bear and that
would get it to move. A couple days later this happened. I asked him, as I
took off my shoe, what he was doing in my path. Then I told him that here
was my shoe, and the bear took off into the bushes. . . . About two days
later, when I was still quite a distance from my campsite, I saw the bear
where I usually hung my food. I shot, it growled at me, but I missed him. I
thought about what had happened that day before I went to sleep. In my
dream, a tall man with a bushy mustache came to me. He asked why I was
shooting at him, and I told him he had brought it upon himself, so he
walked off without saying anything. . . . The next morning I offered the
bear corn pollen. I called him grandfather and told him I was thankful that
he was talking nicely to me. I told him from then on I would not shoot
again. I had already said I would not harm them, and I kept my word, even
though at times they got very close.[5]

Relationships between people and the things of nature are real and
comparable.

The land is no exception, offering a map of relationships, where things
are found, and why they are there. Navajo mythology—especially in the
Mountainway ceremony (Dziłk'ijí)—is replete with teachings about bears
living in the Chuska Mountains and around Black Mesa.[6] As Changing
Woman traversed the land, she had five pet animals that protected her and
her fellow travelers. One of those guards was a bear, who viciously attacked
any enemies that endangered the group. At the end of the journey, Changing
Woman released the bear saying, "Our pet, you have served us well; but we
are now safe among our friends and we need your services no more. If you
wish, you may leave us. There are others of your kind in the Chuska
Mountains. Go there and play with them."[7] He ambled off in that direction,
which explains to the Navajo why bears have been numerous in that area
ever since. Perhaps that is why medicine man Frank Mitchell pointed to
Beautiful Mountain and declared that was where Monster Slayer, in an effort
to destroy monsters that roamed the earth and ate Navajo people, killed
Tracking Bear Monster (Shash Na'ałkaahii) there. This wily bear
disappeared and reappeared through a system of interconnected dens.
Monster Slayer studied the creature's action, determined where the bear
would surface next, then waited outside until the monster's head protruded
enough to be cut off.[8]

Chuska Peak is another site where supernatural bears hold power that
can harm people who do not show respect. Two young men, identified only

as Elder Brother and Younger Brother, met four beings known as "Maiden That Becomes a Bear" and entered their home near the peak. These women's faces were white, but their legs and forearms were covered with shaggy fur. Although their hands were like those of a human, their teeth were long and pointed. These women did not harm the Twins, but showed them how to make prayersticks and then bury them as part of a sacrifice.[9] The men continued with their travels. Washington Matthews, who recorded this story in 1887, told of when he was visiting this area with a group of Navajos who approached within three hundred yards of the base of Chuska Knoll. His companions refused to go any farther because it was the home of these women. Matthews proceeded by himself to ride to the peak by traveling over fallen trees and on loose stones. Once he arrived on top, he found a hollow among the rocks with some carved stone images and shell beads left for offerings. He later joined his companions below, mentioning that his horse was getting lame and that it must have gotten injured while crossing over some of the fallen trees. The Navajos felt differently: "Think not thus, foolish American," they said. "It was not the fallen trees that wounded your horse. The Diyiin [gods] of the mountain have stricken him because you went where you had no right to go. You are lucky if nothing worse happens to you."[10] Apparently, nothing did.

Another story about bears underscores how respect and prayers can lead to a positive outcome, while disrespect and ignorance may end in death. In the 1930s, a bear roaming around Sawmill had "stolen" a five-year-old child who had been missing for days. Family members enlisted the help of a medicine man who knew the chants of the Mountainway ceremony in order to urge the bear to release the child. Four days later, following prayers and songs, the searchers found the child unharmed. Around this same time, a second child disappeared, taken by a bear in the Chuska Mountains. This time some white people organized a rescue party, armed themselves with rifles, and went in search. "They didn't do that in the Navajo way. So the bear slammed that baby girl into some rock walls and killed her. She was dead when they found her. They should have prayed to it; the bear knew they were planning to shoot it and so did that."[11] Navajos also say that bears from the Chuska and Lukachukai ranges should never cross over to Black Mesa or else they will bring bad luck.

Although very little has been written about the Bearway ceremony, Hosteen Klah (Hastiin Tł'ah) discussed with trader Franc Newcomb his experience in learning it. He told of when he was a young boy who, along with three others, served as an apprentice to a relative and medicine man named Bear Face. This man received his name from his face being clawed by a bear he was trying to train for the Mountainway and Bearway ceremonies. The raking claws ripped off much of the flesh on one side of his head, exposing teeth and bones that would never be covered again. Following this incident, the only bears used during the ceremony were in sandpaintings. In order to teach the ritual properly, all of the bears in nature had to be in their dens, which meant that late fall and winter were the only times that the neophytes could be taught. Klah spent two years during this season, learning the words and assisting with the objects needed to perform it. He never obtained his own materials and tools to conduct a ceremony. Only twice in that second year was he able to serve as an apprentice, however, his photographic memory allowed him to later recount the minutest detail of its performance.[12]

Bears and the Bearway ceremony are concerned with power. As noted previously, power in Navajo thought can be used for both good and evil, which holds true in this instance also. On the positive side, bear power can remove problems associated with anger and violence, self-destruction and loneliness, and aberrant behavior while protecting an individual from harm. When abused, sickness, increased psychological issues, and antisocial behavior can become inflamed. The bear spirit must be respected. If a bear's tracks are found, pollen and a prayer are applied; encountering one in the woods means using the right language and might require a ceremony; its meat is only eaten on special occasions and is generally avoided.[13] Tall Woman provides one last example of when she and her sister, Isabel, were young and herding sheep. Isabel found a small carved wooden figure of a bear with turquoise embedded in it. She put it in her pocket and later played with it, but told no one what she had. Soon she became deathly sick, requiring divination and different ceremonies to find a cure but to no avail. Eventually Tall Woman discovered what her sister had kept, and so after returning it to the spot it was first found, the family held a nine-day Mountainway ceremony—the only remedy that brought Isabel back to good health.[14] The cure had now been directly related to the cause.

Bear-ly People

Navajo stories, teachings, and ceremonies, almost without exception, are very specific in identifying geographical sites and animals. These locations are places of power since they are where, for the first time, a cure, protection, or teaching was obtained. By returning to a site or by calling upon its power through prayer, a person is healed or protected by those involved when it happened long ago. Animals play a prominent role in all the stories that serve as a foundation to the chantways from which ceremonies come. The creatures' unique qualities and actions explain how they can help an individual in need when summoned. Rituals make this relationship clear and visible to the patient who, with the help of a medicine man, calls upon the unseen powers to assist. An excellent example of this interrelatedness of land, animal, and ceremony is found in the story of "Killer Bear" (Shash Agháanii), the qualities and characteristics of bears, and the territory surrounding Hesperus Peak and the Chuska Mountains. By using bears and this region as examples, one understands the role played by other animals and different land formations, a topic expanded upon in future chapters.

Animals are far more human than Anglo people choose to believe. To Navajos, bears are considered to be holy people, so even their hide is not touched or used and the meat not eaten. None of their parts, except sometimes the claws in a necklace or wristband in the Protectionway ceremony (Ínáályéél), are used. These holy ones are thought to be like human beings. One day, I saw a skinned bear with the hide and head removed. The carcass looked like a person lying there, which helped me understand what the elders had taught. I felt uncomfortable just to look at the body that seemed so human. A person's hand is similar to a paw with its nails and markings. Elders say it is almost like ours and point out that bears climb trees, pick things up, and eat with their paws. They can also stand upright and walk like people. Humans leave an imprint that is very similar to a bear's footprint when it is standing on two legs. The paws' impression is long and not as rounded as when it walks on all four feet. Bears are compared to humans in stories. The teachings about Changing Bear Maiden and how a woman transformed into a she-bear are the basis for the Evilway (Hóchxǫ'íjí) ceremony.

Bear is the leader of the animals and controls the resources of the mountains. He participates in the natural cycle of mating and birth that takes place each year. October and November are the mating months for many of the animals. The moon and stars keep track of the time when it is best for the animals to get together to prepare for the new year and new life that lies ahead. Bears and the other animals understand this, and so their thoughts turn toward creating offspring and when the best times are to have sex. Their colors change and brighten, body chemistry shifts, and their general attractiveness is at its height. The animals' thoughts are different and they become less predictable, just as the weather in the month of October is unpredictable. Is it summer, fall, or even winter? The animals are going to be roaming all about and looking for a mate, doing all they can to attract a partner with the thought of bringing new life into this world.

This thinking is a gift given to them for the months of October and November. The animals have a newfound charisma, and they dance with it.

They have their own talk and songs that they sing only at this time. Take crows, for instance. They make sounds that say, "I'm ready to mate. I'm attractive and singing for you. I don't know if you like my song, but it is mine." Everything sits in this pattern where animals are mixing up with each other. The colors, plumage, antlers, dancing—whatever it may be—is used to attract females to males. The deer have to show their antlers by cleaning them so that they look nice and are effective in fighting. Eagles really show their white heads and white tails, as they lose their old feathers and prepare a nest for their young. They show off and work at keeping their mate happy. Even the crows spruce up, get rid of old feathers, and have shiny plumage.

The black bear is one of the leaders of the mountain animals and controls much of the medicine found in its homeland. Viewed as having human qualities but also a rough, combative disposition, it plays a significant role as protector in ceremonial performance and traditional lore. (Photo by Kay Shumway)

Another old story tells how animals have a human form within, which is uncovered when they remove their outer skin. One time there was a terrible drought in the land; water had become so scarce that green plants were dying, birds stopped flying, and chaos was everywhere. The dry spell lasted a long time; people, through songs and prayers, encouraged it to rain but without success. As the animals talked among themselves, some said the rain had been stolen. They performed ceremonies, but received no results. Finally, they agreed to have a large gathering in a sweat lodge. They arrived at the appointed time and removed their clothes or outer form before entering and were surprised to see that the inner spirit structure of their bodies was human. The creatures went on to solve the problem with Frog, who as a water creature, played an important role. The point here is that while animals have their different shapes, underneath they are like humans who think, talk, and act. Bears are no exception. Since bears are so like humans in nature, we do not eat their meat.

Bears are often associated with fighting, bravery, and protection. In the Protectionway ceremony, the person having it performed is compared to a bear when the medicine people sing, "The black bear (Shashtso diłhił), the mighty black bear is who I am. I am his boy. I'm the big black bear, black arrowhead is my footprint" (Bee ashiiké nishłį eiyeenaa bee ashiiké nishłį eiyeenaa eleina shashtso diłhił k'ad lá shinishłį goo'ana bee ashiiké nishłį eiyeenaa eleina béésh diłhił náshikéé'go). You are singing about the bear and saying, "I am that bear, that black bear that's how I represent myself as a young man." A lot of other animals are compared to humans because of their qualities; for the bear, those qualities include boasting, fierce fighting, and power. That is why in the Bearway (Shashjí), sometimes referred to simply as Mountainway ceremony (Dziłk'ijí) the characteristics of anger, combativeness, loneliness, suicide, and seizures are corrected.

This ceremony is associated with the mountains, the place where bears live. The songs talk about how on top of the mountain there is a tall, straight pine tree behind which stands a black bear. He is talking to the holy ones, who read the patient's mind and look into his or her past. Through crystal gazing they also tell stories about what will happen in the future. The black bear carries holy medicine and stands before the patient every time there is danger. He is a protector, and so the patient will walk like him and be dressed as he is with holy feet, holy legs, holy body, and holy feathers (ats'os diyinii) on his head. This is how prayers are done for soldiers going into the military service, so that they will not be killed or wounded but will be protected by the powers of this sacred animal. The soldier can stand before his enemy and remain safe through the powers of the bear, then return home without harm.

Bears also understand humans and know when they are not wanted. If a person encounters one in the woods and wants it to leave, words from a Yé'ii Bicheii song—"Whoo-hu-hu. Tu-tu-tu-tu-tu"—cause it to depart immediately because he does not like that song. I did not believe this until the day I was working in the mountains of Kemmerer, Wyoming. I lived in a newly cleared spot with a handful of trailers and lots of bears as neighbors. Every evening the bears pulled trash out of garbage cans, and although we had been warned to be careful, they were becoming a real nuisance and refused to leave. One evening there were eight or nine of them throwing trash around with people trying to keep them away. The residents came to me complaining, "Mr. Robinson, in the Indian way, what do you do to a bear when it keeps coming around? What do you say? How do you chase them away?" I told them that my grandfather had always mentioned singing a Yé'ii Bicheii song and so I would try that. A few days later, there were about six bears in the trash cans. I stood in the doorway of my trailer and said, "Whoo-hu-hu. Tu-tu-tu-tu-tu." They ran about fifty feet, turned around, and stood up. One of them really watched me, and then left, never to return. Grandfather was right.

Places of Power

To best understand the connection of bears to the landscape and the Bearway ceremony, it is good to discuss the narrative "The Killer Bear" from which it comes. The story begins with some of the Bear People leaving Mount Hesperus (Dibé Nitsaa—Big Sheep), Colorado, and traveling through southeastern Utah, into New Mexico, and finally to Arizona. They began their journey by following Little Stream Canyon (Tónits'ósí Kooh), where the water talked to the Bear People saying there were places they needed to go and important things that were going to happen in the future. They traveled through Little Canyon to a dome-shaped rock that looks like a hogan [Church Rock] near the road [Highway 191] between today's Moab and Monticello. There they spent the night. The next day of travel took them to the north side of the Carrizo Mountains and Teec Nos Pos (T'iis Názbąs—Cottonwoods in a Circle), where they camped for a few days by a brook flowing from the mountain. This water also spoke to them in their dreams, urging them to continue their travels to the west to Ugly Canyon (Bikooh Hóchxǫ'ó), then on to Canyon with a Pointed House (Tsé Nit'ááh Hooghan). At each of these stops there were "houses" or places to stay, all the way past the Lukachukai (Lók'a'jígai—Reeds Extend White) Mountains to Tsaile (Tsééh Yílí—Where the Water Enters a Box Canyon) and Sonsola Buttes (Sǫ Sila—Stars Lying Down), which has a body of water nearby. This place is now called The Lake That Sits There but used to be known as The Water That Breathes and Moans. There were no streams feeding in or out of it.

Once the bear couple reached it, they dug a trench that drained the water to the south, into other rivers and eventually the ocean. From the sea came a water monster that looked like a water horse (tééh łįį') but also had the qualities of a cow with its wide nose, big nostrils, and little horns. This creature took up residence in the waters of the lake, where it gave birth to a little boy. One day the bear couple heard a baby crying on top of Sonsola Buttes nearby. The water monster had left the infant in a circular enclosure made of juniper trees, the kind used in the fire dance during the

Mountainway ceremony. This is the beginning of the Tóee or Waterway ceremony because of the boy coming from the tééh łį́į́', and the Mountainway ceremony with the discovery of the baby in the sacred center of the circle within the enclosure. Three different ceremonies— Mountainway, Waterway, and Bearway—have their roots in this one story.

The bears raised this baby until he turned twelve years old. By then he was a very accomplished hunter trained by his bear father, who knew how to track, stalk, and kill game, how to dress it, and the proper prayers necessary for success. The boy also learned prayers that helped protect him, which he used when later confronted by those seeking to harm him during four nights of terror. This geographical area around the Lukachukai and Chuska Mountains is important to the Navajo in the development of the bear-way of hunting, since this is where the young man learned those techniques.

The bears' adopted son was very prosperous for four years, bringing in an abundance of meat every day. The family traveled and hunted about, staying in homes that are now mountains and rock formations. One day, when they had returned to the lake, the male bear went to its shore to get water but never returned. The female bear waited and waited, wondering where her husband had gone. She finally decided to follow his tracks even though the Holy Wind warned against it; she started her search, but also failed to return. The water had captured and taken them deep into the lake.

The young man missed his parents; one night he had a dream that told him to cut the water off that flowed from the south side of the lake. He moved to that spot, where he met another male and female bear. He lived with them for a long time, but as the male bear grew older, his ability to hunt declined. The old bear tried everything he could to obtain food, failed, and grew increasingly desperate; starvation stared at him as he continued to search without success. Finally, the old couple became so desperately hungry that they decided to eat the young man who had been so kind to them. Holy Wind came to him and warned, "You better leave because the male bear is really hungry. He's getting angry about his hunting, so he is going to come and eat you. Since you are not one of the Bear People, he sees you as a possible source of food. He's getting angry, stressed, depressed, and is ready to kill you. You had better go to Mount Hesperus and remain in those mountains. It is the only safe place."

As the young man set out on his journey, he knew that he must go but always had thoughts of returning to the man and woman bears. The Holy Wind persisted, warning not to go back, for they would kill him. Meanwhile, the male bear was tracking his potential victim. That night, the young man camped on a high plateau. Holy Wind cautioned to put fire all the way around him in a circle, because bears avoid flames and will not go over them.

Bear appeared and requested, "Put the fire out. Let me come in, and we can go home. Let's talk about this." The man refused, kept the fire burning around him all night, and in the morning, again started his trip to the mountains in Colorado. The next three nights there were similar challenges but different solutions that prevented harm. For instance, the second night the man climbed on top of a rock with a small flat surface. The bear could not get up it, so he sat beneath and begged his intended victim to come down and go home with him, but he refused. The last night, the man crawled into a large crack in a rock, after putting fire outside of the entrance. Finally the bear gave up and returned home while the young man reached Mount Hesperus, where he became one of the sacred people who live there. The water that runs from behind the mountain (Colorado River) and goes all the way to Moab, then joins with Green River, is also sacred, as is the mountain.

Each of the four times that the bear tried to break down the defense of the man, new sacred prayers and songs given by Air, Night, and the Fire People grew out of the experience and are now part of the Waterway ceremony because this young man had come from the water. He also took actions that protected him, and these prayers are now part of the Bearway. The same is true of parts of the story connected to the mountains and so is part of the Mountainway. From the water to the mountain, the ceremonies came together. There are other elements of this story that are much more detailed and important for medicine people, but this brief summary shows how the land, animals, and ceremonies are tied together.

Teachings of the Bearway

The teachings from these ceremonies help people to get through some real life crises. The bear was physically trying to harm the young man; implied in the meaning of getting him to come home was also sexual abuse. The bear was suffering from anger, frustration, and other behavioral disorders that lead to the destruction of another person. Fortunately, the boy had been trained for twelve years by his adopted parents to understand the behavior of bears and how to avoid problems. When the boy saw the bear's teeth bared, ears up, and claws ready, he recognized what was next and avoided it. Navajos today warn that one should not hit a child with a hand, which is considered holy, because it will knock sense and goodness out of the person struck, and those qualities will not return. The same is true when living with one's wife or interacting with other people. That person will become bad, not listen, and develop his or her own way of bear thinking. If a person returns, persuaded by the abuser, they are told, "You already knew what was going to happen and you came back anyway. So part of it is your fault." That is another teaching.

At the same time that this bear represents evil, other bears are protectors. The bear parents who raised the boy taught him how to defend himself through sacred prayers developed at that time. Everything that the boy learned helped him to overcome the problems that lay ahead. The sacredness of the bear is captured in the Bearway songs whose prayers have become part of the Protectionway, developed as the young man learned to think like a bear. The prayer about protection includes, "wearing black flint shoes to protect my feet, black flint socks going out from my toes to my knees, clothing of black flint that goes from my knees to my shoulders." Then the prayer declares, "Black mirage [flint] is going to surround me (dinoolyínii hiináanii) for my protection, all the way up to my shoulder." Next there is a black flint hat that protects the head, and finally there are twelve black feathers that encircle the person, which nothing can penetrate. "In my hands are two rocks that are very holy. They will protect my hands. Everything that I hold will be against my enemy. Black lightning will go around me twice, lightning and thunder will encircle me four times, and they will protect me for who I am. My enemy will fall before me. Whatever the enemy tries to do against me will not work, and I will defeat him." This is how the prayer goes as a patient dresses himself with the entire image.

Black, blue, yellow, and white flints were part of the young man's protection, each one used on a different night in a different prayer as the bear tried to attack him. The normal color sequence is reversed, starting with black, because the young man represents black flint with scalloped edges, sharp for cutting. This is a prayer taught by his bear father, who was male, and so this prayer is said first. The second prayer comes from the bear mother, who gave him a blue flint and prayer; the third is from the father, protecting the boy with jagged yellow flint; and the fourth is from the mother or female side, represented by white shell in the form of a feather. That is how the prayer was set during those four nights.

Sometimes a grandmother or grandfather may act distantly to their grandchildren. They can choose not to love them. The grandparents may not get along with the grandchildren's mother and father or not like the in-laws. Some of this happened to me in my own life. My grandmother was called The Very Thin Lady (Asdzą́ą́ Áłts'óózí) and she had different fathers, uncles, and aunts. When my mother was conceived, she had a father who belonged to the Salt Clan (Áshįįhí), which meant my paternal grandfather also belonged to them. But my grandmother soon divorced my grandfather during the first few months of pregnancy and married another man named Rock Gap People (clan name—Tsédeeshgiizhnii), who was more prosperous. My grandmother told my mother, "Your real biological father is that person, but I met this other man and he has been with us since you were born. He has become your second father." My mother did not like her biological mother, and so she tried to establish connections with her first father, but he would not acknowledge the relationship. The Salt People had abandoned her. If you look at my biological grandfather from the Salt People, his facial structure is exactly the same as my mother's because they have square jaws, while my other grandfather has different features. He does not look anything like my mother, but he is the one who married her biological mother, and so my mother gives him credit as her father.

My mother never liked her biological mother and felt like she had been pushed away and never taken in with that side of her family. She had not come into this world with love, and she was not finding it in her life at this point. This is how she thought about her mother. One time my grandmother had my mother in a cradleboard on the side of a horse pack as she traveled over a mountain (by this time my mother was about three or four months old), when the cradleboard fell off the pack and was left behind. My grandmother never looked back or seemed to care. Once she had reached the other side of the mountain where her sister's home was located, she started to be questioned, "You just gave birth to a child. Where is she?" My grandmother replied, "Oh, I had it sitting on the side of the saddle, but I lost her somewhere over the mountain." Her sister: "And you're sitting there eating?" My grandmother: "Oh, well. She has probably been eaten by the coyotes by now, so I'll have another child." There was no remorse. My other grandmother got really mad at her sister, yelling, "What is wrong with you?" She took a torch made of juniper bark with piñon sap placed on top and went back over the mountain trail until she found my mother resting in her cradleboard against a small tree. She took her home and never, ever returned her to her sister, telling her, "I'm taking this child. You lost it. I found it. Now she's mine."

This other grandmother had a lot of love, but she could not have any children. She raised my mother as her only child and gave her everything— land and livestock—when she died. My mother loved her and hated her real mother for what she had done to her. My caring grandmother even raised us as children. She was the best grandmother that we ever could have had, but my biological grandmother did not like us because of the way my mother felt about her. As her grandchildren, she always pushed us away saying, "Get out of my house. Go away. You're not my grandchildren." She ended up having an unhappy life and family, and it was all based in her attitude.

My life experience ties in directly to what is being taught in the Bearway ceremony. It is a teaching that explains what happened in my family and shows how these narratives help people to understand life. The adopted grandchild lived with one pair of grandparents in a family of love, while the other grandparents were disconnected and ready to destroy him. Each part of the story has different teachings about people's attitudes and behavior. As I look back, the actions of my two grandmothers with my mother fit exactly into this story of the bears' families and the end results each obtained. Now I understand why one grandmother hated her situation, but it was her own doing. No one told her to have a baby and then leave the father to go live with another man. That was her doing, and in the end, it defeated her. She watched her sister raise a good child, and through that side of the family, all became medicine people.

The children my biological grandmother raised all turned to alcohol, drugs, gambling, infidelity, and broken homes. Many served time in jail and died young, and none of them were happy. They were never taught the good way. This is because they took on their mother's attitude. Her sister, however, coming from the same home and teachings, had just the opposite experience. She worked hard to develop the land, taught us all about traditional medicine—much of what I learned came from this grandmother's side—and all of my mother's children are doing well and are happy. You can still see this big family, when you go to my home down in White Valley, with all of the nice houses and beautiful gardens where there are lots of horses, cows, and sheep. This is all because of one grandmother. If you look on the other side of the family, you'll just see poverty. They have run-down houses, nobody really works, and they ask why they are not like us. It is a different story.

Remembering the Land

The Bearway ceremony is tied to the locations where events occurred. When a person wants to make an offering at one of these sacred sites, a medicine person travels to that spot and calls upon the power and sacredness there. For instance, one might go to Teec Nos Pos, to the camping site by the stream that runs off of the mountain. An offering is placed near the rock formation that served as the first two bears' home when they journeyed south. An offering ceremony can also be held at the pointed "house" that sits on a ridge of the Lukachukai Mountains. If a person really wants to go to the heart of the Bearway ceremony, then they visit Tsaile. That is where the main events of the story occurred. It is good to mark and be specific about where these activities took place. They become special sites where an individual visiting that location for power leaves an offering. Just as when the two staffs meet during the Enemyway ceremony as one travels from the east to the west and the other from the south to the north, there is a crossover

This 1904 Edward S. Curtis photo of Navajo men visiting a shrine of rocks captures the importance of remembering events that take place upon the land. Where something happened holds power—to be either used for good or avoided due to evil. The rock placed by an individual to honor a site commemorates its significance and the spiritual essence present. (Courtesy Library of Congress—Photo 8921)

that happens at these places. A change is made in a person's life, and so the patient leaves a rock that accumulates into a pile as others visit the same site.

This point is critical in the story and subsequent healing and so is referred to as the center of the medicine where a change or crossover occurred. The rock ensures that from that day on, this spot will be recognized as holy. The person who is sick or has problems places it there, showing that he has left the issue behind and departs healed. For instance, the spot where the two bears sat and meditated is such a site. People recognize this as the location where the bears went, scratched around on the ground, thought about their problems, and planned what should be done. Somebody learned where this happened and so left a rock there. He told others, making this an important place for this Protectionway ceremony where rocks have accumulated over the years. People often ask, "Where is the place the bears sat? Where is the rock pile?" After receiving directions, the person responds, "Okay, I'll say my prayer ceremony with the bear right there, as part of my Protectionway. I'm going to this site and will place a rock for my protection." This is a good thing, and so people return to this spot as long as they have a purpose because the holy ones are where there is sacredness. At Blue Gap during an Enemyway ceremony, the staffs crossed over at a place named "The Gathering of the Rocks." The site is a small hill that sits on the south side of the gap and is called Tsé Ninájih—"Where You Place Rocks." If one has a problem, they can pick up a rock and travel there to say prayers and let their issue go before continuing on their way. There are sacred circles like that all over the Navajo Reservation, where people have left behind their problems. This is where their prayers sit. The person walks away with a light, light load.

There are other teachings concerning the land and its animals that come from this story. The bears traveling from Hesperus were brown bears or grizzlies and are bigger than the black bears found around Tsaile and in the Chuska Mountains. They went into the water and never returned, and that is why this type of animal is not found on the reservation today. Black bears from the south are smaller animals contrasting with those in the north. Each has different features and ways of doing things, but still belong to the bear family. Part of this story tells about the brown bears first meeting the black bears in the Lukachukais at Pointed Mountain House. The male brown bear had a dream in which he heard another bear hollering for help. From this the bears made a song that said, "That's one of our relatives. And this is what they're singing about. They need help."

The male bear left that night, went into the middle of the mountains, and approached a pond from the north where a black bear sat waiting to the south. The brown bear said, "We come from Mount Hesperus in the north and are being guided to sacred areas by the Holy Wind." The black bear sitting opposite the brown bear across the pond introduced himself, then responded that all of the different places in this area were sacred. Then these two medicine bears began to teach each other about the deer and how the ones from the north had a white feather for a tail, but those from the south had a black feather tail. Deer, like everything from the north, were bigger, although their rack of antlers was smaller than those found in the south. Then the bears compared the bones, meat, and medicine the deer leave behind for others to use. When these animals eat, they spit medicine back out. People say if a deer chews on plants, then spits them out, a medicine person should pick up that matter, dry it, grind it, then add it to the mountain tobacco used in a smoke ceremony. Good ways of thinking and good thoughts will come to those who use this mixture. This is part of the medicine the two bears developed that night. A lot of what they discussed became part of the teachings for the Deerway ceremony. The bears also compared plants and animals found in their respective environments, even down to the level of porcupines, squirrels, mice, and grass, all of which was part of a bear's diet.

That is how they exchanged ideas. The brown bear, as a visitor, brought the emotional and spiritual side of the teachings. This animal from the north lived outside of the boundaries of the sacred mountains, and like the gods, visited to bring new ways of thinking and doing. The black bear, as the mountain host, lived in the south, represented the more physical side of life, and was open to new thoughts. The same is true of the Navajo people who have had many new ideas and goods introduced on the reservation. The two bears also spoke of bears farther to the north and how they are associated with white, such as polar bears. These animals are considered holy ones and more sacred than the black and brown bears to their south. My grandfather taught about these animals, although he did not see the white bear or buffalo or deer or wolf, yet he knew they existed and could be approached through prayer. He talked about them in a spiritual way. I wonder sometimes what my paternal great-grandfather would have thought if he had seen a picture of a polar bear and all of these other things he thought about.

There are other teachings and practices that come from the story of "Killer Bear." One is when the young man started to realize the male bear wanted to eat him and his eyes began to twitch. This is part of a belief that teaches one's body can sense a problem and tries to warn the individual to be careful. When the young man said that he planned to go to Hesperus, the female bear encouraged him not to go. His throat began to make noises. Later, his intestines did the same thing. These were warnings of danger (hayi'dahadlo'); a person's body is very intelligent and can sense approaching trouble. It will make a sound that warns "No. Don't do it." People need to listen to their own bodies. A parallel teaching tells of when a man's wife died and her family gathered on the fourth night after her death saying, "Okay, we're going to sit here for one hour and listen to the hogan. We're going to sit here and listen. If the hogan makes a song, then we're going to have to give this man a new wife. If not, then he can pack his stuff and go home to his people." Sound can be an important messenger.

Performing the Ceremony

As mentioned previously, the Bearway ceremony is similar to and part of the Mountainway ceremony, both of which are part of the Protectionway. When a Mountainway ceremony is held, the circular corral made of cedar branches is where the Bearway ceremony will be performed, the reason for which will be discussed later. The Mountainway ceremony lasts nine nights, but the more public activities last for five. The Bearway is a one-night performance held on the third of five nights. Part of the reason for the blending of these ceremonies is because of the mountain animals that are

There are many mountain ranges and high-altitude mesas associated with bears. The Bears Ears in southeastern Utah has two stories, one of which is pictured here. When viewed from the south, these two buttes are said to have been the head and ears removed from Changing Bear Maiden after she killed many of her brothers. The events are part of the Evilway narrative. (Drawing by Charles Yanito)

found in both. Take for instance raccoons, coyotes, foxes, and other animals with black markings. They are referred to collectively as Black Bear's Children and are considered medicine people. All are connected to water, and most are identified by having black feet and black markings on their back, representing the prayers that they carry with them. In Navajo this is called atahwiishjin—black stripes or blackening of the body—which is something performed during a ceremony. These animals often act humanlike by standing on their hind legs, holding activities in groups, and being directed by Bear, their leader. This story tells of when Bear's children started to become involved in medicine.

There are four different phases of the Bearway ceremony, the first one beginning with the black flint prayer. This was previously mentioned as part of the blessing of the feet, knees, hips, shoulders, elbows, neck, head, then hand, in that order, for protection. All of these body parts are related to the bear, black flint, and how a person stands behind them for safety. The ceremony sits on the outside of the Evilway, which uses ashes and grease for blackening; here, there is an application of red ochre mixed with grease (yishchííh). Plants from the mountains are used to make the corral and also to decorate a person who impersonates a bear during the second phase. The man, dressed in spruce boughs, is called The Clothes Are Going to Be Made out of Spruce (ch'óyáázh diłhił; ch'ó'éé'). Underneath the vegetation, his body is painted with chííh, representing the inside of the bear, while the spruce represents the outside. Unlike earlier Ute performances, this person would not wear a real bearskin, just four sets of spruce branches tied to the foot, leg, back, and arms, with a fifth on the head like a crown that points to the four directions. An eagle feather is placed in the center of this halo.

There are four different types of spruce—blue spruce is very stiff so that when grabbed, it pokes the skin; there are also white and yellow forms of spruce that hurt and irritate, but the black spruce is soft and the one used for clothing. This tree is also used because it is taller and is set into the ground deeper as it stands on the earth and reaches to the heavens. That is why it is called "The One That Reaches High" (Yá Yiyah Niizíní). Just as the bears have four different colors tied in with the four different directions, so too, do spruces have four different types of bodies. In the east the bear stands with the black spruce tree. Ordinarily in the Navajo color scheme, the east would be white, but this time the prayers that go with it start with black, then blue, yellow, and white, which always serves as the final color. Remember that the White Bear and White Spruce live in the north, and that is the reason they were the last to be called into the ceremony and why the Black Bear was first. These two were the ones that started these rituals and ceremonies and so were switched according to color.

During the ceremony, people chase the "bear" into the arena and sing the songs of the Bearway. The man dressed as a bear walks around the arena, blessing the people by sprinkling acorn pollen and praying for them. Next, he places Mountainway herbs in a basket with water, blesses the medicine, then offers a drink to those seeking to be healed and helped. People line up and make their offering or payment, after which the bear leaves the corral. Next is the healing of a patient through a sandpainting drawn on an unwounded deer's hide. The image is of a corn stalk with six arms and three tassels on the top where corn pollen is found. The tassels are made with yellow corn, the body from white corn, but where the stalks are connected to the ears, ground blue corn is used. On the south side of the buckskin are drawn four footprints extending from the tips of the "arms" of the hide. The person having the ceremony performed has to walk around, putting his foot on those prints before he can sit down on the buckskin. The medicine man then gives him a medicine bundle in a basket, which he holds as he repeats the prayers of the ceremony. The fourth and final part of the ritual is the traditional smoke ceremony.

The Utes have their Bear Dance that is usually held during the spring, but it is very different from the Bearway of the Navajo. Still, the sacredness of the bear to both peoples is similar. I believe it was back in 1988 when I attended a Bear Dance ceremony in which both Navajos and Utes were present. There was an old man named Eldon Neskahi with his family. He and his wife were really holy people who had the dance performed at their home on the outskirts of Cortez, Colorado. At one point, a person brought a tame bear, tethered by a collar and chain around its neck, into the brush enclosure. This really had its effect on the people as the bear walked around the circle and sniffed the participants. After the medicine man led the animal out of the dance area, two people—a man and a woman sitting on opposite sides of the circle—fell out of their chairs with heart attacks. The ambulance arrived and tried to help them, but both eventually died. My understanding is that the sniffing of the bear had something to do with taking their lives.

The teachings from the Bearway show how powerful a bear is. In a fight, when a person growls like a bear and calls upon its powers, he receives additional strength and becomes more deadly. His anger is kindled, he begins to tremble with power, and he focuses on defeating the enemy. Confusion and intimidation of the opponent are also factors. This is why Bearway cures for sickness have a lot to do with hostility, anger, hurting people, disrupting family relations, and losing focus on more positive things. My father taught that in the old days, when a Navajo harmed or killed another Navajo, there were two ways that it could be handled. Western society would send the murderer to prison or execute him. Navajos had a different way to look at the situation. They would say there is still one of the two lives here on earth—nothing can be done for the dead man, but the person still living should receive the help necessary to make him better. Remember that a ceremony is holistic. There is its body, which is internal, and skin that is external. Just as human tissue is fed by the blood stream and controlled by a nervous system, there are parts of the ceremony that serve similar functions when healing. The medicine man sings for the healing moment of all of this through a complete ceremony. Other things may be added for depression or distress. A patient may need a Bearway ceremony to remove anger and frustration before reentering society. Give him a chance to live and redeem himself. My father taught, "A human being is a human being, no matter how you look at it, but you have to heal the ones that are sick." That is what he talked about, using the Bearway as part of the cure.

Two or three years ago, the Navajo Nation devised a program that helped people leaving prison rejoin the general population. The question arose, how do we prepare them? The tribe asked the medicine people for an answer—some type of treatment plan. The answer was rooted in traditional teachings. Depending on the crime and the needs of the individual, there were ceremonies available to remedy the situation—Foot Printingway, Protectionway, Bearway, and others that needed to be held to get the person back into the family circle. This has now become policy and is available as part of the "Reentry Program." While Bearway is still performed and considered part of the solution, those medicine men are shortening it by doing perhaps a two- or three-hour ceremony as part of the Protectionway. One reason for the abbreviated form is that a lot of the younger medicine people do not know much about it, whereas I do the five nights of the Mountainway ceremony, as well as the shortened version of Bearway.

CHAPTER NINE

Sickness, Death, and Evil

In previous chapters, various ceremonies and healing rites have been discussed without establishing clear relationships between them or classifying them in more general terms. Before moving on to the contents of this chapter, it is time to provide an inclusive framework that will not only help in placing them in clear categories based on function but will also identify some of their subcategories mentioned in this study. According to Leland Wyman, there are six main groups, each of which has subdivisions or branches that are attached to the main stalk.[1] Central to all is the Blessingway (Hózhǫ́ǫ́jí) ceremony with four variations based on relatively slight differences. It is considered the oldest and most important of all of the rituals as has been previously discussed. Polar opposite of this is the Evilway (Hóchxǫ́'íjí), which has ten ceremonies, including a male and female version of the Evilway Shooting Branch, and a single version of the Enemyway (Anaa'jí). These rituals deal primarily with war, death, destruction, and other elements considered "ugly." Holyway chants are employed when an individual has done something wrong that offends a particular creature (bear, eagle, snake, coyote, etc.) or element (wind, lightning, ghosts, and so forth), causing sickness to occur.[2] There are seven subgroups, each of which has its own subdivisions, too numerous to entirely name here. A few of the ones Perry discusses include the Shooting Chant (Na'at'oyee—not to be confused with those in Evilway), Waterway (Tóee), and Big Starway (Sǫ'tsohjí); Mountain Chants including Mountainway (Dziłk'ijí) and Excessway (Ajiłee); God Impersonators (Yé'ii Hólóní) including Nightway (Tł'éé'jí), Coyoteway (Ma'iijí), and Big Godway (Haashch'éétsohee); Wind Chants (Niłch'ijí) including Navajo Windway

(Diné Biniłch'ijí) and Chiricahua Windway (Chíshí Biniłch'ijí); Hand Trembling Chant (N'dilniihjí); and Eagle Trapping with two ceremonies. There are a total of twenty-four subdivisions within the Holyway Chant system. The Lifeway group has six subdivisions including male and female versions of both the Shootingway and Flintway, all of which are used to heal injury following a traumatic accident. They have the ability to maintain life and restore the patient back to normal. The last two groupings of War Ceremonials and Gameways are now obsolete and will not be discussed here.[3]

Preceding chapters have centered on mostly positive aspects of daily life and how to help those who struggle. Many of the teachings come from the Blessingway. Now we turn to those traditions, which also solve life issues, but which come from the Evilway and the destruction of negative forces. While each sacred narrative has its own story and hero, two of the major protagonists connected to many of them are the Twins—Monster Slayer (Naayéé'neizghání) and Born for Water (Tóbájíshchíní). While their mother, Changing Woman, is the epitome of kindness and loving care, these two men exemplify the courage and ability of warriors who are constantly on the move destroying evil. Just as the qualities of motherhood and womanhood are embodied in Changing Woman as made visible in the kinaaldá ceremony (volume 3, chapter 2) so too are those of manhood and male protector/fighter in the coming-of-age ceremony for young men (volume 3, chapter 3). The origin of this well-known behavior derives from the Twins' journey to their father and the destruction of the monsters inhabiting the earth upon their return. Since Perry does not go over this iconic story but often refers to its events, a brief synopsis is provided here.[4]

As Big God (Yé'iitsoh) and Gray God (Yé'ii Łibáí) roamed about terrorizing the earth surface people, the Twins set out to meet their father, Sun Bearer, and obtain his powerful weapons to kill the monsters. Their journey was fraught with danger that could only be overcome with supernatural aid received from Spider Woman, Horned Toad, Caterpillar, and others met along the way. Their assistance allowed the Twins to defeat or bypass the different creatures and pitfalls encountered on the Holy Trail to Sun Bearer's home. Not even The Rock That Crushes, Slashing Reeds, Giant Cacti, and Boiling Sands could stop them. Once they reached their destination, there was a different set of challenges, as their father tested them to ensure that they were truly his sons and worthy of his aid. Once their identity was established, the young men received from their father four different types of arrows—two types of lightning, a sunbeam, and rainbow—along with bows to destroy their enemies. Upon returning to the earth by supernatural means, they set about to kill the monsters. First there were Big God and Gray God followed by a host of others including Horned

Monster (Déélgééd), Rock Monster (Tsé nináhádleehké), Kills-with-His-Eyes Monster (Bináá'yee Agháni), Tracking Bear Monster (Shash Na'ałkaahii), and Kicking Monster (Tsédahódziiltaałii). Only four (Old Age, Hunger, Poverty, and Laziness) were left and about to be dispatched before they convinced the Twins to spare their lives. Perry begins his teachings below at this point.

The remainder of this chapter is concerned with understanding the nature of evil, explaining why and how it exists, and using prayer and ceremony to defeat it.[5] Unlike Western Christian thought, the Navajo do not draw a sharp line between the polarities based on a God of good who opposes Satan, the embodiment of evil. Indeed, power to the Navajo is more of a state of being utilized for either good or bad, depending on the intent of the user. Just as electricity warms homes, cooks food, and provides transportation, it can also destroy or maim with apparent ease; likewise, supernatural power exists to both bless and curse those who come in contact with it. Respect, balance, and orderliness become the means by which positive forces are controlled, while evil and witchcraft ('iiníziin) have their rituals based on excess, lack of reverence, and chaos. The power is there; what one does with it determines the outcome. Harry Walters, a Navajo teacher and practitioner of traditional religion, explained it this way:

> In the Navajo world everything is organized in terms of female and male, known as Hózhǫ́ǫ́jí (Blessingway) and Naayéé'jí (Protection Way). The two forces do not oppose but complement each other in the same manner that all female and male species interact in nature. Evil is not a separate quality but is viewed as an integral part of Naayéé'jí. When used appropriately, it serves as protection but where it is abused, it becomes witchcraft (evil). Self-protection is a necessity in nature, so all things have an element of evil. Therefore, one must always go about life with great caution and respect.[6]

Clyde Kluckhohn, in his classic study entitled *Navaho Witchcraft*, identifies four types of evil power—witchery, sorcery, wizardry, and frenzy witchcraft.[7] Witchery depends on "corpse poison" or decayed flesh, bones, or sexual fluids ground into powder and used to curse a person. This material serves the reverse function of corn pollen, which blesses with life and happiness. Diagnosis of the illness through hand trembling, crystal gazing, or other means determines which prayers and ceremonies will protect or heal the sick person. Sorcery creates illness and harm by taking hair, nail clippings, clothing, or some other object that has been in close contact with the intended victim. The item is prayed over so that hardship enters that person's life. Wizardry occurs when an individual magically shoots a stone, bone, or other foreign matter into a victim; the cure is achieved by sucking out the object. Frenzy witchcraft utilizes two forms of delivery: plants, such as datura, or prayers and chants that cause a person to lose self-control and become degraded. Excessive sexual activity or gambling results; the Excessway (also known as the Deerway or less acceptably as the Prostitutionway) usually provides the cure, although there are other ceremonies that may also serve the purpose. While many Navajo people may not think in clinical terms about these four different ways of harming a person, their existence is recognized but not often discussed.

The power—álílee k'ehgo—behind how these forms of witchcraft are delivered, has already been discussed. Applying it to say, wizardry, illustrates how the same principle in healing through song and prayer can also be used to harm someone with the same power. "Shooting" a person with an object fashioned from stone, bone, or wood depends on this supernatural force to penetrate the body with the projectile called an arrow (bik'aa). The individual shooting the object puts corpse powder ('áńt'įįh) on the "arrow" and through chants and prayers, sends the missile into the person. Songs are particularly important. "Skinwalkers chant all the time; the songs cannot stop or their power ceases. Somebody has got to be singing while they are using their supernatural power."[8] Once the object is inserted, the victim remains sick until it is removed or he dies. Jim Dandy, who apprenticed to become a medicine man, explained that this practice was developed by Navajos a long time ago to defeat their enemies from other tribes and later the white man, but now, Navajos have turned it around to use against their own people.[9]

An example of how this all works is given by Tall Singer from Shiprock as recorded by trader Will Evans in the early 1900s. Tall Singer had been chanting over Good Singer's Grandson for some time with no effect. His patient was losing weight, could not eat, and was suffering with intense pain on the right side of the back of his neck. Tall Singer sliced into the swollen area with the sharpest arrowhead he carried in his medicine pouch and began to suck on the large slash. At first there was only blood, but eventually, the medicine man retrieved a piece of charcoal with human hair wrapped around it. "The object was about the size and length of half of the first joint of your little finger. Some witch had secured a piece of charcoal . . . from the remains of a hogan which had been burned because someone had died in it. . . . Then this witch had gone to the resting place of a dead person and plucked hair from the decaying head."[10] Once Tall Singer removed the object, the patient rapidly improved.

After detection comes protection. One of the fundamental assumptions in defeating witchcraft is the ability to turn the bad power to good use. For example, a Blessingway prayer, when said backward, can be used to afflict, but when said in the proper sequence, it can protect by turning the evil. The power associated with Ajiłee (excess) prayers to cure frenzy witchcraft is so strong that they cannot be used in either the wife's or children's home if they are present. When they hear these prayers, "they may go crazy and simply run away."[11] Thus, that which afflicts can cure and vice versa. The holy people developed all of these cures, just as they did the evils in the underworlds. At least thirty-two forms of sickness and death grew from this knowledge with as many remedies. Among the various forms of relief are found white shell, turquoise, abalone shell, jet, iron ore, harebell pollen, "ordinary (corn) pollen," and other types of plants and roots. The holy people inhale these offerings, accept them as gifts, and help effect a healing.[12]

From a theoretical standpoint, the power that drives good and bad are similar and inseparable, although the ends of this continuum result in a duality. The single most important element that gives definition to either end is the quality of order or lack of it. Thus evil is chaos; goodness is a controlled and well-kept existence. When events or natural elements arise in unexpected ways or at undesirable times, it is because of evil. Even excessive good or flamboyant emotions offer the possibility of being out of control. Ritual provides the means by which things out of bounds can be brought back to safety and order.[13]

While anyone can be accused of practicing witchcraft, there are definite patterns or types of people most frequently identified. Kluckhohn provides a quantifiable basis derived from 222 cases of people blamed for practicing the dark art. Of this number 184 were adult men, 131 of whom were classified as "old" as were all (38) of the women. One hundred forty of the men and twelve of the women were ceremonial practitioners, while twenty-one of the men were "headmen" or "chiefs"—a number that Kluckhohn felt as "an exceedingly high figure," given the proportion of leaders found throughout the general population. One hundred fifteen men and women of the total group were considered "rich." All older people wearing medicine pouches at gatherings were feared, and many of the Navajo people surveyed felt that the tendency to practice witchcraft ran steadily through family lines.[14]

Not all difficult events or bad things are necessarily created through evil. Perry discusses the problems associated with death—from the experience at Fort Sumner during the 1860s to lost lives on today's highways. In volume 3, chapter 8, there is a discussion about normal death as part of the human experience, while here, the more traumatic and difficult types are examined. The literature about Navajos is filled with examples of avoiding the deceased, of asking white men to bury a body, or of medicine men performing a ceremony to prevent ill effects. Yet Navajos consistently refer to the handling and burial of the dead as "very sacred." In the past, women and children could not go near the body; the men who buried the deceased had to return by a circuitous route, jump over cactus and bushes with sharp points so that the spirit would not follow, and remain in a separate hogan for four days; the relatives sat at home for a similar period of time but could not lie down until dark; they also could not talk loudly.[15] From the outset, ritual allowed "sacredness to take over. The person was placed anywhere, but there was sacredness with it."[16] As long as people handled the burial according to prescribed formula, there was no danger. Today, however, participants sometimes come to the funeral in truckloads, are inebriated, leisurely lie around with the opposite sex, and do not remain isolated for four days. The result is that death is on the rise, people suffer from physical ailments, and transgressors are plagued by ghostlike spirits.[17] Loss of control has led to chaos.

Jim Dandy, raised near Red Lake, Arizona, was being trained by his grandfather to become a medicine man. Then the instruction stopped. His grandfather urged him to get a white man's education rather than pursuing his present course. He reasoned that many of the traditional practices were fading and that soon there would not be a need for people with these specialized skills. But even more important, he did not want his grandson to have to dabble on the side of evil in order to understand what was necessary to defeat it. Jim remembers him saying, "You have to have some experience with evil before becoming a medicine man if you are really going to be able to help someone. You're going to have to do some evil things. I can't do that to you, Grandson. A real medicine man has to deal with some evil things because that is what you are going to be working against. Without this kind of knowledge you cannot work well."[18]

Monster Slayer and Born for Water: Controlling Evil

Every person has inside of them a spirit, or what Navajos call The One That Stands Within (ii'sizíinii or bii'gistíín). Good and bad affects this spiritual essence every day, with ceremonies directing an individual toward health, safety, and happiness. There are forces and experiences in this world derived from conflict, destruction, and evil that challenge that which is good; the teachings tell how to confront these problems and practice positive behavior to achieve hózhǫ́ or peace. Many of the stories and traditional teachings are about these two opposite sides of existence, why they came about, and how a person should deal with the negative to maintain the positive. The Enemyway (Ana'í Ndáá' or Anaa'jí) ceremony gives a particularly clear picture about overcoming adversity and returning to the path of a balanced life.

The story begins with the Navajo Twins—Monster Slayer (Naayéé'neizghání) and Born for Water (Tóbájíshchíní)—setting out to clear the earth of monsters killing and eating the Navajo people. After receiving from their father, Sun Bearer (Jóhonaa'éí), the necessary weapons, they traveled about to find and destroy the evil beings. One of the first to die from their lightning arrows and powerful clubs was Big God (Yé'iitsoh). To prove to their father that the Twins were really his sons, they cut off Big God's head and left it hanging on the north side of a young juniper tree. When they returned home, their mother asked where they had been, but when they told her that they had visited their father and then killed Big God, she did not believe them. The Twins laughed and responded, "Go look for yourself. He's over there. His head is still bleeding." Changing Woman still did not accept what they said until she located the skull in a tree covered with dripping blood. Later, this symbolically became the first staff now used in Enemyway ceremonies. Big God had yellowish hair and so on the staff, yellow rabbit brush is used, while two ribbons, one long and the other short, represent the blood running off of the head. Two feathers are tied to the staff denoting the protective life feathers of Monster Slayer and Born for Water, on the front of the staff is carved a sacred bow, and on the back side is the image of the traditional hair bun worn by the Twins and Navajo men today. That is how the markings on the staff are set and how the Enemyway started.

The Twins traveled throughout the land killing other monsters until they thought their job was finished. They were mistaken. Four evil creatures remained—one was located near the site of Navajo Dam in New Mexico, another at Navajo Mountain, one at the crossing in Salt Canyon, and another along the Gila River. These enemies continued to harm and kill people, and so needed to be exterminated before the Twins could say they had completed their task. They set out for the first one, The Old Age People, living in the east on the San Juan River near what is now Farmington, New Mexico. When they arrived at their home, they found an old man and woman sitting outside, waiting. Monster Slayer asked if the elderly couple killed people, then said, "Before I slay you, tell me why I should allow you to live." The old ones motioned to them to sit down and listen to the story about the growth and development of humans, who are born and mature into puberty, become adults, then decline in old age. A man and woman will have children and then grandchildren along the way, but eventually become fragile and die. Their eyes will fail, hearing will go, as everything in their life slowly grinds to a halt. "That is how we kill people, but through them there are also

Big God, son of Sun Bearer, was the first of the evil beings killed by Monster Slayer and Born for Water. Using lightning arrows, clubs, and knives obtained from their father, and protected by the life feathers they received from Spider Woman, the Twins were able to remove the evil creatures bothering the People. (Courtesy San Juan School District Media Center)

a lot of their relatives, which they created, left behind. When their first child is born, there was only a man and a woman. Soon that first baby is joined by brothers and sisters, then there will be aunts and uncles and a growing network of relationships. That is how you establish your ground. By the time one becomes an old man, there will be many grandchildren and great-grandchildren, maybe in one, two, or three generations, but four will be the end of that story. By then, a person should be ready to die. Before going, however, there will be good talk about your relations, and people will point at you and say, 'That is my grandfather over there. That is my god. I walk with that god today,' because a lot of good things have been accomplished." The Twins thought about this and felt it was a good thing. Even though Old Age killed people, Monster Slayer allowed them to exist. This part of the story also explains why the San Juan River, where this event took place, is called Old Age River (Sá Bitooh) and is a place where Water Monster/Creature (Tééhoołtsódii) still lives.

Next the Twins traveled to Rainbow Bridge near Navajo Mountain, where another water monster lived with the Hunger People. Monster Slayer and Born for Water inquired of these emaciated beings if they killed humans, to which they replied, "Yes. They die of starvation, but if you allow us to live, people learn to fend for themselves. They will change their food, have better diets with more variety, and prepare what is eaten in different ways. You can live that way if you are not lazy." This made sense to the Twins, who allowed the Hunger People to exist. The Navajo Mountain area today is associated with rainbows and the rainbow road, and is a place of plenty.

Where the Colorado and Little Colorado Rivers meet is called The Crossing of Two Rivers, and that was where the Poverty People lived; they dressed in rags and had only the bare necessities. These beings begged the Twins, "If you allow us to live, people will change their clothes, dress in new deer hides, and look better. They will learn to take care of themselves." My grandfather said that this place was special because there was so much medicine located in the water where the Colorado River (male) and the Little Colorado (female) join together with the female lying on the bottom. People having relationship problems go there and have a lot of prayers said for them to keep them together. There is also a rock beneath the river that, when a person stands on top of it, shows the markings of the staff carried in the Enemyway ceremony. The bow and hair bun sit on the outside of the rock and are visible. If a person ever forgets how these markings should look, they can find the pattern there. It is a very holy place for that reason alone, so the medicine people do not want it changed by future development. As with the other two places already mentioned, a water monster lives there.

The Twins again moved on, this time to the Gila River, where they encountered Laziness/Sleepiness that kills people when they do not have it. Sleep is good because it refreshes people who need time to rest and gives an opportunity to receive dreams. If people cannot recuperate, the functions of their body close down and they die. The Twins also allowed these people to exist. Having traveled in the four directions, they learned that all of these monsters were part of daily life and had a purpose. People are to live through these things to make life better. This last place visited is known for the different Indian groups like the Pima and Papago as well as its saguaro cactus that they use to help them dream and have visions. They are mentioned in the songs and prayers about sleeping and dreaming. There is holiness in that area, especially in the summer. It is said that when temperatures get really hot, there is a mist, and if a person walks through it, there is a coolness that comes upon the individual, who now feels rested and their eyes soothed. This is all part of the dream area and the songs that talk about sleep, meditation, and spirituality. Otherwise, I do not know much

Old Age, like other qualities and forces in the Navajo universe, is personified, making it capable of being influenced. While each of the four "monsters" that the Twins allowed to exist—Old Age, Hunger, Poverty, and Laziness—present formidable issues in life, each also brings with it appreciation for things that are good. (Drawing by Kelly Pugh)

about this region—only enough to understand where the songs are, why they are tied to specific places on the land, and how they heal.

These are teachings from the Enemyway and are discussed to help individuals through life's trials. A person in need may wish to have more goods and move out of poverty or become less lazy. Often the enemy or thing holding us back and making us unhappy is found within—we are our own worst enemy and defeat ourselves. If someone else works hard and obtains more things, then we should not sit there and cry that life is unfair. We make our own success. If we let old age, hunger, poverty, and laziness control us—then they are the foes sitting there and winning. Thus there are two types of enemies that work against people. The first is like Big God and Gray God, who were physically killed by the Twins. There may be spirits attached to similar events in our lives where death and destruction in combat is concerned, but there is also the second type of problem that exists mentally that has to be defeated. The two may be connected and can destroy a person. I feel that one of today's greatest enemies is the one inside of us because we refuse to take responsibility for pushing ourselves. By blaming other people or circumstances, we become impoverished.

The other day I was performing the Enemyway to heal a man who had lost the use of his legs, long after the actual wounds had occurred. Suddenly he was wheelchair bound or dependent on crutches, requiring his son and others to carry out many of the functions he had been able to do for himself. The performance of the ceremony with its songs, prayers, and herbs were to help overcome this physical challenge by restoring mobility once again. Still, there was more to it than just the ceremony. There were actually two different parts of the same force working against the veteran. The ceremony took care of only one of them. The experience that had harmed this individual and left physical disabilities were the most obvious—the one that I could work against with my healing practices. But the invisible one—what the man was feeling and thinking internally—also needed to be defeated. This second form of poverty required both of us to work together to improve his health.

So I spoke openly, telling the veteran that as a healer, I was working as hard as I could but that the wounded warrior was depending too heavily on what was taking place outside of him and not working on the inside to effect a cure. "I don't see you pushing yourself; instead you expect your son to meet your needs. Try getting off that seat by yourself. You are strong inside; push yourself." The man nodded and told his son to back off. Gathering his strength, he slowly pushed himself from the wheelchair and stood there tottering. "Good, now take a step. One step is good, but four is best. The patient began to slowly shuffle around the room and then moved to his chair. I told him I was pleased saying, 'That is what I want from you. I might be the medicine man and know the prayers and songs, but you are the one who is sick. Don't sit there and think I am going to do all of the work. You are going to heal yourself, not me.'"

By the end of the ceremony, the man had gotten up a second time, walked around the room, and then went outside under his own power. By the time we started to eat, he was walking by himself. That was the healing part, the enemy that we needed to overcome; it appeared in two different forms. I see the enemy every day, and when I teach people in the traditional way, I tell them that there are two black bows (eyebrows) that sit on top of their eyes, the better to see the enemy. They are both inside and outside and need to be defeated. I told him, "The enemy comes in two different ways. Yes, there is an Enemyway ceremony that we do, but at the same time, there is an enemy inside of you that doesn't want to make you do things. That has to be overcome, otherwise, it is beating you. Poverty comes from this type of thinking." Sometimes a person has to question or push themselves in order to succeed.

There is an old saying associated with the account of Changing Woman seeing for the first time Big God's scalp and head brought back by Monster Slayer and Born for Water. It says, "I'm going to bite into the tendons of badger," referring to Changing Woman checking to see if she could believe what her eyes told her. She did not want to be worrying and dreaming about something that was not real. To prove that it was real, she bit the scalp. This reality check suggests there may be a tough struggle ahead filled with negative consequences, but it is still something that has to be done. More hardships will appear and there is regret for having taken the "bite," but it is real. There are still other enemies (hunger, poverty, etc.) that will continue to be a problem. "I wish it was all a dream but it is not. I should have never bitten into it."

Dealing with Death

Death is a difficult event for Navajos. My Grandfather shared a good explanation about what it means and why it happens. He said, "You are here because of the holy people and not because you wanted to be; nobody asked you to be born or what name you wanted. You were just given it. But you are here today to improve your life and learn more about being a warrior and defending your family." One day I was really grieving for the loss of my father. Grandfather noticed how I was crying and feeling sad, so he explained that my father was in two places—inside me because I am made up of half my mother and half my father, and he was also in the spirit world.

Monster Slayer is a man of action and is identified with protection, the killing of enemies, and unbounded male energy, while his brother, Born for Water, is contemplative, prayerful, and calm. Each has necessary talents and skills important to Navajo manhood. (Courtesy Library of Congress—photo 101844)

By carrying my father's bloodline and my mother's sensitivity in teaching, I had the same qualities that I missed in them. This also helped me to appreciate and understand myself. This is one reason I do not go to his grave to place memorial flowers, because he is with me.

Grandfather also explained that there is a spirit world beyond this earth, and that at night some of the stars in constellations sparkle more brightly because they are the homes of people who have gone before. Dark is when they are seen and when the dead communicate with the living. "One day, when you really feel distant from your father or a loved one, go outside, watch the stars, and think about the person you are missing. Suddenly, there is going to be a star that is moving and sparkling, and you will know that is where the loved one is. When you talk to them, they will send an answer back through your dreams. That is how you will be connected." There is a constellation called The Ancient One (Azázígo Haz'á) or The One That Used to Live Here (Iizází) or The One Who Left This World. When it comes at night, all the animals know the holy ones are present, and so they lie down and show respect. They do not make songs but are meditating and resting. This is also when night ceremonies take place so that the holy ones can listen to prayers and give direction. As soon as the sun rises, it is a different world with people talking and moving around.

My father shared another way to think about death and those who have gone before. There was a man named Small Water Man (Toniiyázhí), because of his size, who was an accomplished Yé'ii Bicheii singer. He sang loudly and performed the music better than anybody else. He was well known on the Navajo Reservation as one of the lead singers for this ceremony and everyone wanted to accompany him. Following his death, my father and some men were traveling on their horses through the mountains to a Yé'ii Bicheii dance, when they heard something crying. They stopped to listen, then recognized what they thought was someone singing Yé'ii Bicheii songs. The men became curious, followed the sound over some hills until they recognized the voice of Small Water Man and the song he used to sing. They tied their horses and climbed a small hill to watch. There sat a coyote singing. Everybody looked at each other, took out their corn pollen, blessed themselves with it, and walked away. This was the first time they had ever seen something like that. They never talked about it, but they knew it was part of the holy way.

When my oldest brother passed away, we buried him next to my father's grave. At the end of four days a coyote came and lay beside the burial site. We sat there and watched. He went in a circle four times, then waited for another coyote to come out from the far side of a hill. They joined each other, sang, then left together. Family members asked a medicine man how he interpreted these events, and he replied that it was my father coming for his son to take him back.

This was not a bad thing. The coyote actually has more of the good way stories than people realize. Some think that just because a coyote crosses their path that things are going to be bad, but the coyote is a messenger that says, "Look in the direction I am traveling. It might be east. It might be south. It might be west. It might be north. Whichever way, it will indicate something good for you. Going to the east is about critical thinking, south is about planning, west is life, and north is about hope and charity. That is how you are supposed to relate to me, and I will give you a message. I am the first born from the emergence of the people. You have to think of me in those terms."

In the old days, if a person died in a hogan, it was abandoned and left alone until it caved in. The deceased's spirit is believed to travel to the north, where things that have been used are said to go. Family members took their belongings and moved south, following the same pattern as the sun and away from that which lives in the north. The sun travels 102 trails during a year, the same number of years considered a full life for humans. The sun and people move together in the same pattern, from the east to the south, and finally to the west. After an initial move by the family to the south, the direction for the next move is not critical.

While Navajo people avoid interacting with the dead, it can still happen and is viewed as a very real thing. One of my uncles used to have a saying, "I don't want to chop wood for the beavers." He used it one time when some of my relatives asked him to cross a river that was flowing high and fast. My mother heard him say that and got really angry. No one dared ask her why she was so upset, but later, when a family member passed away, the question of what this phrase meant arose, and so we asked. Mother answered that if a person tried something different or difficult, it might kill him or her. Becoming a slave of the beaver, who lives under water and underground, was a way of talking about what happens to those who die. The dead also live beneath the earth and can become slaves to those who rule there, thus "chopping wood for the beaver," could be for an eternity. This was what my uncle referred to before crossing the river, suggesting it might kill him, lead to his burial, and then force him to spend his afterlife enslaved to the dead.

Mention of the dead can have a real effect on a person and can cause bad things to happen. I had an experience at Bosque Redondo or Fort Sumner that underscores just how close the deceased can be. This happened when I was heavily involved with alcohol during my younger years. I had been with some friends who decided to visit this place of sorrow and death for the Navajo people. When we arrived, we saw nothing on the ground except for a few markings and signs. As I walked about, my eyes suddenly closed, and

I felt like I had entered into a spirit world. People were crying, kids were screaming, and a heavy sadness settled into me. Pictures in my head started to focus as I stood there with tears running from my eyes. When I awoke, I felt as if I had gone through a treacherous experience, filled with the suffering of the people who had lived there. A friend helped me walk away because I felt as if I was stuck to the ground. He took me about fifty yards to a road, and then I looked back. Prior to this I never had any dislike for white men, but at that point I suddenly hated Anglo people and felt like I wanted to do something with this hatred. I stayed there for a day and half, sitting in my vehicle thinking about these feelings. After a while, the anger and frustration went away, I was afraid of the emotions I had felt, and I decided that I needed to stop using alcohol and get healed so that I could become a good person. The whole event was scary.

When the Fort Sumner experience ended for the Navajo people in 1868, medicine men drew a line during a ceremony called "A Line Coming Out" (Ch'íhoodzoh), which contained the evil in that place so that the people could leave it all behind and not carry it with them into the future. This closed off all of the sadness and pain, ending the whole experience with the understanding that the people would never return. The evil ones would not come to the people and the people would not return to visit the evil ones. Once the ceremony was performed, this place should not even be mentioned. To do so is just as bad as talking about a sickness that one has and how it is adored and enjoyed. If that happens, all of the evil and sadness returns to those talking about it. Instead, it should be left alone, and people should never return. That is what the ceremony did: "Now you are here, but let's not visit this again; whatever happened leave it behind. From here we learn to heal and have a better life."

Now, people reverse the thought and say, "Those were my loved ones, my people, and I cannot forget that. I'm going to take a stone from home, bring it over there, and put it down as a memorial for those who suffered, then pray for them." Navajos adopted this thinking from other people and felt it was a good way to show respect for the dead. People started taking stones from family sites and celebrating that their ancestors had gone to a better place. The old people say, "You can't go back. You can't do that. If you go back you will cause more bad things that happened there to take place now. You are bringing it back into the inner circle of the reservation where good things are supposed to happen. Don't go back. Why are you doing that?" Still the younger people, who are not aware of traditional teachings, persist and ignore the elders. They feel there must be a memorial, that they should do things in a modern way—"I have a reason to do this and that." Now everything is about memorials—gravesites, rodeos, athletic events,

The stone knife and spearpoint (both approximately seven inches long) are most likely of Anasazi origin and have been handed down for generations in Perry's family. They are held by the patient during part of the Protectionway ceremony and are used by the medicine man to draw a straight line to keep evil away. This practice goes back to the killing of Yéiitsoh and the necessity of preventing his two streams of blood from uniting. Monster Slayer kept them separate by carving a large ditch with his knife. At Torreon, New Mexico, the black "flint" pinnacle still sits on the ground. The ceremony performed at Fort Sumner is another example of this practice. (Photo by Kay Shumway)

historic places—"put my flag, my feathers over there for the little ones that we left behind."

Because of this kind of thinking and teaching, our reservation roads are marked by crosses, signs, and flowers where someone has had an auto accident and died. Relatives put a little cross near the road as a memorial site, but the medicine people say, "You can't do that. You can't pick a place and say there was a body that died there and replace it with a flower or sign.

You are going to ruin your road. All the roads are supposed to be replenished by rain, air, and pollens. That's why the spirit people come, and they address that." As I travel down the road, my children and grandchildren start asking, "Grandpa, why do they have a cross on the road? Why do they have flowers there?" I say, "Don't talk about it. Crazy people put their stuff there. There's something you don't even want to visit. Don't talk about it. We're on a good road here. We're going to a good place. We don't want to talk about the side of the road." The people who put those things there have no respect for the road. They do not have any respect for their elders. They do not have respect for the medicine, and that is why everything is in a state of confusion. This is why things have gone astray today and are working against us. We defeat ourselves because we do not know how to let go anymore, and so people suffer from stress.

Levels of Power and Prayer

Sickness, death, and suffering may come in other forms. During the creation, starting in the Black World, there were four levels of holy people who held different types of power. There were those who dealt with animals or beings on or in the ground and water. This group also included the god of night and one for day as well as those associated with the seasons. A second cluster of holy people existed and interacted at the level that humans breathe, while on the third level there were the birds and other creatures who lived in high places and fly. The fourth level of holy beings was where Talking God (Haashch'ééyałti'í) lived in the heavens. At the beginning, the gods of night (black) and day (white) did not have the ability to fix anything on this earth. Those holy people existing on higher levels made a deal, offering to allow these two to haunt people or make them sick. The higher level gods watched as humans became ill and died, but the earth surface people did not know why. Some of them asked the holy beings, "Can you talk to the air people? Can you talk to the lightning? See what's going on?" So the gods talked to the people, telling them, "There was an agreement with these two on the bottom. The white (day) and the black (night) gods are the ones who do this." The holy people, Day and Night, then spoke to Talking God, who chided them saying, "You are supposed to be helping people. Why are you doing this?" The two gods said, "We needed recognition. We don't want to stay down here. We want to be higher." Talking God counseled, "You're given the task to be with the people because they will need help. Unlike us gods, they cannot just float around, but have to remain tied to the earth. You are the gravity gods (Ni' Yiyah Niizíní, Yá Yiyah Niizíní). You control night and day, the seasons, and keep these humans closer to the earth. Every time you do something wrong, people will leave the earth, and their feet will not be on the ground any more. They're going to get sick. You can't do that." This is one of the ways that sickness first occurred with humans. Illness still arrives with the changes of season, a person becomes wobbly and loses balance both physically and mentally, their temperature changes, and their feet are not flat on the ground.

This began in the worlds beneath, but has been brought into the White and Glittering Worlds. The day and night gods continued to develop their influence on humans, involving the stars, air, light, and wind by listening to what they said, observing what they did, and combining their powers. This was done through strong connections with meditation and their medicines. All of these powers in nature have the ability to help or harm and are controlled through words. Take for instance the word "pááh," which can be used when a storm is approaching or to turn an object being shot at a person through witchcraft. By saying this word, there is protection. The practice developed in the beginning when an uncontrollable storm began harming people and striking homes. Some of those affected went to White Shell Woman and questioned, "The storm that arrived yesterday came very close to my house. I'm in good standing with all of these storms, and so why does it now threaten, and how do I prevent it from harming me?" White Shell Woman answered, "One way the storm will excuse itself is if you take cold ashes from a fireplace, put some in your mouth, and then open your door. Face wherever the storm and lightning strikes are coming and say 'pááh!' spraying the powdery ash in that direction.[19] The storm will turn and go away. Do the same thing for twisters, but use a fire poker to pull the ashes from the fire, flick them in the storm's direction, and chase him [the storm] away. Ashes are also used on a child's forehead when they are having a bad dream and on the bow of a cradleboard as one says 'pááh.'" This scares bad thoughts and evil away and is why White Shell Woman gave it to the people.

Witchcraft

Witchcraft is a difficult topic to talk about. I have not personally experienced it, but my siblings still discuss it and say, "I don't think people like me for who I am because I have many horses and cows. They don't like the way I'm living, so there's a bad vibe that's coming in from the north or somewhere. They are doing it to me, not you, because you don't have horses and other things, and that's why you're successful." I think that in the old days, like the 1930s to 1950s, there were a lot of people who practiced medicine differently and understood how to control those powers. Today, much of that information and many of the ceremonies are extinct and so are not practiced much anymore. Many of the old medicine men and elders who knew about it are now gone, leaving only a minimal amount of it left behind.

Skinwalkers are a form of witchcraft that continues from the worlds beneath to this day. I have heard tell of a young twelve-year-old boy who, with his father, visited some distant relatives in Page. They took him to the Navajo Mountain area where there were a lot of rock formations. Many people were there praying and performing rituals, and his father went off to join that group. The boy was camped nearby and, with two friends, decided to follow his father to find out what was going on. The three boys reached a small cave where a lot of people were dancing outside. They saw some in this group putting feathers in bunches, some making sandpaintings, and others being initiated to run with skins. Nearby guards watching for unwelcome visitors caught the three boys. They brought their captives in and reported, "They were watching so we can't let them go. We have to do something; they can't just walk away from this." The discussion led to either the three boys being sacrificed or joining the group in secrecy. The boy's father had to make the final decision: "Which way do you want to go with this? If he gets sacrificed, then you will have more powers and you get to keep the blood, the heart, and everything." The father answered, "No. Just let him be part of it. Let's initiate him."

These medicine people gave the boy everything—patterns drawn on his body, a feather, and instructions. Next he sat in a large, old wedding basket woven backward or counterclockwise with stars in the design. Suddenly the container started moving, which scared him so much that he passed out. When he next opened his eyes, he was almost halfway dressed in a coyote skin that kept enclosing him more. The medicine person performing this walked up to him and struck him with a rattle on the head. "I want you to stop that. If you close and then open your eyes again, we're going to have to put you in a different area. So do not open your eyes, and let this thing fall away as it is supposed to." The boy's father told him, "Just do what he says. Don't open your eyes again." The group started singing and moving him; soon he was inside of the skin and joined with the others, many of whom had their own skins. They announced, "We're ready to run, just follow us. We are going to be running and getting exercise."

That evening, people started leaving, moving very fast, almost like flying. He followed and was so amazed that he could sprint along without even touching the ground. Before he realized it, he had gone past Navajo Mountain and into Kayenta, where he could see lights and old-fashioned power poles, the type that were put in every quarter mile to bring electricity from one city to another. He traveled right underneath these wires so fast that the poles went by like a flash. The group arrived in Canyoncito near Albuquerque in a wooded area where others were holding a ceremony. They took off their coyote skins, hung them up, walked down to the performance, and started dancing the Yé'ii Bicheii. Here the medicine people initiated the young boy into this ceremony as a Water Sprinkler (Tó Neinilii), the clown who ends up dancing behind everybody. The entire performance came naturally to him. None of this was done in the manner of witchcraft with the intent to hurt people, but only as a means of traveling from place to place for a ceremony. This was how this type of medicine was used, not to hurt people or do bad things.

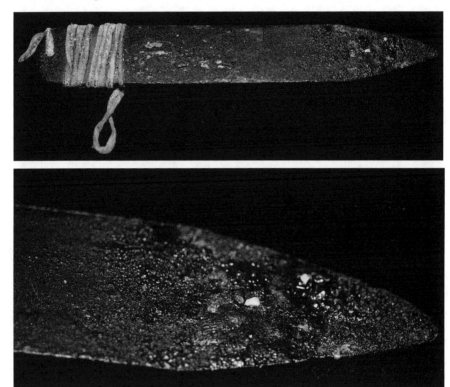

This bullroarer (tsindi'ni') is a good example of how negative power can be used in positive ways by those who control it. Made from a lightning-struck piece of wood, covered with melted pine pitch colored by charcoal, with two inset turquoise eyes and a mouth (one eye is missing), this object, when twirled, makes a whirring sound that keeps evil at bay. Some say that it is heard most distinctly on the north side of the hogan, the direction from which bad things come. (Photo by Kay Shumway)

Many of these practices concerning witchcraft and associated supernatural powers came from the Hopi in the underworlds. For instance, using a basket that was woven in a counterclockwise instead of clockwise fashion, just mentioned, and the concept of reversing normal procedures involved Coyote and the choosing of corn. The Hopi people were in some ways very smart when they reversed some Navajo teachings. Following the emergence of the people, the Hopi brought corn to the Navajo from the worlds beneath. Coyote suggested that the Navajos take it from them, but the people felt that they should not act that way. "We cannot live like that. We can't take things from people. Let them give us the medicine." So the Hopis talked about it, allowing the Navajos to choose what end of the broken cob lying in a woven basket they wanted. Coyote jumped up and grabbed the bottom end, exclaiming, "Here is the root, the closest to the ground [stalk] so we're going to be more stable this way." The Hopis took the top part, where there is growth of new things. When Hopis planted their seeds, the corn grew only about a foot high but had many stalks, which impressed the Navajos. "How did you do that?" The Hopis replied, "It's the growth that you gave us when we took the top because there is corn pollen there as it reaches toward the sky. We can connect with the holy one easier than you can." To add to the dissatisfaction, the Hopis warned, "If we can do this, we can also reverse whatever you are doing." The Hopis decided to redo the baskets obtained from the Navajos and wove them in reverse or in a counterclockwise manner, took the cloud design out of the basket, and embedded stars instead. They also placed these baskets on their chests as a protective shield when fighting and used it as a hat worn during certain ceremonial dances just as they wear buffalo horns in other performances. The Hopis travel with a gourd cut in half or use feathers instead of a coyote skin when practicing witchcraft. The Navajos were really surprised by what the Hopis did and told them to live up on the mesas in the desert where there was no water and everything was dry. At the same time, Navajos developed their own form of medicine, and when the two came together, there were a lot of shared similarities. To this day, the Navajo and Hopi are competitive.

The Coyoteway ceremony features this holy person as a human, just as he appeared at the time of emergence. Coyote is seldom portrayed as he looks today. He is the one who introduced skinwalking as a means of travel, when it was used to move as fast as possible overnight to get to ceremonies or conduct business. In each of the worlds beneath, however, he traveled to the four directions very quickly, returning each time with some type of physical or mental disorder that caused problems. He was this world's first "teenager," constantly challenging and upsetting established rules of conduct. Much of what is today considered antisocial behavior or issues with mental health are connected to this being. Of course, he blamed all of these problems and disorders on others, excusing himself with, "I learned it over there [in one of the directions] and that is how they do it." By the time he had traveled in the four worlds and four directions, there were sixteen physical or mental issues, the same number of positive hogan songs used to correct problems.

The previous example of medicine men traveling as a group to a Yé'ii Bicheii ceremony shows how they had been given this ability to travel as a positive power. But there are always people who will take a good thing and reverse it to do wrong. This is true of skinwalkers. I have heard that in the old days, there were those who would cut across the Colorado River at Marble Canyon near Page, then travel to Kanab and as far as Salt Lake to steal livestock, then drive them back to the reservation at night. They used their medicine power to cover the long distances quickly. These men would go to the Salt Lake area where ranchers lived, take their animals, and immediately herd them away that night. The horses and cattle were so scared they would run full speed with men dashing beside them and four other herders behind them until they reached the mountains around Kanab. There the thieves had hidden their horses. I personally have no knowledge of these things and stay away from this side of medicine practices. The real important power is in doing things in a helpful, sacred way. Everyone has to make a choice.

Not everything that happens to people can be blamed on witchcraft. There are many physical illnesses that occur because of the things we do, and there is no magical cure for them. People have to accept their own consequences and cures and not point their finger to blame others for problems. Still, there is a dark side to everything. There are evil people who do wrong and need to be controlled. If I believe a person has really been a victim of black magic, I can reverse the evil and have it returned back on the person who is causing the problem. For instance, if a man buries things belonging to the individual he is working against, saying prayers and performing actions that leave a curse, he will suffer for whatever he is doing. The evil will fall back to him, perhaps two- or threefold. If he buries something in the ground, that means that he put his hand there and maybe he will be buried himself. A lot of times I tell people, "We're not going to go dig it up. It's not our place to do that. We're all here, clean on this earth. The bad person put something in the ground and that's his responsibility, but we're going to put a stop to it. If he likes things in the ground, maybe we'll put him there. We will give this problem back to the Creator and let him take care of it." The prayers and the songs are reversed, and they will bury him. The final part of curing a person who has been cursed ends with the Blessingway and a restoration of happiness.

Notes

Chapter One

1. J. Gerald Kennedy, ed., *The Life of Black Hawk, or Ma-ka-tai-me-she-kia-kiak: Dictated by Himself* (New York: Penguin Group, 1833, 2008).

2. Charles Eastman, *Indian Boyhood* (Alexandria, VA: Time-Life Books, 1902, 1993); *From Deep Woods Into Civilization: Chapters in the Autobiography of an Indian* (Mineola, NY: Dover Publications, 1918, 1997).

3. John G. Neihardt, *Black Elk Speaks: Being the Life Story of a Holy Man of the Oglala Sioux* (Lincoln: University of Nebraska Press, 1932, 2014).

4. Charlotte J. Frisbie and David P. McAllester, eds., *Navajo Blessingway Singer: The Autobiography of Frank Mitchell, 1881–1967* (Tucson: University of Arizona, 1978, 2003); Charlotte J. Frisbie, ed., with Rose Mitchell, *Tall Woman: The Life Story of Rose Mitchell, A Navajo Woman, c. 1874–1977* (Albuquerque: University of New Mexico Press, 2001).

5. Frisbie and McAllester, *Navajo Blessingway Singer*, 193.

6. Emily Benedek, *Beyond the Four Corners of the World: A Navajo Woman's Journey* (Norman: University of Oklahoma Press, 1995); Walking Thunder with Bradford Keeney, *Walking Thunder: Diné Medicine Woman* (Philadelphia: Ringing Rocks Press, 2001); and Kay Bennett, *Kaibah: Recollection of a Navajo Girlhood* (Self-published, 1975).

7. Alexander H. Leighton and Dorothea C. Leighton, *Lucky: The Navajo Singer*, ed. Joyce J. Griffen (Albuquerque: University of New Mexico Press, 1992).

8. Robert S. McPherson, ed., *The Journey of Navajo Oshley: An Autobiography and Life History* (Logan: Utah State University Press, 2000).

9. Louisa Wade Wetherill and Harvey Leake, *Wolfkiller: Wisdom from a Nineteenth-Century Navajo Shepherd* (Salt Lake City: Gibbs Smith Publisher, 2007).

Chapter Two

1. Gladys A. Reichard, *Navaho Religion: A Study of Symbolism* (Princeton, NJ: Princeton University Press, 1950, 1990), 476.

2. Gary Witherspoon, "Language and Reality in Navajo World View," in *Handbook of North American Indians: Southwest*, vol. 10, ed. Alfonso Ortiz (Washington: Smithsonian Institute, 1983), 570–78, quote on p. 578. For a more complete study, see Gary Witherspoon, *Language and Art in the Navajo Universe* (Ann Arbor: University of Michigan Press, 1977).

3. For different versions of this creative process, see Pliny Earle Goddard, "Navajo Texts," in *Anthropological Papers of the American Museum of Natural History*, vol. 34, part 1 (New York: American Museum of Natural History, 1933), 127–79; Berard Haile, *The Upward Moving and Emergence Way: The Gishin Biye' Version* (Lincoln: University of Nebraska Press, 1981); Aileen O'Bryan, *Navaho Indian Myths* (New York: Dover Publications, 1956, 1993); and Paul G. Zolbrod, *Diné bahane': The Navajo Creation Story* (Albuquerque: University of New Mexico Press, 1984).

4. Gladys A. Reichard, "Human Nature as Conceived by the Navajo Indians," *Review of Religion* 7 (May 1943): 360.

5. Ibid., 575.

6. Harry Walters, personal communication with author, January 28, 2012.

7. Reichard, "Human Nature," 354.

8. Witherspoon, "Language and Reality," 577–78.

9. See James K. McNeley, *Holy Wind in Navajo Philosophy* (Tucson: University of Arizona Press, 1981), for a complete evaluation of the functions of níłch'ih.

10. Mary C. Wheelwright, *Myth of Willa-Chee-Ji Degínnh-Keygo Hatrál* (Santa Fe: Museum of Navajo Ceremonial Art, 1958), 1–2.

11. Marilyn Holiday, discussion with author, September 23, 2007; Jim Dandy, discussion with author, September 24, 2007.

12. Robert S. McPherson, *The Journey of Navajo Oshley: An Autobiography and Life History* (Logan: Utah State University Press, 2000), 99.

13. Gladwell Richardson, *Navajo Trader* (Tucson: University of Arizona Press, 1986), 161.

14. Karl W. Luckert, *Coyoteway: A Navajo Holyway Healing Ceremonial* (Tucson: University of Arizona Press, 1979).

Chapter Three

1. There are many excellent versions of the creation story and beginnings of Navajo culture, including the emergence and the events surrounding Changing Woman, Monster Slayer, and Born for Water. Here I have included, in alphabetical order, some of the most readily available examples. This information is equally relevant for both this and the next chapter. See Stanley A. Fishler, *In the Beginning: A Navaho Creation Myth*, Anthropological Paper no. 13 (Salt Lake City: University of Utah, 1953); Pliny Earle Goddard, "Navajo Texts," in *Anthropological Papers of the American Museum of Natural History*, vol. 34, part 1 (New York: American Museum of Natural History, 1933), 127–79; Berard Haile, *The Upward Moving and Emergence Way: The Gishin Biye' Version* (Lincoln: University of Nebraska Press, 1981); Jerrold E. Levy, *In the Beginning: The Navajo Genesis* (Berkeley: University of California Press, 1998); Washington Matthews, *Navaho Legends* (Salt Lake City: University of Utah Press, 1897, 1994); Don Mose Jr., *The Legend of the Navajo Hero Twins* (Blanding, UT: San Juan School District, 2009); Franc Johnson Newcomb, *Navaho Folk Tales* (Albuquerque: University of New Mexico Press, 1967, 1990); Aileen O'Bryan, *Navaho Indian Myths* (New York: Dover Publications, 1956, 1993); Mary C. Wheelwright, *Navajo Creation Myth: The Story of the Emergence by Hasteen Klah* (Santa Fe: Museum of Navajo Ceremonial Art, 1942); Leland C. Wyman, *Blessingway: With Three Versions of the Myth Recorded and Translated from the Navajo by Father Berard Haile, O.F.M.* (Tucson: University of Arizona Press, 1970); and Paul G. Zolbrod, *Diné bahane': The Navajo Creation Story* (Albuquerque: University of New Mexico Press, 1984).

2. John Holiday and Robert S. McPherson, *A Navajo Legacy: The Life and Teachings of John Holiday* (Norman: University of Oklahoma Press, 2005).

3. Gary Witherspoon, *Language and Art in the Navajo Universe* (Ann Arbor: University of Michigan Press, 1977), 48–49.

4. O'Bryan, *Navajo Indian Myths*, 2.

5. Ibid., 5–6.

Chapter Four

1. Leland C. Wyman, *Blessingway: With Three Versions of the Myth Recorded and Translated from the Navajo by Father Berard Haile, O.F.M.* (Tucson: University of Arizona Press, 1970), 4–5.

2. Ibid., 104.

3. Ibid., 40.

4. For further discussion of the arrival of the Navajo in the Southwest, see William B. Carter, *Indian Alliances and the Spanish in the Southwest, 750–1750* (Norman: University of Oklahoma Press, 2009), 3–23.

5. Deni J. Seymour, *From the Land of Ever Winter to the American Southwest: Athapaskan Migrations, Mobility, and Ethnogenesis* (Salt Lake City: University of Utah Press, 2012).

6. John Holiday and Robert S. McPherson, *A Navajo Legacy: The Life and Teachings of John Holiday* (Norman: University of Oklahoma Press, 2005), 264–65.

7. Robert S. McPherson, Jim Dandy, and Sarah E. Burak, *Navajo Tradition, Mormon Life: The Autobiography and Teachings of Jim Dandy* (Salt Lake City: University of Utah Press, 2012), 176–77.

8. Robert S. McPherson, *Viewing the Ancestors: Perceptions of the Anaasází, Mokwič, and Hisatsinom* (Norman: University of Oklahoma Press, 2014).

Chapter Five

1. See Alexander H. Leighton and Dorothea C. Leighton, *Gregorio, the Hand-Trembler: A Psychological Personality Study of a Navaho Indian*, Reports of the Ramah Project, no. 1 (Cambridge, MA: Peabody Museum of American Archaeology and Ethnology, Harvard University, 1949); also, Robert S. McPherson, *Dinéjí Na'nitin: Navajo Traditional Teachings and History* (Boulder: University Press of Colorado, 2012), 13–43, portions of which are reproduced here. It also has an extensive list of sources in the endnotes.

2. Gladys Reichard, *Navaho Religion: A Study of Symbolism* (Princeton, NJ: Princeton University Press, 1950), 99.

3. Ibid., 99–100; Charlotte J. Frisbie and David P. McAllester, ed., *Navajo Blessingway Singer: The Autobiography of Frank Mitchell, 1881–1967* (Tucson: University of Arizona Press, 1978), 163; William Morgan, "Navaho Treatment of Sickness: Diagnosticians," *American Anthropologist* 33 (Summer 1931): 390–92.

4. John Holiday, interview with author, September 9, 1991.

5. Ibid.

6. Susie Yazzie, interview with author, August 6, 1991.

7. Guy Cly, interview with author, August 7, 1991; Ella Sakizzie, interview with author, May 14, 1991; Ada Black, interview with Bertha Parrish, June 18, 1987.

8. George Tom, interview with author, August 7, 1991.

9. Harvey Oliver, interview with author, May 14, 1991.

10. John Norton, interview with author, January 16, 1991; Cecil Parrish, interview with author, October 10, 1991; Holiday, interview.

11. Susie Yazzie, interview with author, November 10, 2000.

12. Ibid.

13. Ibid.

14. Don Mose, interview with author, June 7, 2011.

15. Leland Wyman, "Navaho Diagnosticians," *American Anthropologist* 38, no. 2 (April–June 1936): 238.

16. Franc J. Newcomb, *Navaho Neighbors* (Norman: University of Oklahoma Press, 1966), 183–98.

17. On March 27, 2018, Perry and I met with professional geologist Dr. Clay Conway at his home in Blanding where we showed him the "single terminated quartz crystal" and the "igneous shallow intrusive andesite" with feldspar, which caused the sparking. Conway was "surprised" that a crystal had been found on top of Mount Hesperus, but explained how it could have happened with very hot water dissolving silica.

Chapter Six

1. Franc Johnson Newcomb, *Navajo Omens and Taboos* (Santa Fe: Rydal Press, 1940), 70–74.

2. Charlotte J. Frisbie, *Navajo Medicine Bundles or Jish: Acquisition, Transmission, and Disposition in the Past and Present* (Albuquerque: University of New Mexico Press, 1987).

3. Charlotte J. Frisbie, "Talking about and Classifying Navajo Jish or Medicine Bundles," in *Navajo Religion and Culture: Selected Views— Papers in Honor of Leland C. Wyman*, edited by David M. Brugge and Charlotte J. Frisbie (Santa Fe: Museum of New Mexico Press, 1982), 103.

4. Frisbie, *Navajo Medicine Bundles*, 109–12.

5. Franciscan Fathers, *An Ethnologic Dictionary of the Navajo Language* (Saint Michaels, AZ: Saint Michaels Press, 1910, 1968), 396.

6. Gladys A. Reichard, *Social Life of the Navajo Indians, with Some Attention to Minor Ceremonies* (New York: Columbia University Press, 1928), 147.

7. Gladys A. Reichard, *Navaho Religion: A Study of Symbolism* (Princeton, NJ: Princeton University Press, 1950, 1990), 308.

8. Kenneth E. Foster, *Navajo Sandpaintings* (Window Rock, AZ: Navajo Tribal Museum, 1964), 6; Clyde Kluckhohn and Dorothea Leighton, *The Navaho* (Cambridge, MA: Harvard University Press, 1946, 1974), 213.

9. Leland C. Wyman, *Blessingway: With Three Versions of the Myth Recorded and Translated from the Navajo by Father Berard Haile, O.F.M.* (Tucson: University of Arizona Press, 1970), 65–66.

10. Foster, *Navajo Sandpaintings*, 6.

11. Franc Johnson Newcomb, Stanley Fishler, and Mary C. Wheelwright, *A Study of Navajo Symbolism*, Papers of the Peabody Museum of Archaeology and Ethnology, Harvard University, vol. 32, no. 3 (Cambridge, MA: Peabody Museum, 1956), 4–6.

12. Foster, *Navajo Sandpaintings*, 6.

13. Mark Bahti, *A Guide to Navajo Sandpaintings* (Tucson, AZ: Rio Nuevo Publishers, 2000); Nancy J. Parezo, *Navajo Sandpainting: From Religious Act to Commercial Art* (Albuquerque: University of New Mexico Press, 1991).

14. Will Evans, "The Twins Who Were Raised from the Dead, A Navajo Folk Story," *Southwestern Lore* 14, no. 3 (Summer 1948): 63–65.

Chapter Seven

1. Stephen C. Jett and Virginia E. Spencer, *Navajo Architecture: Forms, History, and Distribution* (Tucson: University of Arizona Press, 1981); Cosmos Mindeleff, *Navaho Houses*, Bureau of American Ethnology, 1895–1896, Seventeenth Annual Report (Washington, DC: Government Printing Office, 1898).

2. Georgiana Kennedy Simpson, *Navajo Ceremonial Baskets: Sacred Symbols, Sacred Space* (Summertown, TN: Native Voices, 2003); Clyde Kluckhohn, W. W. Hill, and Lucy Wales Kluckhohn, *Navaho Material Culture* (Cambridge, MA: Harvard University Press, 1971).

3. Robert S. McPherson, Jim Dandy, Sarah E. Burak, *Navajo Tradition, Mormon Life: The Autobiography and Teachings of Jim Dandy* (Salt Lake City: University of Utah Press, 2012).

4. The roof of the first hogan built by the holy people was made, in its spiritual form, with a rainbow.

5. Jim Dandy, interview with author, October 8, 2007.

6. Wanda Ketchum, interview with author, September 11, 1993.

7. Betty Yazzie as cited in Georgiana Kennedy Simpson, *Navajo Ceremonial Baskets*, 51.

8. Geno Bahe as cited in Simpson, *Navajo Ceremonial Baskets*, 52–54.

9. June Blackhorse as cited in Simpson, *Navajo Ceremonial Baskets*, 54.

10. Kluckhohn, Hill, and Kluckhohn, *Navaho Material Culture*, 317–21.

11. Ibid., 321.

Chapter Eight

1. Leland Wyman and Clyde Kluckhohn, *Navaho Classification of Their Song Ceremonials*, Memoirs of the American Anthropological Association, no. 50 (Millwood, NY: Kraus Reprint Company, 1938, 1976), 4–5.

2. Franciscan Fathers, *An Ethnologic Dictionary of the Navajo Language* (Saint Michaels, AZ: Saint Michaels Press, 1910, 1968), 139, 174.

3. Charlotte J. Frisbie, ed., with Rose Mitchell, *Tall Woman: The Life Story of Rose Mitchell, A Navajo Woman, c. 1874–1977* (Albuquerque: University of New Mexico Press, 2001), 40.

4. Franciscan Fathers, *Ethnologic Dictionary*, 444.

5. Robert S. McPherson, ed., *The Journey of Navajo Oshley: An Autobiography and Life History* (Logan: Utah State University Press, 2000), 88–89.

6. An excellent study of the importance of bears and how they fit into this nine-night ceremony is found in Leland C. Wyman, *The Mountainway of the Navajo* (Tucson: University of Arizona Press, 1975).

7. Washington Matthews, *Navajo Legends* (Salt Lake: University of Utah Press, 1897, 1994), 155.

8. Frank Mitchell, "Version II," in *Blessingway: With Three Versions of the Myth Recorded and Translated from the Navajo by Father Berard Haile, O.F.M.*, ed. Leland C. Wyman (Tucson: University of Arizona Press, 1970), 430; Don Mose Jr., *The Legend of the Navajo Hero Twins* (Blanding, UT: San Juan School District, 2005), 68–70.

9. Washington Matthews, *The Mountain Chant: A Navaho Ceremony*, Fifth Annual Report of the Bureau of Ethnology (Washington, DC: Government Printing Office, 1887), 407.

10. Matthews, *Navajo Legends*, 39.

11. Frisbie, *Tall Woman*, 454.

12. Franc Johnson Newcomb, *Hosteen Klah: Navaho Medicine Man and Sand Painter* (Norman: University of Oklahoma Press, 1964), 108–9.

13. Malcolm F. Farmer, "Bear Ceremonialism among the Navajos and other Apacheans," in *Navajo Religion and Culture: Selected Views—Papers in Honor of Leland C. Wyman*, edited by David M. Brugge and Charlotte J. Frisbie (Santa Fe: Museum of New Mexico Press, 1982), 112.

14. Frisbie, *Tall Woman*, 268–69.

Chapter Nine

1. Leland Wyman and Clyde Kluckhohn, *Navaho Classification of Their Song Ceremonials*, Memoirs of the American Anthropological

Association, no. 50 (Millwood, NY: Kraus Reprint Company, 1938, 1976), 5–7.

2. Leland C. Wyman, "Navajo Ceremonial System," in *Handbook of North American Indians: Southwest*, vol. 10, edited by Alfonso Ortiz (Washington, DC: Smithsonian Institution, 1983), 544–45.

3. Ibid., 542–43.

4. See chapter 3, note 1 for an extensive list of books that recount, in detail, the story of the Twins and their struggle to make the earth safe for the Navajo.

5. What follows are excerpts from a lengthier study I wrote called "Sacred Evil: The Dark Side of Life along the San Juan," in *Dinéjí Na'nitin: Navajo Traditional Teachings and History* (Boulder: University Press of Colorado, 2012), 72–99.

6. Harry Walters, personal communication with author, January 28, 2012.

7. Clyde Kluckhohn, *Navaho Witchcraft* (Boston: Beacon Press, 1944, 1970), 22.

8. Jim Dandy, interview with author, September 26, 2007.

9. Ibid.

10. Will Evans, *Along Navajo Trails: Recollections of a Trader* (Logan: Utah State University Press, 2005), 231–32.

11. Karl Luckert, *A Navajo Bringing-Home Ceremony: The Claus Chee Sonny Version of Deerway Ajiłee* (Flagstaff: Museum of Northern Arizona Press, 1978), 186.

12. Berard Haile, *The Upward Moving and Emergence Way: The Gishin Biye' Version* (Lincoln: University of Nebraska Press, 1981), 24.

13. Gary Witherspoon, *Language and Art in the Navajo Universe* (Ann Arbor: University of Michigan Press, 1977), 77, 185–86.

14. Kluckhohn, *Navaho Witchcraft*, 59.

15. Florence Begay, interview with author, January 30, 1991.

16. John Norton, interview with author, January 16, 1991.

17. John Begay, interview with author, May 7, 1991; Margaret Weston, interview with author, February 13, 1991; Jane Silas, interview with author, February 27, 1991.

18. Dandy, interview.

19. The word "páóh" is used in the Blackeningway ceremony ('Ant'eesh) to blow away evil and send it to the north, a place of death, evil, and harmful things. In the ceremony, a person holds an arrowhead covered with ash in his palm and blows on it, saying this word to push maleficence away.

Index